TRAIL
of 32

PAUL REGA

*The True Story of a Youthful Spirit
That Knew Not of Defeat*

Also by Paul Rega

12 Steps to Freedom

How To Find A Job: When There Are No Jobs

Dedicated to my Scoutmaster, Jerry Risting and fellow Scouts; Steve Mahoney, Jeff Anderson and the late Ray Bender, for without their spirit and quest for adventure, this trip would have never taken place. My special thanks to Anthony Zoubek for his invaluable contribution.

"Life is nothing more than getting along with others and appreciating the animals. Nature in itself is a neat thing, and then you add the animals."

Jerry Risting, (Former BSA Leader) 01/27/09

ONE

SHUTTING DOWN MY RECRUITING BUSINESS even for a few days was always a difficult task for me. Owning a small business for nearly 23 years was grueling enough. Taking a vacation and trying to mentally check out from the demands of my business was extremely difficult. It was late October and the fall season was fast approaching. There was usually a day or two during this time of the year, when the weather would cooperate and I'd be able to get away to fish and reflect on my hectic life.

Indian summer had not yet arrived and I began to think it would never come, but the weatherman miraculously changed his forecast at the last minute to a sunny, 75°F day. I would have to act quickly, as I was sure another day like the one predicted would not come again until next year. It would be perfect fishing weather and I was determined to go and try to rejuvenate my work torn mind and body.

I was particularly excited about the prospect of a fishing trip this year, as I had missed my annual outing to the river the year before, because of a difficult time I was having with my family. Earlier in the week, when the unpredictable Midwestern weather didn't seem to be cooperating, I started to think about what other options I might have to get away on a fishing trip before another harsh winter set in. I began to have visions of my previous fishing trips in the warm gulf waters of the Florida Keys once again. I had taken a much needed trip a few years back in February 2002, in an attempt to cope with a difficult family situation, and avoid a burnout from the rigors of my business. My dream had always been to be in Florida, sitting on a beach somewhere in the Keys, writing a book.

The Keys had always been a place for me to go where I could gather my thoughts and connect with my father, who had passed away a number of years ago. In an effort to cope with my life, and recharge my internal batteries, I decided to take the trip alone and reflect on my life's future. This was unusual for me, as I have a relatively large family of four boys and we would normally travel together. This particular year however, had been much different from the past and some time alone was exactly what I needed to save my sanity, and potentially my marriage.

We had lost our only daughter, Jennifer, in the summer of August 1998, in a tragic car accident, and our family was never quite the same afterwards. Jenny was not my wife's biological child and she did not live with us at the time of her accident. My wife did not quite understand the pain and extreme level of emotion I was feeling. It was having a negative impact on my ability to function or even run my company.

Relieved by my decision to take a fishing trip by myself, I was still somewhat lonely and missed my family. Nonetheless, I was determined to enjoy myself on my vacation while writing my book and trying to relax in the warmth of the Keys. I decided to explore an expansive white sandy beach in a beautiful state park called Bahia Honda. The warm clear blue ocean waters and sound of the gentle surf began to calm my soul. This incredible park is located on Bahia Honda Key, approximately eight miles south of the town of Marathon and Key Vaca. To get to the park via automobile, you need to cross an enormous bridge that spans nearly seven miles into the ocean, before coming to rest on another small island and piece of the Keys. If you're heading south toward Key West, the "Seven Mile" bridge, as it is called, is situated between the Atlantic Ocean to the east and the Gulf of Mexico to the west.

The Keys are literally comprised of hundreds of tiny islands, the largest of which are connected by several man-made bridges and are primarily made up of coral deposits. As a result, very few natural beaches are present in this part of Florida. A much older bridge, that was originally built in 1912, as an overseas railway by industrialist Henry Flagler, runs parallel with the newer more modern bridge. Large sections of the original bridge were destroyed by a massive hurricane that killed hundreds of people in the Keys on Labor Day, in 1935.

I fished for the first time in the Florida Keys on that trip; somewhat ironic since my father had owned a townhouse for many years in Marathon on Key Vaca. I didn't catch many fish despite having an excellent guide, but I came to admire the beauty and serenity of the backcountry. The pristine blue waters and the thousands of exotic birds that often congregate in the shallows of the Keys were magical. I had dreamed of going to Africa for many years, and as I sped across the crystal blue waters of the Gulf of Mexico and parts of the Everglades in my 16 foot skiff, piloted by Captain Charlie Owens; I was in Africa that day.

As I sat on the beach trying to relax on a cheap lounge chair I had bought at Wal-Mart for ten dollars, I felt the warm white sand between my toes and a gentle breeze start to caress my face. I soaked up an abundance of sun and began to visualize leaving my business and writing full-time. I was on a special mission during that trip, as I was trying to prove to myself that I could write and relax at the same time. I was anxious to try my hand at backcountry fishing. Both writing and fishing have always been passions of mine, and unless I scheduled time to do either one of them, often constraints due to my business and family life seemed to get in the way. That particular trip to

Florida had special significance and meaning for me, and I was sure it would be one I would remember for the rest of my life.

A Midwestern fishing trip, like the one I was beginning to plan for, nearly always eluded me. This year however was somehow different and no matter what, I was determined to go. The previous destination for my trip was the Vermilion River in a beautiful part of South Central Illinois. It's a rather unusual river as it flows north on its journey to meet up with the Illinois River. The fact that the Vermilion runs north is a feat shared with only a few other rivers in the world, one such being the great Nile of Egypt. The Vermilion is a very old river as its many twists and turns are evidence of the time spent cutting through its rocky and sandstone banks. Many miles of beautiful and untamed sections of whitewater rapids and pristine wooded shoreline dotted with massive boulders, can be seen having been deposited by the last great Ice Age. Wildlife is abundant, while any real industry is rare, and not a single house can be seen for many miles at a stretch.

As a young boy, my father would take me canoeing and fishing at the river and we would often camp along its lush wooded banks. He loved the area so much that he would later purchase a small farm on the river above the dam near Streator, Illinois. He used it as a refuge to get away from the demands of his own business. My trips to the Vermilion during later years of my life were often bitter sweet after my father's passing in June of 1997. My memories of him and our many times together, either fishing or canoeing the river, lay heavy on my mind. I missed being with him. My personal trips to the river as an adult were a time and opportunity for me to reflect on my own life and the challenges that lay ahead of me on my own journey.

An area of the river where I planned on fishing during this trip had a very significant and special meaning to me. It was also rife with a vivid memory of a near tragedy. My father and I had been canoeing the river many years ago, when I was only nine years old. The river seemed rather high for that time of the year and the water was moving at a very fast pace. I was wearing a bulky, oversized lifejacket my father had purchased from a Navy supply store. I think he thought the bigger the better, but I remember not being able to move or even paddle very well. He had added an extra level of security by tying a half inch piece of rope around my back and securing it with a large square knot in the front of the jacket.

The military issued lifejacket was very constricting, but I was sure it would hold me up in the water and probably one other person should I fall into the raging rapids. It had only been my second time down the river and I could sense a certain amount of concern on my father's face. He was desperately trying to keep our canoe afloat as we dodged numerous rocks and submerged boulders. I recall his anguish as he commented that the river was a lot higher than he had originally thought and the current was moving faster than he could ever remember.

My father was an expert canoeist and former Boy Scout, having canoed numerous rivers across the country including the Vermilion and several others in Illinois. For whatever reason, he decided to run a rapid on the far left side of the river in an area known as the Rock Garden. I think he wanted me to experience the thrill of running a real rapid. Strewn across entire sections of this part of the river are numerous jagged rocks and massive boulders, some partially exposed. When the water is higher than normal, the Rock Garden can be rather treacherous and deadly, as many a canoeist, both novice and experienced, have discovered over the years.

My father had purchased a Voyageur canoe that had fallen off a delivery truck and was severely damaged. He was able to buy it for a reasonable price and quickly learned how to repair it with fiberglass. The canoe was maroon in color, and the bow and stern of the boat rose up and curved at the top resembling an Indian birch bark canoe. It was unlike any canoe I had ever seen. Its extra wide body and keel were well suited for whitewater and almost never tipped. Over the years, the canoe would take on a new dimension and weight, as we would need to repair it after several bouts with the Vermilion. The canoe became so heavy due to all its repairs and added amounts of fiberglass, that it would take four men just to carry it to the launch site near Englehaupt's property.

On a previous trip with my father, Mr. Englehaupt, who lived in one of the few homes on the banks of the Vermilion warned us that if you're not familiar with this river or are a novice canoeist, this section can be very dangerous during times of high water and should be avoided. He was right, and we were just about to run this part of the river and try to navigate through some of its most treacherous rapids! I began to feel my heart beat faster as we got nearer to the Rock Garden. I could see and hear the water swirling and crashing violently against the rocks. My father yelled to me, "Get down on your knees, Paul, stay low and paddle!" Because I was in the front of the canoe, I could see clearly as we approached what appeared to be a massive amount of whitewater and a five to six foot drop off. We were heading straight into the center of this incredible whirlpool of swirling whitewater.

The front of our canoe hit the rapids first and we began to drop off the edge of the waterfall. I heard a loud crash as the bottom of the canoe scrapped hard against the rocks below the surface and the fiberglass began to buckle. Our canoe shook violently from side to side and just as I thought we were about to tip over, my father steadied our canoe and we continued to move swiftly through the rapid. Then, without any warning, there was a loud crushing noise followed by an eerie almost deadening sound of what must have been solid rock ripping through the bottom of our canoe. As our small craft came to an abrupt stop in the middle of the raging rapids, it began to shake more violently as waves crashed hard against its sides. With our canoe on the verge of being eaten alive by the rapids, I heard my father cry out in pain. When I looked back at him, to my horror I saw a steady flow of his fresh blood clearly visible against the gray bottom of our canoe. His left knee had been split open from a jagged rock that that had punctured a section of our boat where he had been kneeling.

We were now being held in place by a large jagged rock in the middle of a churning mass of whitewater. The rock had just ripped a gaping hole in our canoe severely injuring my father. His face was grimacing with what had to be excruciating pain. His massive body and tired arms tried desperately to keep our small canoe afloat. He yelled to me, "Stay low, and don't panic!" I don't remember panicking, but I was worried about my dad and wondered how we would manage not to sink and be swept down river in only our lifejackets. Even at nine years old, I was a pretty good swimmer, but questioned my ability to swim with any chance of survival in these types of waters.

As more and more water rushed in from the large rip in the bottom of our canoe, huge whitecaps crashed over the sides completely soaking our bodies in cold river water, threatening to sink us. I could feel our canoe begin to shake violently once again as my father desperately tried to free it from the grips of the rock that had punctured our boat, and ravished his knee. Suddenly, I heard another loud scrapping noise and our boat catapulted forward and was finally free from the grips of the rocks. My father yelled to me, "Bail Paul, bail!" I quickly dropped my paddle into the canoe and began to frantically bail the water out of our nearly swamped boat with a plastic milk container.

Our only hope to survive this incredible mishap was to try and make a quick sharp turn across the river and shoot for the right bank. I could see that the left bank of the river was completely washed out by the high water and there was no sign of dry ground. A massive concrete and steel bridge that spans across the Vermilion at this section of the river has hash marks on its immense columns, indicating the height of water in the river. As we came closer to the bridge, I could see that the river was well past the six-foot marker on the columns, nearly reaching the seven-foot mark, an extremely dangerous water level for this river. At an eight-foot level, the Vermilion looks like a branch of the Colorado River.

As we desperately tried to keep our canoe afloat, I thought that if we missed getting out of the river at this point, we might be washed further downstream without much hope of getting out for several miles. I was worried about my father's knee and his ability to continue paddling. If we were to save ourselves, we would have to safely steer our small canoe around the massive bridge columns, make a sharp right turn and head for the far right bank of the river. Not a very easy task with a boat nearly filled with water and my father's severe injury. Still kneeling, he tried desperately to stop the profuse bleeding from the gash in his knee by wrapping his drenched shirt around his wound. As he applied pressure, I could see his face grimace in pain. It was a first aid technique I'm sure he must have learned while in the Boy Scouts. It was apparent that he was in agony and was the only one paddling, as I continued my desperate attempts at bailing.With each movement forward, our canoe continued to take on more river water. The water rushed in through what appeared to be two large jagged rips in the bottom of our canoe.

As I struggled to bail, mustering every ounce of energy left in my body, I could hear my father groan in pain as I felt our weighted down canoe start to slowly turn toward the right bank with each powerful thrust from his paddle. His last orders to me on the river were, "Stop bailing, Paul, now paddle, paddle hard!" Somehow through our incredible determination to save our lives, my father and I were able to make it safely to the other side of the river without sinking and being swept down the Vermilion River. It's a vivid memory of how determination, teamwork and the sheer will to live, which saved our lives that I will never forget. I often reflect on this amazing tale of courage, as I continue to fish and canoe that very part of the river as an adult.

TWO

I COULD FAINTLY HEAR the weatherman on the radio in our family room once again revise his forecast for the day of my trip. It would be a mostly sunny day with a high temperature of 82°F, he claimed. It was late October and this improved forecast would certainly set a record. I continued searching for my fishing gear in the basement. It had been some time since I had last used any of my equipment. I desperately needed this time alone to gather my thoughts and be away from my family and business troubles. The Vermilion River was always a place I could go to and reflect and connect once again with my father.

After searching for nearly an hour through a mountain of plastic storage bins, most un-marked since our last move, I spotted a large bin with a small piece of yellowed masking tape on the top corner. The label's faded blue ink lettering read, "Camping and Fishing Gear." It appeared to be the most dust covered bin in the basement. It was clear that it had not been opened in a long time as dust and cobwebs nearly obscured the label. As I started to pull up on the top corner of the bin, I wondered when the last time I had actually seen the contents of this particular bin or even had fished at the river? Had it been more than a year, I wondered. It seemed like it. My consulting business and family life had suffered since our move to Yorkville, Illinois in late 1995. My family life was wrought with frustration from a slowdown in business and my debilitating grief as the result of my daughter's tragic accident. The toll shook my family by its core and threatened to break us apart. Unfortunately, what I had hoped to be a positive move to the country, proved to be a major strain on everyone.

The top of the bin popped off and my eyes were immediately drawn to an old washed out khaki green Boy Scout backpack. It was partially stained from the ravages of time and what appeared to be dirt and grime accumulated from many years of camping. The Boy Scout insignia was located on the outer top flap of the backpack and was faded and badly worn. An inscription that encircled the emblem was barely legible and read, "Boy Scouts of America, Be Prepared." Most of the seams of the pack were intact as was certainly an indication of the workmanship at that time. Barely a stitch was out of place or missing. I noticed a brown plastic name tag on the back of the backpack with the inscription, "PROPERTY OF" at the top of the tag and "No. 573 Haversack," and a place below it to write your name, address and troop number. Hand written in black ink was the name, Billy Lonergan, 2153 N. Melvina. Billy was my best friend and fellow Scout at the time, and we would often borrow each other's camping gear. It was apparent I had never returned his backpack. I felt a certain sense of guilt for my actions and wondered how he was doing. He, unfortunately, had lived a difficult and often trying life as a young boy due in part to a rather tragic family life.

Digging further into the bin, I quickly came across some of my fishing equipment that I had been looking for, including an old Flambeau brand Adventure Tackle Box. It was one of the first tackle boxes my father had given to me as a boy and it still appeared to be in good shape. I immediately opened it and found it nearly intact and completely filled with several fishing lures, bobbers, extra fishing line, weights and hooks. Rummaging further, I spotted one of my old silver Zepco Reels. It was a great find and I was certain I had not seen this fishing box in a number of years and feared it had been lost during our move. Excited, I continued to dig deeper into the bin and found more of my old camping equipment. Much of it I had used as a Boy Scout, including two cooking kits, one with a partially blacked frying pan, an old percolating coffee pot, and a green battery-powered lantern. Everything looked to be in excellent, almost preserved condition.

Sifting further through my Scout backpack, I noticed that the cloth material was very rigid from what must have been the result of applying a great deal of waterproofing material. It sat upright on the floor without any support. Inside the pack I discovered a well-preserved Boy Scout Fieldbook, whose printing date was 1972. I was shocked to think that it had been nearly 34 years since I had actually used this book, as I had been in the Boy Scouts for almost five years from 1968 to 1973. Looking further into the pack, I found a well-equipped Swiss Army Knife, and more fishing tackle. I enjoyed collecting all types of fishing gear as a boy and used my own money either from my allowance or from my rabbit and grass cutting businesses.

Excited about my recent discoveries and happy that I wouldn't have to buy new fishing gear, I continued to look through the plastic bin pulling out a few other pieces of camping equipment. As I neared the bottom, I noticed what appeared to be my old Boy Scout uniform partially wrapped in a black plastic bag on a metal hanger. There were two khaki green colored belts with partially tarnished brass belt buckles attached to the top of the hanger. Carefully pulling off the plastic bag, I could see that my uniform was fully intact and only somewhat wrinkled despite having been in storage for so many years. Most of the badges and metals were still securely sewn on the uniform, except for those signifying Troop 65, and Wood Dale, Illinois. They were barely holding on with a few remaining threads and rusty safety pins. Fitted across the shoulders and wrapped around the front of the uniform was a bright red vest with tassels at the top of each shoulder. The vest was a part of the Boy Scout uniform and used to display badges and awards.

I had been awarded a total of ten merit badges throughout my five years as a Boy Scout, signifying that I had achieved the rank of Life Scout. It was one rank below an Eagle Scout, the highest rank that can be achieved in Scouting. Becoming a Life Scout was a significant achievement. I marveled over the fact that I had kept my uniform in such good shape for all these years. I had introduced my oldest son to the Scouts at an early age and hoped to be able to show him my uniform as he progressed through Scouting. Unfortunately, he decided after only a few years in the Cub Scouts, to pursue other interests.

My merit badges were sewn onto a green sash that was typically worn with the uniform. It was also in excellent condition. My mother is a wonderful cook, but she hated sewing and it was never quite her strong suit. In her apparent haste and desire to use her new sewing machine, she agreed to sewn all 10 of my merit badges onto my sash. The badges are round and rather small and only about an inch and a half in circumference. To stitch each one individually would have taken a good amount of patience and time, all of which my mother was in short supply. Maybe she didn't think I would notice, but she had sewn three badges next to each other never lifting her foot off her sewing machine pedal, or miss a single stitch across the entire span of three badges. When she was done, you could see parallel stitching across the entire width of the sash, spanning across three badges on the upper and lower parts of each badge. To make matters worse, she used white thread for the entire project instead of a color that would match the badges. As I looked more closely at my green sash full of merit badges,

I marveled at this sewing masterpiece. I wondered what she must have been thinking, or worse what did my Scoutmaster or fellow Scouts think!

In all fairness to my mother, she had been actively involved with me during my early Scouting days as a Cub Scout and I am sure sewed on many patches for me by hand. I suppose as a Boy Scout, I should have been able to sew on my own badges and would suspect that I probably started to do so after this incident. It was yet another lesson about self-reliance that my mother had so vividly taught me.

Pushing further into the bin, I was finally reaching what I thought must be the bottom. I could see something about the size of a large book, that appeared to be wrapped securely between a red bath towel and several pieces of yellowed newspaper. As I picked up the object from the bin, I could almost feel what might be glass through the towel and began to carefully unwrap it. Glancing further into the bin, I noticed another red towel with something wrapped tightly between several pieces of newspaper and sections of a corrugated box. Curious, I quickly removed the first towel. To my surprise, I discovered a well-preserved but slightly yellowed Boy Scouts of America certificate that was encased in glass, with a black lacquered frame.

I anxiously sat down and began to read what had been inscribed on the certificate. It was dated July 22, 1972 with the caption typed in italics. The official certificate was trimmed in gold with the Boy Scout insignia at the top and read, BOY SCOUT TROOP 65 - Boy Scouts of America - TAKES PLEASURE IN AWARDING THIS - Certificate of Appreciation To - Paul Rega - IN RECOGNITION OF - *Exceptional performance in carrying out his assigned duties and providing good discipline and high morale for the thirty-two Scouts and leaders on the*

*most adventurous expedition in the history of Troop 65 on a bicy-
cle trip from Wood Dale, Illinois to the State of Florida.* Inscribed
below this statement were the dates July 22, 1972 to August 20,
1972. The certificate was signed by Jerry Risting, my Scoutmaster at the time, Michael Terese the assistant Scoutmaster and E.
L. Malick, Committee Chairman.

Tears began to well up in my eyes as I started to reread the
inscribed words on the certificate. My emotions were filled
with an overall feeling and sense of amazement for this great
accomplishment. I felt a deep level of reverence for the 32
Scouts and leaders that had embarked on this incredible journey nearly 33 years before. A great deal of time had passed
since this fantastic trip. I was now an adult, almost 50 years of
age with the responsibilities of a family and a business. I
started to wonder about my fellow Scouts. What they had accomplished during this incredible journey was remarkable. I
was in awe over their great feat of courage and strength. I began to recall some of their names and see their boyhood faces
and tried to visualize them as adults. I wondered what their
lives must have been like over past several years.

As I started to study the plaque in more detail, my eyes were
once again drawn to the bottom of the storage bin and the
other red towel. Without hesitation, I reached into the bin. I
picked up what felt like a solid object wrapped tightly in a
towel-like cocoon of old frayed newspaper and rigid cardboard.
The object appeared to be about the dimensions of a large book
and light green in color. It was trimmed in gold with the words
"Scrap Book" inscribed in large cursive gold letters on the front
cover. The cover had been partially crushed under what must
have been the weight of my camping gear resting on top of it
for so many years. I carefully opened the scrapbook, cautious
not to further damage some of the pages that were partially

torn and yellowed with time. To my surprise, my mother had hand written on the inside corner of the scrapbook the words, "Trip to Florida July 22, 1972-August 20, 1972.

I started to carefully turn the delicate pages of the scrapbook, viewing its aged contents. I felt a level of excitement and curiosity similar to that of an archeologist discovering the tomb of an Egyptian pharaoh. It was an emotional feeling as I began to read the many newspaper articles and look at the other pieces of memorabilia my mother had so carefully preserved, chronicling our journey. Our incredible expedition began in Wood Dale, Illinois and continued as we bicycled through eight states before arriving at our final destination of Jacksonville, Florida.

I had completely forgotten about this amazing scrapbook and the wealth of its contents. Time has an extraordinary way of turning what was surely an important event and an amazing feat of courage in 1972, to something even more meaningful in today's fast paced world. Time I was certain, had surly continued to march on and exert its influence on all of us, who had partaken in this momentous journey.

There were 32 of us in all, mostly boys ranging in age from eleven to sixteen years old, chaperoned by six adult leaders. Nearly a month passed, as we traversed through a total of eight states covering nearly 1,400 miles on our 10-speed bicycles known as Free Spirits. We all displayed an amazing degree of courage, often fraught with physical pain, but mostly a sense of what I have determined to be blind ambition, fueled, and driven by a youthful spirit that knew not of defeat.

THREE

A S I ANXIOUSLY continued to prepare myself for my fishing trip to the Vermilion River, I could recall my father's own account of his first experiences in Scouting. It was late fall of 1946. My father was nine years old at the time and had just joined the Cub Scouts. A rather gentle soul by the name of Ann Walters, who happened to be my father's next door neighbor was also his den mother. She was often his guardian angel. Due to a rather tumultuous home life, Ann provided a needed safe haven for my father and his siblings for many years. His family was often in turmoil. In addition to her obvious community service as a den mother, Ann was also my grandmother's best friend, mentor and occasional drinking partner.

My father's many fond memories of Ann, or Mrs. Walters as he would always refer to her as, surrounded stories of their many fishing and camping trips. Ann was a rather small framed woman whose facial features were clearly that of a mostly Czechoslovakian descent. She had pitch black hair that she parted down the middle and usually wrapped tightly in a brightly colored babushka. Her dark brown eyes were of a caring nature, but also told of a darker story of the pain and anguish she suffered as the result of an abusive, and often drunkard husband. She was a rather muscular person and despite her small stature could single-handedly carry a canoe on her back. She loved to fish and would often take my father out in her rowboat fishing in nearly every lagoon in Chicago. She was also an excellent cook and taught my father how to properly clean and prepare his catch for cooking. Ann loved the outdoors and would take my father and his Scout troop on numerous fishing trips.

As a young boy living in my grandmother's basement, I remembered Ann and her kind and gentle ways. I often witnessed my father's special bond with her as they spoke to one another across fence lines. It would be a relationship that would last for many years. Sadly her long and courageous battle with colon cancer would tragically end her life in the early 1960's. My father, as well as the world of Scouting, would deeply miss a great and dedicated woman that helped to shape the lives of many young boys on their journey toward manhood.

Despite my father's initial love for the Cub Scouts, his days and future as a Scout were nearly cut short due to an unfortunate accident that occurred while he was at a den meeting at Mrs. Walter's house. In one of my father's letters to me, he described the mishap as follows:

"I was nine years old and a Cub Scout at the time and Mrs. Walters was our den mother. The organizational structure of the Scouting movement at the time allowed that each den mother would have a den chief, who was an older Boy Scout. Our den chief was Jack Garner, a 13 year old Scout who proudly wore his blue and gold braid on his shoulder which indicated that he was a leader of young boys. And I did admire him. One day we were sitting in Mrs. Walters's basement on the cold, damp concrete floor. We were working on a Father's day present which was an ice cream keg being wound with twisted crepe paper that would ultimately turn into a waste basket. It was in this uncomfortable position that I peed in my pants. Initially it was a gloriously pleasing experience but the feeling was only temporary. The puddle of murky urine spread beyond the area of my seat on the floor. It became apparent to at least one other person that the big kid had just pissed in his pants. That person was Jack, our den chief. Quick thinking and ever resourceful, he said, "Okay everybody, up and outside and pick up all the itsy bitsy pieces of garbage in Mrs. Walters's yard. Except you, you stay there."

"The other Scouts jumped to their feet and ran whooping and hollering out to the yard. As soon as they made it to the basement door, I leaped to my feet, went up the interior stairs into the front room and ran frantically out of Mrs. Walters's house toward home. On the way, I was very creative and discovered an ideal disposal method for one pair of pissed in underwear, socks and pants.

"The following Friday afternoon I did not go to the Cub Scout meeting. I didn't want to face a group that knew I had pissed in my pants. I had decided to quit the Scouts. The following Friday afternoon, Jack stopped by and said, "Thought I'd pick you up for Cub Scouts."

"I'm not going," I said.

"Why not?" Jack replied.

"I don't know I just don't want to go," I said.

" I didn't tell anyone you pissed in your pants," he replied.

"Why not?" I said, somewhat in disbelief.

"I don't know, it just never came up," Jack responded.

"I decided to go to the Cub Scout meeting that day despite my fears of being ridiculed. I looked suspiciously into the eyes of my other den brothers and they returned dull unknowing glances and wondered where I was the week before. Repairing a bent ego would have been my reply had I been a philosopher at the age of nine. Instead, I just shrugged my shoulders and tried to pretend that the incident had never happened.

"It passed and from then on, Jack became the proverbial leader that I would follow down the barrel of a cannon. When I graduated into the Boy Scouts a few years later, all the shit jobs on campouts were the ones for which I volunteered willingly.

27

Our fearless leader, Jack would ask, "Who wants to get up at 6:30 a.m. and cut firewood and start the breakfast fires?" "I will," said I. "Who wants to dig another hole for an outhouse?" he said. "I will," said I. "Who wants to get up through the night and keep the fire going because it's going to be colder than hell out this weekend?" he asked. "I will," said I. And on and on it went as there was no task too mundane, too ugly or too exhausting that I would not volunteer to do.

"Jack stood at my side often and our friendship became strong and fast. We created together, concocted and built an Indian dance team while we were members of a branch of Scouting called the Order of the Arrow. We learned and studied the backgrounds of Indian tribes including the Sioux, Blackfeet and the Oglala and talked philosophy over campfires."

Scouting for both my father and his loyal friend and leader, Jack Garner, was as much a place to go and experience camping, fishing and the great outdoors, as it was an escape from a harsh childhood both endured as boys growing up on the South Side of Chicago. In the beginning of my father's early Scouting experience, Mrs. Walters initially provided the outdoors experience and loving refuge my father so longed for as a nine-year-old boy. Yearning to experience the outdoors and camping, Jack also sought out the Boy Scouts as he desperately tried to flee a dirt poor existence growing up in Chicago's Englewood ghetto.

His father, an unskilled laborer, was barely able to provide the basic necessities for Jack and his family's existence. An occasional day trip with his family to Fox Lake, Illinois would often end abruptly when his drunken father forced him to drive home at the age of 12 because he was too inebriated. Disgusted with his family life and a boyhood desire to experience the outdoors, Jack, began his Scouting adventures when he was 12 years old. He joined Boy Scout Troop 670.

It was late 1945, and World War II the most widely fought war in human history had just come to an end. A young Army sergeant by the name of Butkus had completed several tours of duty. He had honorably served his country in a war that had been fought across several nations of the world. He possessed a strong desire to continue serving his beloved country. He wanted to give something back to the Boy Scouts of America, an organization that had been called upon by the US government for help in its war efforts.

Earlier that year the BSA had conducted their largest single war effort that supported General Dwight D. Eisenhower's Waste Paper Campaign. More than 700,000 Boy Scouts and Cub Scouts gathered 318,000 tons of paper. In addition to the Scout's recycling campaign, they were also instrumental in distributing 1.6 million defense bonds and stamp posters, planted victory gardens, collected millions of used books for our service personnel and helped the American Red Cross in their efforts.

Sergeant Butkus, after returning from the war, was well aware of the incredible efforts put forth by the Boy Scouts and felt compelled to give something back. He decided to start a local Boy Scout troop on Chicago's South Side. He felt strongly that he would be able to provide value based leadership and visualized a group that would benefit the lives of young boys. He sought to attract boys who had a desire to join the Scouting movement based on a foundation of morals and a value system established by the Scouts. A group of boys that would be able to experience the things they longed to do like camping, fishing and hunting. The new Scout troop would be structured around the twelve principles of the Scout Law.

Sergeant Butkus soon became the Scoutmaster for Troop 670 and the Scouts went camping nearly every weekend beginning with their first outdoor adventures at Camp Kiwanis, an old CCC camp located near the Indiana and Michigan border. The sergeant was a very dedicated man that had survived a horrific war and only wanted the best for the boys. He structured and ran the new troop similar to that of a military operation, instilling a great deal of discipline into the boys who desperately needed and sought out a sense of direction in their lives.

Unfortunately, the Scouting movement at the time suffered as a result of a country that had been ravished by a war lasting several years and a loss of 416,800 US military personnel. In those days, the Scouting organization was not very popular and lacked sufficient leadership. Although the young sergeant made a major effort toward recruiting more boys from local schools, his troop did not grow. Somewhat disillusioned with the lack of attendance, Jack's enthusiasm for the very things that had drawn him to the Scouts would eventually lead him to Boy Scout Troop 621.

The neighborhood had been troubled for some time and was quickly changing for the worse, as racial tensions mounted. After a period of time, Jack's, new troop also began experiencing attendance and leadership problems. Disappointed but still dedicated to the spirit of Scouting, Jack sadly would leave this troop too, and join Boy Scout Troop 656. His previous Scoutmaster, Sergeant Butkus would soon follow. Fortunately, this troop's efforts in recruiting other boys was more successful and the small group grew in number over a three to four year period.

My father, who was three years younger than Jack, would eventually join the same troop and both boys later became members of an elite division of the Scouts called the Order of the Arrow. Because of his devotion to Scouting, Jack would be-come an assistant Scoutmaster at the age of 18. He would re-main dedicated to the Scouting movement for 60 years, where he served as a Scout leader for more than half of those years. "The Boy Scouts have been my life," he would later tell me.

FOUR

WHETHER OR NOT my father or Jack had realized it at the time, the Boy Scouts of America also known as the BSA, had already been in existence in the United States for some 35 years. During that period, the BSA had established a rather long history and tradition of helping their fellow citizens by doing good turns. The organization would become one of the most successful youth movements in history. The Boy Scouts of America was first established in the United States and incorporated as a business in Washington, D.C. by Chicago newspaper publisher, William D. Boyce on February 8, 1910.

Born on June 16, 1858, Boyce grew up on a small farm in rural Plum County Pennsylvania where he developed an incredible work ethic and love for the outdoors. Educated at Wooster Academy in Ohio, he would later travel to Chicago, beginning his long career in publishing as a salesman for a local magazine. Having great success and a love for traveling, Boyce moved to Winnipeg, Canada where he co-founded a weekly newspaper about the Northwest Frontier. He would eventually move back to Chicago where he established several other weekly newspapers including the Saturday Blade in 1887. An enterprising man, Boyce hired approximately 30,000 boys to deliver his newspapers and developed a great understanding and compassion for the needs of America's young men.

Boyce was a multi-millionaire by the early 1900's and had developed a very successful publishing empire throughout many parts of the United States. Because of his vast business ventures and love for the great outdoors, he continued to travel throughout the world, often embarking on big game hunting adventures. By the time he reached the age of 51, Boyce became less interested in his pursuit of making money and began to focus his energies and great wealth toward community service.

According to historical accounts, Boyce was en route to East Africa to embark on a safari and had stopped in England in 1909. He became lost in London's dense fog while attempting to locate his hotel when out of the murkiness, a young boy in uniform appeared. Noticing that Boyce was lost, he offered to lead him to his destination. Afterwards Boyce tried to tip the young boy for his assistance but he refused, saying, he was only doing his duty as a Boy Scout and could not accept the gentleman's money for a good turn.

Boyce was so impressed with the young man's kindness that he asked him to tell him more about the Scouting organization. The "Unknown Scout," as Boyce would later refer to him as, directed the American publisher to the Boy Scout headquarters. He would soon make a personal visit and obtain information about the organization, including a copy of "Scouting for Boys," a handbook written by its founder and British war hero General Robert Baden-Powell or B-P as he was often referred.

"Scouting for Boys" was first published on January 15, 1908 and became the heart and soul of the Boy Scout movement in England. The Boy Scout handbook was the culmination of at least two of General Powell's earlier military training manuals he had written for his British Army Scouts. "Reconnaissance and Scouting," was first published in 1884. "Aids to Scouting," was later published in 1899 and became an instant hit with soldiers as well as boys interested in Scouting.

B-P's training manuals were used to teach his young military scouts basic frontier skills and survival techniques including camping, navigation, tracking and first aid. He emphasized the importance of leadership and self-reliance. Resourcefulness was a key element in each of Powell's training guides focusing on being prepared.

In July of 1899, B-P was on leave in London when he was given orders to return to South Africa to defend against a possible attack from the Dutch Boers. He strategically stationed his troops in the South African town of Mafeking. Anticipating an imminent attack from a military force much greater than his own which consisted of only 300 trained British soldiers and 300 volunteers, B-P took a defensive stance. He quickly established and fortified a six-mile perimeter around the town.

On October 13, 1899 the Boer Army launched a massive attack on Mafeking, besieging the British garrisons with over 6,000 soldiers equipped with powerful long range cannons. Colonel Powell utilized all of his resources, including a group of young boys called Cadets, for various duties as orderlies, messengers and lookouts. The Cadets ranging in age from 11 years and up had been organized into a group called the Mafeking Cadet Corp by a police sergeant. The Cadets grew into a group of nearly 40 boys and were led by an outstanding young man, 12-year-old Sergeant-Major Warner Goodyear. B-P made sure the boys were equipped with their own khaki uniforms including black stockings and wide-brimmed hats.

The boys were extremely proud of their contribution to the war effort and proved to be courageous as they carried out their assigned duties. They routinely would act as lookouts warning the town of an attack and delivered messages and mail in town and to outlying forts. The Cadets chose bicycles as their mode of transportation for their deliveries. The bicycle became a symbol of the Mafeking Cadets brave service to their town and a new postage stamp was created commemorating their fearless leader Warner Goodyear on his bike.

Baden Powell was so impressed with the Cadet's courage and performance that he would later praise them for their bravery in "CAMPFIRE YARN NO. 1" in the first chapter of "Scouting for Boys." The publication marked the beginning of the Boy Scout movement in England. In a conversation he had with one of his Mafeking Cadets, B-P writes: "I said to one of these boys on one occasion, when he came in through a rather heavy fire, "You will get hit one of these days riding about like that when shells are flying." And he replied, "I pedal so quick Sir, they'd never catch me."

After the war, Powell was surprised to find that his military training guide, "Aides to Scouting" was being widely read by boys and used by other youth group leaders across the country to teach the merits of scouting. His interest in helping the youth of his time had already been spurred by his involvement with the Mafeking Cadets. He realized that although young, the boys had a willingness to serve with useful enthusiasm and vigor. It was those traits that both intrigued and inspired B-P and became the driving force behind his formation of the Boy Scout movement in England.

Other influential men including Ernest Thompson Seton, and Daniel Carter Beard, were concerned about the youth of their time and the many young boys who were destined to poverty. In 1896 after having traveled throughout the world pursuing his passion for wildlife, Seton settled down in the United States and began writing about nature. During his travels, he had developed a knack for the outdoors and a deep respect for Native American Indian traditions. He wrote tirelessly about their lifestyle as well as his findings on nature, wildlife and living on the frontier.

In July of 1902, Seton formed a group called the Woodcraft Indians that organized boys into tribes, fashioned around his studies of American Indian lore. He would later write a guide for his Woodcraft Indian movement published in 1906 called, "The Birch-Bark Roll of the Woodcraft Indians." His writings and vision for his organization would eventually lend itself to the content and spirit of the Scout movements in England and the United States.

Having written the beginnings of his training guide, "Scouting for Boys," Baden Powell was now prepared to move forward with his campaign for the Boy Scout movement. He would hold an experimental camp on August 1, 1907 at Brownsea Island, England. The Scouts were issued khaki scarves and presented with a brass fleur-de-lis badge signifying the first use of the official Boy Scout emblem. After passing tests on camping and other outdoor skills, the Scouts were awarded another brass badge in the form of a scroll with the words, "Be Prepared," which would be adopted as the Boy Scout Motto.

On January 15, 1908 Powell would publish his Boy Scout handbook "Scouting for Boys." It became an instant success as thousands of enthusiastic boys and youth leaders across England and other countries devoured the material written by the celebrated war hero. The first part of the book was titled, "A Handbook for Instruction in Good Citizenship" and was organized into what he called Campfire Yarns.

B-P knew it was vitally important for the continued success of the new organization that he had to appeal to a boy's sense of play and adventure. His formula for success was working and by the end of 1909, there were more than 100,000 registered Boy Scouts in Great Britain. As Chief Scout of the World, B-P continued to be actively involved with the Scouting organization he had founded, and traveled to the United States in 1912 in an effort to help promote Scouting in America.

William Boyce had been inspired by what he had learned about B-P's Boy Scout organization and incorporated the Boy Scouts of America on February 8, 1910 in Washington DC. He believed strongly in the movement and was committed to making it a success. The YMCA had already established a few Scout troops using Baden Powell's manual "Scouting for Boys." Edgar Robinson, an executive with the YMCA, convinced Boyce to allow their organization to help structure the BSA and provide the needed leadership. Boyce was impressed with Robinson's dedication and extensive youth work and readily agreed to help fund the organization.

On June 1, 1910 Robinson opened a small one room national office for the Boy Scouts of America next to his own office at the YMCA building in New York City. Through his summer camp work, Robinson had become friends with Ernest Thompson Seton and asked him to merge his Woodcraft Indians into the BSA.

A new handbook was needed for the growing organization and Seton was the obvious choice to write it. He was instrumental in creating what has been called the first official Boy Scout of America handbook. Seton promoted a more naturalist way of teaching a Native American Indian method of Scout craft. Included in the original edition of the handbook are 50 pages taken from General Baden Powell's, "Scouting for Boys," and 100 pages of Seton's writings, from his earlier book, "The Birch-Bark Roll."

FIVE

I T'S UNCERTAIN whether or not young Scouts like my father and Jack in 1945 ever realized the incredible influence
men such as Baden Powell and William Boyce had on them. As
a young boy, I can vividly recall my father's stories of his
Scouting expeditions and the many camping trips with Jack.
Their incredible tales of adventure were magical. I listened in-
tently about how they traversed the hills and forests across
many parts of Illinois, Indiana and Wisconsin, with only a map
and compass to guide them.

My father's stories would be told at night under a starlit sky,
while sitting around a campfire after a day of fishing and hiking in the woods. He would reflect on his exploits of the past
while in the outdoors as a young boy. Both my father and Jack
would express their love and deep respect for nature and
stressed protection of the environment. They reminisced about
their intense involvement with the Scouts and their sacred experiences while in the Order of the Arrow. Proud of all its
pageantry, they danced wildly around a blazing campfire
dressed in their Indian costumes and headdresses.

My father and Jack's involvement in the Boy Scouts from an
early age was intense, and it was what they lived for. It was a
way of life for them. Their dedication to Scouting was evident
from the very beginning, when Sergeant Butkus first volunteered his time to the movement. Jack's compassion toward my
father had led to a lasting friendship and brotherhood formed
by furthering their Scouting experiences through the Order of
the Arrow. It was a bond that would last throughout their entire time spent in the Scouts and for a great many years as

adults. Jack would later tell me that he and my father, "Lived the Scout Law."

As a young boy, I could remember my father stopping on numerous occasions to help a stranded motorist who was stuck in a ditch after one of our Midwest's nasty snow storms. He would always have a large heavy duty chain in his car, and without hesitation would stop and help any poor soul who had managed to get themselves stuck. He did this good turn having learned the lesson of good citizenship as a Scout.

My father's involvement in the Scouts and the Order of the Arrow, molded his ideals toward nature and the manner in which he conducted his life. He had a great respect for nature and guarded the sanctity of it. He continued to practice and teach what he had learned from his many experiences with the Scouts the rest of his life. He was a pure environmentalist and some of his earliest teachings taught me and my siblings how to respect and protect nature. We learned to never harm or destroy it in any way and certainly never to litter. If my father ever saw you drop as much as a candy wrapper on the ground, you had better pick it up as instantaneously as you had dropped it, or face dire consequences.

We were on a family vacation in the early sixties and had gone to see the Hoover Dam. It was a period in our country's history before littering seemed to be a crime. I was with my father and the rest of our family on top of the dam overlooking the expansive beauty of Lake Mead. I heard my father ask another young boy to please pick up a candy wrapper he had witnessed the boy throw on the ground. The boy replied in a rude tone, "No!" and quickly ran away. My father not being a shy man, proceeded to follow the boy several steps to an area where his parents were standing. In a calm voice, he asked the boy once again to please pick up the candy wrapper he had just dropped. The boy refused and scampered away hiding behind his mother. At this point the boy's parents apparently not aware of what had occurred were starting to get upset with my father's gestures toward the boy. I could hear the boy's father raise his voice directing his anger toward my father.

A few minutes passed, and everyone seemed to settle down and my dad and the boy's father shook hands. Soon afterwards, the boy finally went over to where he had rudely dropped his candy wrapper and promptly picked it up off the ground and deposited it into his pocket. He then walked over to where my father was standing and apologized for his behavior, promising never to litter again.

The Order of the Arrow is an advanced level of Scouting based on the culture of the Delaware Indians. Jack was 16 years old when he was first inducted into the Order of the Arrow. My father was only 13 at the time. Paul Price who lived on the South Side of Chicago was in charge of my father's Order of the Arrow group. He was a rather gruff man and uncompromising in his ways and insisted on running the organization his way. He had no interest in anything the boys wanted to do.

In an effort to express their individuality, my father, and Jack started their own chapter of the Order of the Arrow. They called it the "Garrison Chapter." The new chapter was established for the Scouts that lived in the South West District. Each Boy Scout troop belongs to a lodge and the Scouts of the newly formed Garrison Chapter under Jack's guidance were of the Owasippe Lodge. They created a fantastic Indian dance team and performed many of their elaborate dances at Marquette Park in Chicago, while hundreds watched in amazement during Scout camporees.

The two young men had courageously started the chapter with only six boys and would build the group to over one hundred boys. Dressed in their impressive Indian garb, including colorful headdresses and war makeup, they performed intricate dances around huge bonfires they had built in Chicago's sprawling South Side park. As the crowds watched in awe, the Indians danced wildly through hoops of fire coated with heavy fuel oil citing their lines. The show was bolstered by a massive sound system my grandfather had set up. Both young leaders were disciplined in their guidance of their young braves. They always insisted that they memorize their lines and dance moves so that their performances would be the best it could be. The dance team became well known throughout several districts and would often draw large crowds.

Jack was the mighty chief of the Owasippe Lodge and proudly wore a full Indian headdress signifying his place in the order. My father was known as Meteu, the medicine man. The medicine man was considered the number two man who always had the chief's ear. He wore a large dark brown beaver fur hat with two large elk horns protruding outward. His fierce look was even more pronounced with his face painted black on one side and white on the other. Members of the Order of the Arrow are called Arrowmen, and are further identified by a white sash with a red arrow worn over their right shoulder.

They followed the Scout Law in its strictest sense and developed numerous work camps providing a useful service to their growing South Side community. They believed wholeheartedly in the principles of brotherhood and service to others and their community. These were teachings of Indian lore passed down to them throughout their time in the Scouts. "What goes around comes around" was one of the many lessons learned in the Order. "Reap what you sow," my father would often say to his young followers.

During the early years of Jack and my father's Scouting career, they were inseparable and went on numerous camping and fishing expeditions together. Later in life, they would continue to camp nearly every weekend involving both families. My father's lifelong friend Jack of whom I had known ever since I was a young boy, was now considered my "uncle Jack." It was said by many who knew them both, that my father and uncle Jack were mentally connected somehow and could feel each other's pain and often each one's sorrow. They were truly brothers.

My father's deep love and appreciation for nature was clearly passed on to me and my siblings. My uncle Jack, now an old warrior was always at our side as both families camped and enjoyed the outdoors. My uncle would later become very active in both of his own son's Scouting careers and would be their Scoutmaster for many years to come. David, the oldest, would eventually become an Eagle Scout, the highest rank bestowed upon a Boy Scout.

The mid to late 1900's were considered by my uncle Jack as the "changing years" where he felt that the Boy Scouts were basically the same organization but were starting to develop a major flaw. The Scouts were originally designed to be a youth run organization. The senior Scout leaders during this time began to take that important aspect away from the Scouts. "It seemed to be more about what the adult leaders wanted and the medals they might personally earn," he would say almost in disgust. The shift away from a "youth run" organization disturbed him as he recalled a similar struggle for freedom of expression during his youth when he and my father had been involved in the Order of the Arrow. "It's all about morality," he would later tell me, with a strong sense of conviction.

During the final days of my father and uncle's time together in the Order of the Arrow there were serious racial tensions beginning to erupt. Some troops were all white and some consisted of all black kids. It was a rather tumultuous time in Scouting and the South Side of Chicago seemed to harbor a growing sense of it. Tensions amongst black and white Scouts escalated. After my uncle relinquished his position as the chief of his lodge, he stayed on as a senior advisor to the Order of the Arrow for nearly two years. My father would then become the chief and assume his duties over the next two years. In an effort to further integrate the races and calm a growing racial divide, a colored man was assigned the task of senior advisor to the Order. Sadly, racial tensions became even more heightened. This is when my uncle made the difficult decision to get out. He was only 19 years old at the time.

Camping became a big part of my life growing up as the "son of a chief." Our family seemed to camp nearly every weekend, and most of that time was spent camping alongside my uncle's family. Throughout the many years that would follow, we camped in many states and in nearly every Illinois and Wisconsin state park. We started sleeping initially in tents and eventually graduated into a hotdog stand that my father and uncle converted into a crude camping trailer.

As time passed, my family purchased a 35 foot Yellow Stone trailer. We camped in it for many years, until one day when my father and I were nearly killed heading to White Pines State Park. It was a very windy day and my father was concerned that the trailer was beginning to sway back and forth on the road. He instructed me to get into the back seat. There were no seatbelts back then and even if there were, no one wore them as they were almost always buried under the seat cushions. As I was getting ready to jump over the front seat, we rounded a sharp corner, and someone in a hurry passed us at a high rate of speed nearly clipping the front of our car. My father grumbled some explicative as the trailer began to jerk back and forth in a wild almost Slinky-like motion. I was thrown over the front seat hitting my head on the back seat cushion. Unable to control the trailer, our Ford Station Wagon was violently jerked off the road into a ditch where we came to an abrupt stop, jackknifing the trailer. The crash shook up my father so much that he sold the trailer shortly after the incident, and our days of camping in a trailer abruptly ended.

After the accident, we started to tent camp again but that only lasted for about a year since my father's back began to act up on him. It wasn't too long afterwards that he would purchase a house trailer. He had convinced Chuck, the owner of Holiday Hollow Campground to let him park the trailer on a plot of ground next to a small stream. We all called the campground, "Chuck's Place" and it was located about a 100 miles southwest of our hometown of Wood Dale, Illinois. My father's house trailer at Chuck's Place became our summer home. It was a stark difference in camping styles, since having started our camping experience sleeping in tents. The main campground where our trailer was located was accessed by driving through several fords formed by a small creek that meandered throughout the property. The creek was a tributary of the Vermilion River some 10 miles to the south.

When the rains first started, my uncle Jack yelled over to me to put all of our camping chairs under the trailer to keep them from getting soaked. My father was in the trailer watching the Bears game. It was raining harder than I could ever remember and it didn't stop raining for nearly two hours. When the deluge finally seemed to subside, another wave of heavy rain hit the already water logged campground and the creek began to flood over its banks. The water continued to rise some 40 to 50 feet over its sandy banks engulfing nearly everything in its path. It was no longer a small creek and looked more like the mighty Vermilion.

The torrent of brown foamy water heading toward the Vermilion carried everything down with it, including folding chairs, coolers and even a few smaller trailers. My father's Bears game had been interrupted as water rushed unabated under the entire length of the trailer as the creek had now risen some 60 feet over its banks. In a desperate attempt to save the trailer from being swept down the rapids, he chained the metal hitch to a large nearby tree. The camp chairs I had carefully stored under the trailer were long gone. We had all evacuated the trailer and both of our families were standing soaked on higher ground. Several campers who realized that the flooding had completely cut them off from the rest of the campground, began to panic and made frantic attempts to call for help on their CB's.

My father had been trained in the Boy Scouts to never panic. He calmly told us that there was plenty of high ground and that the water level would never reach such heights. My uncle's Nomad trailer was parked on higher ground away from the raging creek and wasn't affected by the flooding waters. The 100 year rain event had started to subside and my father asked me to place a branch next to the creek's bank. Then we waited. After about 30 minutes it was clear that the water level was beginning to go down. The fords were still well under water and could not be crossed with a car. Chuck would eventually drive his John Deere tractor through the fords and rescue those that were upset and anxious to leave the campground.

Our house trailer had been spared up to this point as most of the debris floating down the creek had hit several small saplings shielding it from getting damaged. Just as we thought the trailer would be safe, a massive tree some five feet in diameter was heading straight for the center of the trailer at a high rate of speed. Without any hesitation, the huge tree rolled over the saplings like a bowling ball striking its pins. The giant tree with its massive girth tore through the center of our trailer like a hot knife in butter. This created a gigantic hole for the raging creek to begin its immediate assault on the interior of the trailer. It destroyed the center bedroom where my younger sister would normally sleep. My uncle Jack ran to the other side of the mangled trailer and yelled out to my father, "Good news, Paul came out the other side!" We were thankful the storm had not hit in the evening and no one was seriously injured.

The house trailer was a total loss and would mark the last time we would ever camp in a trailer. My mother, a year later, would locate a beautiful 15 acre piece of property located along the Vermilion River about five miles above the Streator Dam. The property had been owned by Nick Plane, an old railroad man. The small, white, one bedroom ranch sat high above the banks of the river.

We called our new summer place, "Rega's Riverview Ranch," and built a massive sign over the driveway with 30 foot telephone poles. It was the type of sign that you might see at a 200 acre spread out West somewhere. The Ranch would prove to be our family's opportunity to forge a new beginning, having left our damaged trailer behind on a hilltop overlooking Chuck's Place. Over the next several years, we would create many lasting memories at the Ranch. It was a wondrous place with many hiding places for an adventurous young boy to grow up. It signified our family's continuing and everlasting love of nature and the outdoors.

SIX

I T WAS EARLY MORNING on August 6, 1957 when I was faced with my first real challenge and struggle in life. I was born about a month premature and only weighed five pounds twelve ounces. An ounce or so before the doctors considered placing me into an incubator. Rather critical for the times and a scary thought as the medical technology of the mid 1950's was certainly archaic compared to what's available in today's modern world.

After surviving my initial brush with fate, my parents brought me home from Chicago's Garfield Park Community Hospital in my father's pizza delivery car, a late 1940's Chevy painted with the same colors as the Italian Flag. I think he must have thought it was a smart advertising move in an effort to help generate more business for his fledgling pizza parlor. My dad made a great pizza and won several awards for his master cookery. However, he had not yet honed his business skills in the early days of his career. To make matters worse, an unscrupulous business partner was stealing money from him. As a result, his pizza place soon went out of business and he was faced with trying to find another job to support his new family.

After suffering the loss of his first business, my father was able to secure a job at a corrugated box company and initially worked as a utility man in the factory and would later move into a sales role with the same company. My father, the oldest of five children had grown up on the South Side of Chicago in what was at the time a mostly Italian neighborhood. My mother had grown up in the small town of Evergreen Park, dominated by mostly people of Irish and German descent. My parents first met when they were both 19 years old while attending the Chicago Teachers College. By the early age of 20, they decided to get married as they were expecting me. My mother had been studying nursing at the time but soon dropped out to raise her new family. My father had been enrolled in a business curriculum but due to the financial pressures of raising a family, also dropped out of college. Most people got married very young in those days with an average age being in the early twenties. For the most part, people stayed married even if the couple was miserable, as divorce was very rare and carried a stigma for both men and women.

During the first few years of my life my family lived in a small two bedroom apartment on the South Side of Chicago and later moved to the tiny village of Crete, a far south suburb of Chicago. As the result of a failed business and the monetary pressures of a family beginning to grow in numbers, my father's finances began to suffer. In an effort to survive, my parents decided to move into my grandmother's basement apartment located on Hermitage Avenue on Chicago's South Side. At four years old, this is where the memories of my earliest childhood and the lessons from my father, a former Boy Scout would begin.

I was surrounded by excellent cooks, and from an early age helped to prepare many different and exotic foods influenced by my father's Italian heritage, and my mother's German descent. Raw clams, squid and homemade Italian sausage, with ravs and a variety of other pastas smothered in red and white sauces were part of the menu. It was my family's custom, upon turning five years old, to suck down a raw clam from its shell and swallow it whole. The tradition always followed a toast with my father and uncles. I can remember gagging a bit on my first experience, but have enjoyed this custom around the holidays ever since. Living in my grandmother's basement had its benefits. My aunt Liz, who was only six years older than I was and more like a big sister, would walk me down to the corner store and allow me to fill up my brown paper bag with penny candy. A dollar back then bought a lot of candy of all shapes and sizes.

We always seemed to have enough money for our jaunts to the candy store and most other things, but money was tight for my parents during this time. My grandfather, Paul was born in America in 1910, and was one of 24 kids born to my great grandparents, Luigi and Josephine Rega. Tragically, a number of his siblings would soon die having been afflicted with the 1918 flu pandemic, otherwise known as the Spanish flu that killed an estimated fifty to one-hundred million people. Most were young, otherwise healthy adults, making it one of the most deadly natural disasters in human history.

"There seemed to always be a coffin in the family's living room," one of my father's aunts would later say as she described the horror to me. My grandfather escaped death from the flu and was the youngest of four boys and twenty girls. Unfortunately, he would pass away at the age of 47 after battling heart disease for several years. He had suffered rheumatic fever as a young boy and it was suspected that his heart had been damaged by the disease.

My father's aunt Annie married a relatively ambitious Sicilian by the name of Pete Ambrosino who first ran alcohol for Capone and later graduated to making wine in his bathtub. That built him a stake to start his own business, and when my father was nine, the Ambrosino Italian Market was a landmark in Little Italy on the South Side of Chicago.

The store was walking distance from my grandmother's house. With our red Radio Flyer wagon in tow, I would sit impatiently during a several block trek to where my grandmother would do most of her grocery shopping. My great aunt and her husband, Uncle Pete would look forward to me and my grandmother's weekly visit. When my aunt Liz turned nine, she would often bag groceries at the store and she would already be working when we arrived. She loved the store, especially since she could snack on Lu Lu Beans, an Italian delicacy the size of a quarter and an occasional Italian Ice.

It was an old store in the heart of what was mostly and Italian neighborhood. Its wooden planked floors creaked as you walked across them releasing a pungent aroma of oregano, basil and garlic into the air. Many other dried spices and exotic Italian seasonings were everywhere stored in open bins. Several large wooden barrels of fruits and vegetables, as well as olives, peanuts and beans were stored in large wooden barrels strewn throughout the store.

Uncle Pete, who was rather slim, had quite a different build than his wife, and at 5'5" had a pretty ferocious temper. He had dark brown eyes and jet black hair that was always combed straight back with gobs of grease. He watched over the open barrels of peanuts like a hawk, waiting to catch anyone that dared steal anything, while my aunt tended to the customers. When he suspected that a theft had occurred, he would rush over and stand with his arms crossed, yelling at the kids to get the peanuts out of their pockets.

There were several wooden barrels of live snails throughout the store. As I walked down the aisles, I would have to step over some of them that had crawled out of the barrels. One of my aunt Liz's dreaded jobs was to arrive about a half hour before the store opened so she could collect all the snails that had escaped from the barrels. Numerous kinds of cheeses and lunch meats were aligned in neat rows, stored behind a glass encasement. Dried and salted Bacalhau, along with several varieties of cheeses and salami hung by thin white string from the rafters, permeating the air with the pungent smells of Italy.

Customers would fill their own brown paper bags full of spices, some falling to the ground and disappearing into the cracks of the wooden floor. I had my first experience eating a whole cucumber when my aunt Annie, who was quite a cook, offered me a cucumber out of one of the wooden barrels. She cut off the end and sprinkled it with salt and said, "Here Pauly, take a bite!" The fresh taste of cucumber and salt exploded in my mouth.

My father's memories of his aunt and uncle's store were not as fond as my aunt Liz's however. He was often instructed as a young boy by my grandfather to take his wagon down the streets of old Chicago and pick up some of the rotting fruits and vegetables that couldn't be sold in the store. This trip would prove to be different. The ritual always seemed to be the same -- across Paulina, down two alleys, up to the side yard where the rotten vegetables were stored, ready for the garbage truck the next day. Heaped on my dad's wagon could go three, four or sometimes five bushels of tomatoes, peaches, and peppers.

This time, my father had been instructed to go into the store and ask Aunt Annie for a package for his daddy. As he entered into the store, my aunt, all 300 pounds of her, was behind the counter where she rarely left her oversized chair. "My father says you have a package for him," he said quietly, hoping Uncle Pete wouldn't hear him. Looking like a fugitive and noticing Uncle Pete across the other side of the store, she quickly passed the package around the other side of the counter and said, "Ok, now go!" Before my father could make it out of the store, Uncle Pete came running over and snatched the package from his hands, tore it open, and started throwing the ends of dried out, old salamis, at Aunt Annie screaming, "Beggar, beggar, beggar!"

My father, now crying, ran out of the store through a side door, leaving his wagon full of rotten fruit and vegetables behind. He didn't stop running until he got home where he would encounter my grandfather who wasn't pleased that he had failed to bring home the package. My father wanted desperately to escape the old neighborhood, and erase the memories of a young boy growing up poor in Chicago. The early lesson would serve to shape his thinking as an adult, and motivate him for the rest of his life.

SEVEN

I N MY FATHER'S EFFORT to save enough money to purchase a house, my family continued to live in my grandmother's basement until the early part of 1963. With the
arrival of my new sister, Robin, I think my grandmother was at
her wits end with three young kids living in her basement.
With her help in the form of a small loan, my parents were
able to purchase their first house.

The move was rather traumatic for me even though I was
only five years old at the time. I was attending O'Toole Elementary School on Seeley Avenue, a short seven block walk
from my grandmother's house. My aunt Liz, who was only 11
years old would escort me to school every day where we had
to cross Chicago's busy Damon Avenue. If I behaved myself
during our walks, she would often buy me a large piece of taffy
after school from the corner store for five cents.

It was mid-afternoon and I was taking a nap on my rug next
to a cute little blond girl I had become friends with, when my
mother walked in, and rather abruptly, picked me up from
school. My parents had apparently decided to pull me out of
kindergarten before the day had ended. I never returned to
O'Toole Elementary or even had an opportunity to say good-
bye to my friends. After our move, my mother, never enrolled
me into another kindergarten class.

Our family of five, including my younger brother, Mark and
new born sister, moved to the small town of Oak Forest, Illinois
that year. It was a tiny suburb about 24 miles southwest of
downtown Chicago. The house my parents purchased was
brand new construction but was only partially finished. My father being very handy was able to save a substantial amount of

money by completing the necessary interior work needed to finish the house. He and my uncle Jack, who was an electrician, worked on the house diligently nearly every day. They completely finished building the house by doing all the necessary electrical, plumbing and drywall work so we could move in. The small two bedroom, one bath, ranch was mostly wood construction with white aluminum siding and dark brown wood trim. It was built on a concrete slab with a one-car garage where we kept our washer and dryer and an extra refrigerator.

We had one black and white TV in the living room in a beautiful dark mahogany wood cabinet in a single unit that was combined with a radio and record player. With the exception of Saturday mornings, when our favorite cartoons such as Bugs Bunny and The Road Runner were on for a few hours, my entire family watched the same TV programs. If there had been a remote there was little use for it since there were only a handful of channels.

Since we only had one TV in our house, we almost always watched the programs my father wanted to see when he would get home from work. My dad's favorite programs were Perry Mason and the Honeymooners, and we almost never missed a Chicago Bears game. If a channel needed to be changed, I was the one assigned to the task since my father trusted me around his prized TV. I didn't watch very much television as a young boy, as I was always outside running around playing army with the Bollinger kids or in the sandbox building roads for my matchbox cars with my metal Tonka Trucks.

I loved to watch The Three Stooges, but my father was a very strict disciplinarian with high morals and hated the show. He thought it would contribute to us becoming juvenile delinquents. It was widely reported at the time that juvenile delinquency amongst teenagers was on the rise. The epidemic was thought to be caused by an increase in violence on TV and in comic books. My father so despised The Three Stooges that he once removed the picture tube in the TV so we couldn't watch it.

Our television entertainment was very limited in those days with only a handful of channels. If you wanted to see a new movie, you had to go to the movie theater. The VCR wasn't introduced until 1972. On rare occasions, my dad would pull out his home movies that he had shot using an 8 mm camera. If we behaved through the movies, he would run Woody Wood Pecker, the only kid's movie with sound my father owned. It was a great movie and I really looked forward to watching it despite having seen the same movie dozens of times. I can still hear Woody's crazy cackle and laugh and reflect back to those days when we appreciated what we had, and seldom asked for more.

The fifties Baby Boom was closely followed by a housing boom, where homeownership rose dramatically. The tiny town of Oak Forest was in the early stages of a population explosion. Our neighborhood of Fieldcrest was comprised of very modest two and three bedroom homes built on slabs. A sodded yard was not one of the options the builder provided. Our yard was mostly dirt and sparsely covered patches of grass. My father built a small swing set for us out of heavy metal pipes that he painted bright red. It had a few swings, a ladder and a metal battleship gray glider.

In an attempt to save as much money as possible, my father was quite industrious and very self-sufficient with most of his projects. He was an accomplished carpenter as well as an excellent handyman and knew how to use many different types of tools. He would often tackle huge jobs, which only a few people today would even dream of attempting. Throughout my entire youth, he taught me the proper use of tools and why using the right tools for the job was important. One such project my father and I tackled was the construction of a massive sandbox we built with seats on each corner and a sloping shingled roof. We would often use the sandbox as a fort while playing our endless games of army. When we would eventually move from our house in Oak Forest, my father tried desperately to take the sandbox with us but it was so large that it didn't quite fit in the truck.

My father's early lessons with tools would serve me well throughout the rest of my life. As a young boy, I would often enjoy building everything ranging from a tree fort to a skateboard made out of a section of two by four and old roller skate wheels. As early as five and six years old, I was already handy with many basic tools and was always tinkering with my old bicycle, trying to keep it in tip top shape.

I played army with my friends and dreamed about being a soldier someday. My younger brother and I played nearly every day in the large open fields behind our house. I would strategically position myself on top of the dirt hills wearing my green plastic army helmet, firing on the enemy below with my machine gun. At five years old I was already pretty independent and even somewhat of an explorer. I can remember being very mobile and, unbeknownst to my mother, would often walk quite a distance away from our house exploring my surroundings.

For a young curious boy of five, there was a lot to explore ranging from new home construction to what laid behind the Oak Forest Hospital. The hospital was a massive complex bordered by 159th Street to its north and Cicero Avenue to the west. It was hot sticky day in July, sometime before my sixth birthday. I had never ventured this far away from my house or so close to the hospital before. Strewn across a large open field of overgrown grass and weeds near the back of the hospital were what looked to be hundreds of green plastic bags. Some were stacked on top of each other and others were torn open reveling garbage and rotting food from the hospital's cafeteria.

I found myself getting so close to what I thought must be the back of the hospital that I could clearly see two small metal doors, one on each side of the reddish brick exterior. Above the doors were several large white windows where I could see interior lights shining through. There was a large plume of black smoke streaming out an old brick chimney attached to one side of the hospital. I could smell a heavy, nauseating stench that must have been enhanced by the 95°F heat that day.

My heart began to beat faster as I got closer to the back of the hospital. I started to crouch down closer to the ground and began to crawl on my belly the same way I had seen soldiers do it on TV. As I got closer to the hospital walls, I came upon more green plastic bags. Moving ever so slowly, I started to stand up in an effort to get a better look at the hospital. My entire body was immediately swarmed by dozens of huge black flies. Swatting the flies away from my face, I started to move quickly toward the hospital having to step over several more bags of garbage that obstructed my path.

Most of the bags close to the hospital had been ripped open by what I thought must have been a raccoon or some other large animal in search of food. The garbage was scattered everywhere and I could see amongst the decaying food, plastic surgical gloves covered with brownish dried blood and used syringes some with their needles still attached. I could hear in the distance an older man's voice yelling something, but was confident he hadn't spotted me as I quickly darted around the plastic bags crouching and hiding behind a small clump of bushes.

I sat motionless, not making a sound for several minutes, until I didn't hear the man's voice any longer. With my curiosity now heightened, I wanted to get a better look at the hospital. As I turned away from my hiding place, my right foot struck something hard. I stumbled forward nearly falling over a large black dog that must have been dead for several days. Flies and other insects were swarming over it and covered its stiffened body. The stench of rotting flesh immediately sickened me and I nearly threw up. I started to run as fast as I could back toward my house trying not to trip over other bags of garbage and debris that littered the area. It was a frightening experience and I never dared to venture back to the hospital or even share my harrowing experience with my parents. I was sure that the dog had died as the result of ingesting something poisonous.

My father having been in the Boy Scouts for many years was also an explorer and was always seeking out new wilderness fishing and camping adventures for us to go on. I was sure I had inherited this exciting but potentially dangerous tendency from him. I had learned to love and respect nature during many of our early trips together. I was determined to be the best outdoorsman and camper possible. As a young boy, I started fishing from the banks of several small lakes in the area using a large bamboo pole that my father had given to me. My younger brother, Mark, and I had a rather unique fishing style as I can remember squatting very low to the ground with our long bamboo poles firmly in hand. We had a serious look on our faces with all the intent in the world on catching a fish. Usually our boyish impatience of a three and five year old never seemed to lend itself well to catching many fish in the early days of our adventures. We had a lot of fun trying though.

Our family started camping together in a large eight-person canvas tent my father had purchased at Sears. The tent always seemed to leak whenever it rained no matter how much water repellant my father had applied to it. In the early days of our camping adventures my family would often camp with my uncle Jack and his family. My uncle and his wife, who we affectionately called Aunt Gail, were also my godparents and had two boys of their own close in age to my brother and me. We camped together nearly every other weekend and I became very close friends with my uncle's two boys and would later canoe and camp with them as young adults. David, the older of the two brothers, became very active in the Boy Scouts and achieved the rank of Eagle, the highest level of Scouting possible.

My father was getting tired of sleeping on the ground in our leaky tent and had always wanted a camping trailer similar to the comfortable Nomad my uncle Jack had bought. Unfortunately, his finances were still very tight since he had just purchased a house. However, my father was a very resourceful and industrious man and despite his tight budget was determined to buy a trailer. Later that year, he purchased an old 1950's hotdog trailer and decided to convert it into our new camping trailer. The trailer was in pretty bad shape and was only about 12 feet long with a single axle and two balding tires. It would be rather small for a camping trailer especially for a family of five, but my father was pretty ingenious and would make it work. The trailer had one large window located on the front side that was used to serve its previous owner's customers their hotdogs and soda. The exterior of the trailer was constructed of mostly wood, and was bolted onto a rusty metal chassis. Parts of the wooden frame had started to rot. The exterior was painted mostly red and white with a large picture of a hotdog and all of its colorful condiments on the front of the trailer.

The help and skills of my uncle Jack were called into action once again as my father's plan to convert a hotdog stand into a camping trailer had begun. It was another major project as the entire inside of the trailer had to be gutted and rebuilt. They built two sets of bunk beds, one considerably larger than the other to accommodate my father's large stature. He was a big man and quite an intimidating figure with jet-black hair and dark brown eyes that protruded from their sockets. His massive 6'2''frame, weighed some 300 pounds, and his loud booming voice demanded your attention.

My uncle replaced the door that was nearly falling off its rusty hinges. He cut new holes for additional windows and added an adjustable dome type vent in the roof for added air circulation. My father was on a mission and had declared a deadline to complete the renovation as he had plans to take the trailer on its maiden voyage. It would be an ambitious trip that would take us completely around Lake Michigan. My uncle had talked my father into covering the outside of the trailer with a bright silver colored aluminum siding to protect it from the elements. It was a great idea except for the fact that on the day they had planned to side the trailer, a total solar eclipse was about to occur.

It was an amazing sight as my mother tried in vain to push me inside the house so I wouldn't go blind as I tried to watch this rare event. The sun's intense rays bounced off the bright aluminum siding like giant mirrors, nearly blinding my father and uncle. "The Silver Trailer" as we frequently called it was born, and our first major camping trip, an adventurous journey around Lake Michigan was soon approaching.

We left in early August, sometime before my sixth birthday, and headed east toward the Indiana Dunes State Park located along Lake Michigan. I had never seen sand dunes before. I was stunned by their immense size, some rising 125 feet above the lake, appearing like small mountains planted in the Midwest. For the next several days we traversed north traveling into the state of Michigan, through several small towns, and up the eastern shore of the lake. The further north we got, the more wooded and desolate sections of our path became, dotted by sparsely populated towns.

Crossing the massive five-mile Mackinac suspension bridge that connects the upper and lower peninsula of Michigan was a spectacular but terrifying experience. My father told us that five people had fallen to their deaths during construction. The bridge was an engineering marvel and was relatively new when we crossed it, having only been open for service since 1957. It's the longest bridge of its kind in North America and sits some 200 feet above the cold windswept waters of the Straights of Mackinac, where Lake Michigan and Lake Huron connect.

Having successfully crossed over the great bridge, we were now in Michigan's Upper Peninsula and the landscape had changed dramatically. We camped in the Hiawatha National Forest, a majestic wilderness rich in wildlife including white tail deer, turkey and black bear. My father cautioned us not to wander off alone as the bear population was rather high in the area. It was early morning and we had just finished a hearty breakfast of pancakes, Italian sausage, and scrambled eggs that my father had cooked on a two burner Coleman stove.

My parents were anxious to take off, so we quickly broke camp and were heading west toward our next destination driving slowly up a steep, curvy section of the road. Suddenly my ears were deafened by a loud and high pitched screeching noise. The back of our 1953 Plymouth station wagon began to shake violently nearly jerking us off the road. My father uttering some explicative I had never heard before, immediately pulled over to the side of the road. He quickly jumped out of the car to check for any apparent problems. To his shock the entire left wheel of our trailer had nearly fallen off and a dense cloud of black smoke started to surround the wheel and undercarriage of the trailer.

My father yelled, "Get out of the car!" He rushed to get his fire extinguisher that he had always carried in the trunk. Thankfully, he was able to extinguish whatever fire may have started as a result of the wheel nearly falling off. Although I never saw any flames and my father never said there was an actual fire, I was pretty certain there had been one. Whatever had burned, had stung my eyes and was now inside my nose and sickened me. He was pretty shaken by the experience and threatened to leave the trailer by the side of the road and continue on without it. I could hear the fear in my mother's voice, as she whispered in my father's ear saying that she was thankful no one had been seriously injured. She was relieved that the accident hadn't occurred while crossing the Mackinac Bridge. Apparently, the problem with the wheel was the result of a bad axel that predated the trailer itself and had to be completely replaced before we could continue on our journey. Fortunately there was a small town nearby where a mechanic had access to spare parts at a local junkyard and was able to repair the old trailer.

The rest of our trip went relatively well, until my father announced that we were starting to run out of money due to our axle mishap. He explained to us that we had to carefully budget our money so we would have enough for gas to get us back home and still be able to buy enough food to feed our hungry brood. After finishing another one of my father's great breakfasts, he stood up and said that we had two choices. We could make the decision to eat better by spending two dollars a day and stay for a shorter period of time, or spend a dollar a day and not eat as well, but could stay longer. Nearly everything cost much less in those days. Gasoline was only about 30 cents a gallon, and milk cost just 49 cents a gallon.

We all made the decision to stay longer and despite the near tragedy with our trailer, had learned some valuable lessons in life and how to always be prepared for potential problems. My father had taught us how to stay calm, and act quickly in a difficult and potentially life threatening situation. He had also taught us how to budget money, and as a result of our experiences that summer, we had one of the best and most memorable vacations of our lives.

EIGHT

———————————

I HAD TURNED six years old while on our trip around Lake Michigan. Soon after we returned, I started first grade at Highlands Elementary School in the small town of Hazel Crest, Illinois. It would be my first experience riding a school bus. I was a bit apprehensive about going back to school after having been so abruptly pulled out of kindergarten. My new teacher was an older lady who was quite large in stature that intimidated most of the students with her loud bellowing voice. She had been teaching school from what must have been the beginning of time I thought. She appeared much older than even my own mother. It was a large class of twenty-five students consisting of mostly boys and seven girls. A real handful for any one person and I am sure it's why my teacher, who looked more like a linebacker on the Chicago Bears, was assigned to this class.

For our class picture, several of the boys wore ties and some even had on suit coats, while all the girls wore dresses and curled their hair. All of the boy's haircuts were very short, with mine among the shortest, sporting a crew cut. It was my father's favorite style of haircut and he always cut mine and my brother's hair with his own barber's clippers that he had purchased at Sears. My great grandfather, Luigi had been a barber in Italy, and I think my father thought he had an inherent talent for cutting hair.

My father was always looking to better himself professionally. He had made a major career move into sales with the same boxboard company he had been working for over the past several years. His boss, a Greek by the name of Angelo Minotis, encouraged him to take several business courses at

Northwestern University. There he would meet Maynard Garfield who owned a consulting business and was teaching a few business courses on sales technique. My father did very well in Mr. Garfield's classes achieving nearly perfect grades and was soon offered a job with his company. The sales position my father accepted required a great deal of travel and he needed to be close to a major airport. It was March 1963, when my parents once again made the decision to move. This time we moved to Wood Dale, Illinois and it would be an even more traumatic event for me, as I had only been in first grade for about seven months. I did not want to transfer to another school in the middle of the year.

Despite my apprehension of going to a different school, I was excited about moving into our new house located at 243 Harvey Avenue. My father was concerned about the cost of our new house saying that he thought $25,000 was far more than he had ever expected to pay for a house. Our move would take us quite a distance north, passing several towns along the way. I was sure I would never see my friends or neighbors, the Bollinger kids again.

Our new two-story house was constructed of mostly brick and dark brown wood trim with a large picture window in the front. It was considerably bigger than our ranch, although it had the same number of bedrooms. It had one bathroom, a living room, and a dining room that was directly off the kitchen. At the back of the house we had a sunroom where we put our only TV. My parents loved this part of the house because they could observe the wildlife often present in our backyard. Unfortunately, it was the coldest part of the house, since it was a tile floor and situated over a part of the basement that wasn't insulated.

It was the first time since having lived with my grandmother Rega in Chicago that I had been down in a basement. It was much larger than my grandmother's basement with several small cavernous rooms separated by old wooden plank doors that creaked as you opened them. I would soon explore nearly every corner of our new basement on my quest to find even more hiding places. On the upper level of the house, there was a massive attic that spanned the entire structure of the house. The attic was one of the main reasons my father had purchased this particular house as he saw a great deal of potential for expansion.

A good friend of my father's by the name of Mel Damesworth, looked a lot like Elvis Presley, with his slicked back jet black hair. Together, they would eventually transform this dusty attic into a huge dormitory style bedroom. It featured separate sleeping quarters for my brothers and me, a private bedroom for my sister and a second bathroom. Not only did Mel look a lot like Elvis, he talked like him too, as he was originally from the hills of Kentucky and had a very distinct southern twang. He and his wife, Helen, were very genuine people having come to the Chicago area several years earlier in search of better jobs. Helen worked for the Wilson Sporting Goods factory in the city and would always give us new basketballs and other sporting equipment for Christmas. Mel had worked aside my father for many years in the boxboard factory in the maintenance department. He was as my father described him, "The most talented and skilled mechanic I have ever seen."

Our new yard was immense and nearly an acre in size. It was bordered with tall thick bushes on nearly every side of the property and several massive evergreens that rose up over a hundred feet into the air. The thick green needled branches at the bottom of the tree sprawled several feet from the trunk covering the ground. It would be another perfect hiding place, I thought. I wanted to quickly unpack my army gear and begin to explore my new surroundings. Near the back of our house, we had a brick two car detached garage with several paned windows. A large double wooden door swung upwards on huge metal hinges that squeaked as the old springs labored to open the door. Toward the back of the yard was an old grape arbor that was still producing grapes. The thick shaggy grape vines were supported by several large green four inch steel pipes connected like giant tinker toys spanning across the yard. This was truly a magical place and offered boundless possibilities for an adventurous six-year-old boy on a mission.

Our massive shed that looked nearly as big as our last house, was directly behind the garage. It had originally been used as a chicken coop and was completely constructed out of old World War II ammunition boxes. I decided that the shed would be one of my first forts because of its long military history literally written on the walls. The wood from the boxes were mostly uniform in size and only about a foot and a half in length and an inch thick. It appeared very old and brittle with very little dry rot even though it had been exposed to all the elements for years. I marveled over the giant jigsaw puzzle of ammunition boxes that made up the ceiling and walls, spanning several feet across and nailed to old two by fours. We stored everything in our new shed from my mother's gardening tools to our bikes and my father's Gravely lawn tractor.

One of my father's first projects was to build a massive fire pit some 20 feet in circumference surrounded by huge boulders. It was our burning pile, as my family would call it. It was strategically placed behind our shed and surrounded on two sides by tall thick bushes you couldn't see through. It was a perfect spot for the many nighttime ghost stories and tales my father and uncle Jack would tell us. As we sat around the raging bonfire, often roasting hot dogs and marshmallows, our eyes would be wide open in anticipation of the many wilderness stories soon to be told. I imagined real Indians dancing around the fire, as my father and uncle spoke of their Indian dance team and how they would dress up in their costumes and perform at their Order of the Arrow campouts. My uncle scared us numerous times as my father would begin to tell a tale, usually of a massive man eating bear in the woods. Just at the right moment, my uncle who had secretly slipped away, would jump out of the bushes and scare the living daylights out of us.

Wood Dale was a great place to grow up. It was small, quiet Midwestern town with a population slightly above 3,000 people with very little industry. The Winnebago Indians originally from the central and north Atlantic coast were being forced further and further west but refused to move beyond the Wisconsin River. They made claim to the area in the early 1800's and would often establish camp near Salt Creek and set fire to the surrounding prairie forcing the animals into the nearby forests where their hunters lay waiting.

The first white settler, Hezekiah Dunklee, a native of New Hampshire was drawn to the area because of its rich farmland and boundless wildlife. He arrived in the area in 1833 making claim to both prairie and forest near Salt Creek and Irving Park Road. His initial attempts to farm the prairie were futile as he soon realized the ground was nearly impossible to penetrate with his crude farm implements. In order to grow crops and survive the harsh prairie winters, he was forced to cut down trees and farm the fertile soil of the forest.

Like the early settlers, my parents were also drawn to the area because of their love for nature including the forests and wildlife. The tiny village of Itasca, bordered us to the west, while Bensenville, a larger town was to our east. We were relatively close to O'Hare Airport and could hear many of the jets fly overhead as they took off or prepared to land. The people of Wood Dale were friendly and the town offered a good wholesome and safe place to raise a family. My father was only 28 years old when we moved and began what would be a life-long career as a business consultant working for Maynard Garfield. As a young boy during the 10 years that my family lived in Wood Dale, I developed many close friendships in the town and would later become very active in sports and various Scouting organizations, including my father's beloved Boy Scouts.

Soon after our move, reality struck early Monday morning when I realized that I had to go back to school. I had never even seen the school, but was told that I was going to be attending Westview Elementary, about a half-mile walk from our house. I figured a school bus like the one I had just gotten used to riding, was not going to be picking me up any time soon. My first day would prove to be a very traumatic experience. I didn't want to go to another school and be the new kid again. I resisted and my mother had to drag me across several of our neighbor's acre sized yards in her quest to get me to go to school. Unfortunately, she succeeded, and suddenly I was the new kid sitting in a classroom being stared at by all the other kids It was a frightening and humiliating experience, but I had always been an outgoing kid and soon made friends.

During the earliest days at Westview Elementary, I was mostly concerned with how many cat's eye and blue boulder puris I had in my marble bag. We played marbles nearly every day we went out for recess. When I wasn't playing marbles I had developed an elaborate road system in the dirt for all my Matchbox cars and trucks. I loved recess and getting outside and always dreaded when we had to go back into the school.

It was also during this time of my young life that the neighbor boy, Scott Cesar who was almost two years older than me would tell me that Santa Claus was in reality, my parents. His older sister had apparently broken the news to him at an early age. I was devastated by his admission and ran home almost in tears asking my mother if what he had said was true. My boyhood innocence of having just turned seven had been deflated and I was no longer a believer.

My father disliked Scott from the beginning. He thought he was a juvenile delinquent and a bad influence on me since he was from a broken family, often running wild throughout the neighborhood. He lived with his mother, who worked during most of the day and his older sister. Divorce in those days was still quite rare and seen as a taboo, and those involved were often shunned. I never saw Scott's father, who was an electrician, in all the years we lived in Wood Dale. Their house and property around it was usually in poor condition and mostly unkempt. Scott's yard would provide excellent hiding places, and his dad had left an old Cabin Cruiser we would play pirates on.

With his dislike of Scott, my father tried for months to keep us from playing with each other, but found it nearly impossible. My father was desperate to keep us apart and one evening when he caught Scott and I playing a game of hide and seek, he cornered him between our shed and the garage. It was a place my father had chosen carefully because no other eyes or ears would be present. He warned him that if he continued playing with me, he would kill him and cut his body up in little pieces and distribute them under our shed where no one would ever know of his whereabouts. A warning, I think Scott must have taken seriously, as there were several months where we didn't play together. After some time had passed, despite my father's ominous threat and often harsh discipline toward me, Scott and I continued to play with each other. We would remain good friends throughout the many years we lived in Wood Dale. After a few years, my father seemed to soften his approach toward Scott and took him with us to the YMCA and helped to teach him how to swim.

My father was a very strict disciplinarian and some of my first experiences with his belt across my bare ass were experienced as the result of my defiance toward him in regards to playing with Scott. Discipline was rather harsh in those days and it was common for your dad to use a belt or even a stick. I would be instructed to pull my pants down and place my hands on my father's bed, as he would proceed to strike me repetitively across my small and mostly bony bottom. I can remember screaming, "No more!" and he would yell in response, "One more time!" I feared his wrath and the severe pain he would often inflict on me to such a degree that anytime I found myself in trouble, I would often cry and tremble in anticipation of an impending beating.

My father was a large man, some 300 pounds, and his leather belt was thick. The unmistakable sound of his belt as he pulled it out of the belt loops was nearly enough for me to pass out before any beating even began. His fierce temper had been inherited from my grandmother and he adopted her harsh disciplinary measures. The nuns were typically the front lines of discipline at the Catholic schools where my father had grown up. His brother, Joe, had experienced their brutality, when a stick wielding nun dressed in a traditional black habit broke his hand.

As a young student of Catholicism, my father had been roped into being an altar boy for Father Angelo, a Catholic Priest at St. Mary's of Mt. Carmel, who had salami breath and a bad temper. When my father misbehaved, he would be marched into Father Angelo's office and be instructed to bend over and grab his ankles. This 5'7" two-hundred and fifty pound priest would then unleash his brutality on my father's ass.

Father Angelo's beatings were becoming more regular and the ferocity was increasing. One Sunday morning after the last mass of the day, a beating my father was about to endure, would be his last. He had been caught earlier using his pocketknife to carve the words, "God slept in the park last night, because the church was locked," into the metal of one of the bathroom stalls. After being escorted up to Father Angelo's office by Brother Don, my father bent over in what was now a familiar position.

This devil of a man removed his belt and began whopping and whopping until the beating would be too much for my father to bear. Screaming, "No more, no more!" he stood up and ran as quickly as he could out of the church across 67th street and through the alley. Following closely behind was Brother Don, a slave of Father Angelo. When my father got home, he retreated to his basement, where he thought he could hide. There was no phone, but the message came quickly to his mother who took up the beating where Father Angelo had left off.

Discipline continued to follow me throughout my childhood and early days of school, where large thick wooden paddles made of oak and painted with black lacquer were crafted in our middle school shop class. These ominous looking paddles had several holes drilled through them enhancing the pain and increasing the speed across ones derrière. They were common-place in most public and Catholic middle schools often hanging on a hook in clear view near the blackboard. I personally became to know this fact all too well. My friends and I, mostly out of fear during our early childhood, learned quickly to respect all authority figures, including our parents and teachers. We were taught to listen and obey them without question or debate. It never occurred to me to talk back to my father or a teacher, as I knew a beating might follow.

NINE

IN THE early part of August 1965, I turned eight years old and my mother promptly enrolled me in the local Cub Scouts, Wood Dale Pack 34. Maybe she thought she would get rid of me for a few hours a month. During our first pack meeting, she was asked to be a den mother. She had always enjoyed volunteering for various events while we lived in Oak Forest. Not able to say no, she became my first den mother. She apparently didn't know what she was getting herself into, and was not mentally prepared to deal with a brood of eight and nine year old boys, as they descended upon our house during our first den meeting.

Scouting was in my father's blood and someone in his family was going to be involved in the Scouts, it just wasn't going to be my mother. She was not den mother material, as she could barely handle my younger siblings or me, especially since I had adventurous tendencies. She lasted just two or three den meetings and proclaimed that she couldn't handle the pressures of being a full-time mom of three young kids and a den mother at the same time.

My mother never worked outside the home, although I believe she wanted to and I can vividly remember her and my father engaging in some ferocious arguments as the result of her interest in seeking a job. Her pleas were always followed by my father's threats to end the marriage if she decided to work outside the home. A married woman who worked at that time was often perceived as a weakness within the husband. A real value system was established and maintained by both of my parents. Rules were often enforced by my stay-at-home mother, while a strict set of manners were routinely discussed and practiced with my father at the dinner table.

My adventures in Scouting, that would last for nearly eight years, had begun with Wood Dale Cub Scout Pack 34. Our pack was relatively large even though the Cub Scouts and the overall Scouting organization had suffered a significant dropout rate during the 1960's. This was a difficult time for Scouting, as its value system was under attack due to a sweeping cultural change that enveloped the country. Scouting represented a conservative and wholesome way of life with a reverent respect for authority. It was an organization based on several principles of goodwill and morality. The disregard and lack of those virtues were quickly emerging in the 1960's and were attacking the Scout's core values and principles.

Pack 34 was run by den mothers and a few fathers in the community acting as pack leaders. There was no camping to speak of due to rules set down by the Boy Scout organization prohibiting it. We marched in several town parades and were involved in a number of community service projects, cleaning up some of our local parks such as the Salt Creek Forest Preserve. As an eight year old boy, I was already setting up tents, chopping wood and helping my father start campfires and was even doing some experimental cooking. For most of my early Scouting years, I was stuck doing craft projects in our den mother's house, along with an occasional pack meeting.

White Pines State Park in Oregon, Illinois was one of my parent's favorite parks. It's a fantastic 385 acre park with a history rich in Indian culture. My father's reverence toward the Indians and the many lessons he had learned as a Boy Scout and as a chief in the Order of the Arrow would leave an indelible mark on his mind. He would often tell us stories around a blazing campfire of the Sauk Indians and their terrible plight as the settlers forced them out of the Rock River Valley during the Black Hawk War of 1832. You could tell from listening to my father's voice, as he told his tales, that he had a deep respect for the Indian's way of life.

This incredible park has the largest stand of natural White Pine trees left in Illinois. Several small one to four room log cabins with flagstone fireplaces dot the landscape originally built by the Civilian Conversation Corps in the 1930s. The campground was rather primitive and had no electric hookups or shower facilities and usually kept the numbers of campers to a minimum. It was a chance to experience real camping without the crowds. The park has a beautiful stone and wood lodge with an enormous fireplace. We would often use it to warm our hands and feet after a day of sledding during many of our winter outings.

The high rocky bluffs that soar a few hundred feet above Pine Creek are abundant with White Pine and Cedar trees, many growing directly out of the limestone. They seemingly defy gravity and hang precariously several hundred feet over the creek. Pine Creek has a mostly rocky, sandy bottom and is usually pretty shallow and only about 25 feet at its widest point. In the spring, it would often flood its banks closing the fords and other parts of the park.

As a young nine year old Scout, I would hike along the creek's banks and become to know its many twists and bends as it meandered throughout the entire park. Many miles of winding trails existed, some rising several hundred feet above the creek. Many of the trails took me deep into a dark green fern covered forest with thick brush and dense white pine and oak trees. An occasional small cave and jagged rock formation along the trails provided me with many hiding places. I played my Indian war games and visualized the Sauk Indians walking along the same paths.

Several concrete fords covered in green algae span the creek throughout the park. The water bridges allow people to access different parts of the park in their cars.The algae that grew across nearly every inch of the concrete fords were usually very slippery, if a person tried to walk or bike across it. Despite the many warning signs, I would always walk across the fords as I was pretty agile, even at nine years old.

I would sometimes slip a box of Cracker Jack into my knap-sack before one of my big hikes or fishing expeditions into the woods. It was one of my favorite snacks that I would treat my-self to along the trail. It was surely one of the first junk foods at that time.The best part of Cracker Jack was that there was always a real toy inside the box. I can remember dumping out the caramelized popcorn and peanuts into a bowl just to get to the prize, as it was usually at the bottom of the box.

During one of my excursions into the pine forest, I had stopped to rest and have some of my snack. To my surprise, I discovered what was to be my first real compass. It was round with a shiny metal base about an inch or so in circumference with a small needle tipped at one end in red that my father had instructed me pointed north. It was a great find and the best prize I had ever found in any of my treasured boxes of Cracker Jack. With my father's help, I began my first instruction in the proper use of map and compass.

Fishing in Pine Creek was one of my greatest memories as a young boy. Small and largemouth bass, crappie and bluegill were plentiful in the creek at the time. I often caught fish as I would cast my line using my new Zepco reel. I found a place under a tree and soon found that the fish loved the shade as much as I did. Cheddar cheese was one of my favorite baits and apparently the fish liked it, too, because I caught several fish using it.

My father got me started with my first tackle box filled with a few fishing lures, hooks and weights. But, as I soon found out, Pine Creek was pretty unforgiving with its rocky bottom. Despite my best efforts to salvage my prized lures, I lost a lot of them that year. It then became my responsibility to replenish my dwindling tackle box and I bought much of my own fishing gear with the money I had earned raising rabbits, shoveling snow and cutting grass. When I was 10 years old, I landed my first paper route and cut several of my neighbor's lawns. I was taught responsibility and how to work hard and earn money at a very early age. We would often work in our yard on projects with my mother and father, sometimes tending to my mother's massive garden.

I was literally left to run wild and run I did throughout many of the forests, fields and pastures, sometimes terrorizing the local cattle. I would often play a dangerous game where I would jump a barbed wire fence wherever we might be camping and get a bull's attention. As it turned to chase me, I would run as fast as I could and leap high over the barbed fence. Safely on the other side, I would lie on the ground and watch a really pissed off bull exert its frustration as it snorted and stomped its hooves into the ground agitated over my taunting.

The Pinewood Derby was the highlight of my experience in the Cub Scouts. Each Scout is provided with a small cardboard box filled with four wheels, two axles, and a block of balsa wood. He is then supposed to design and build a racecar with a weight not to exceed five ounces. The derby is supposed to be a family project to encourage the spirit of working together, fostering a closer father and son relationship and to promote craftsmanship and good sportsmanship through competition.

It was evident that as I arrived at my first Pine Wood Derby race that most of the kids did not build their cars by themselves, but rather had lots of help from their fathers. Some of the kids and their fathers were pretty nuts, even to the point of building elaborate storage boxes for their cars. The day of the race was electric, as the excitement and anticipation of the big race was building throughout a good part of the day. Everyone scurried to make last minute changes to their cars hoping to become the fastest down the wooden track that spanned a good part of the Holy Ghost Church basement in Wood Dale. The Pinewood Derby was great, as I always had a love for race-cars.

My first Pinewood Derby car is one that I really don't recall making myself or even having any say in its design, because I didn't. My father made it himself one evening in his shop, while I was sleeping. My car was dark green with yellow and orange flames painted on each side. It was a pretty slick design and got a lot of compliments from my other Cub Scout buddies. It was definitely the only dark green car. Despite my many urgings, we were running out of time to build the car due to my father's work schedule. It miraculously appeared on our kitchen table one morning. The dark green and yellow paint was still wet. Despite the cool design the car failed miserably and we lost nearly every race, but it was still a fun event that I would participate in the years to come.

TEN

WHEN WE FIRST arrived at our new house in Wood Dale, I was so excited, that as soon as my father parked our car, I jumped out and began to run around exploring our yard. Running was part of my genetic makeup. My mother was a naturally gifted runner in high school and had won numerous medals. Running for me usually took the form of chasing my friends and siblings through several of our yards and was a big part of the outdoor games we played. We ran, and then we ran some more, until we dropped from exhaustion. Having this many hiding places and grapes as a built in food supply, was great! I almost never had to go into my house. My mother would often say, "If you need a drink, don't bother coming into the house, there's a hose."

We played a game we simply called the "Chase Game," where the playing field spanned across three adjoining yards. Each yard was nearly an acre or more surrounded on three sides by massive bushes, so thick that you couldn't see through to the other side. The Chase Game would sometimes even spread into a few of our neighbor's yards that were adjoined, but were fenced. My brother, sister, and all of our friends played the game well into the evening, only to reluctantly end when my mother would call us in. My neighbor, Scott, was the fastest and I was second fastest. I could catch him on occasion, but only if I caught him off guard or cornered him in an area where he couldn't get through the bushes. I was, however, a better hider than he was, a skill I had learned from playing my endless army games.

My best friend, Billy Lonergan was fast, too, but not quite as fast as Scott or me. Billy had lived in the neighborhood his entire life and knew all the best hiding places. His sister, Kathy, was also pretty fast and like her brother, knew all the best hiding places. My brother's best friend was a kid by the name of Steve Neuman. Steve was a big stocky kid for his age and a pretty good football player. He was not very quick on his feet though and I rarely picked him for my team. His was of German decent and had jet black hair that looked like his father had cut it using a bowl. His dark brown eyes seemed to match his mild mannered demeanor and quite determination. Although he wasn't as fast as I was, he would never give up in any game we played.

Tony Peters was probably one my brother's strangest friends, as he had an annoying lisp when he spoke and would stutter when he got mad. Frankie Lullo, from down the block, was small but fast, and I always wanted him on my team. Bob, from the back, was a stockier kid and a pretty tough character. His rugged demeanor would be tested, as I chased him out of our house one afternoon. I feel terrible about what happened to Bob that day.

I was chasing him through my house after an argument we apparently had. He flew down our steep stairs from my attic bedroom almost falling as he tried to clear more than one stair at a time. We ran through our kitchen and out through the back door into our mudroom. I was gaining on him, and all Bob had to do was go through one more door to escape to the outside. I almost caught him and just as I went to grab his left shoulder his right arm went through the paned glass storm door completely severing an artery. The ruptured vessel in his arm began to immediately spurt blood into the air. We both looked at each other somewhat in shock at what had just happened. Bob was a pretty cool character and was able to stop the bleeding at least for a moment by placing his hand over his wound. He just ran home and I didn't see him for several weeks after the incident.

The Chase Game was really just a hide and seek game but with a twist since we all liked to run so much. There were two teams that we picked amongst ourselves based mostly on our running and hiding abilities. Scott and I were never on the same team since we were the fastest. We would always argue whose team Billy would be on because he was athletic and the third fastest. Usually whose ever team was the fastest won the game of chase. We started the game by flipping a coin to deter-mine who would hide first while the other team counted to one-hundred. Once you found someone hiding on the other team, you had to run him down and try to tag them. We would dart between the trees and the bushes, sometimes running through the grape arbor dodging all the steel posts in an at-tempt to elude your chaser.

A favorite escape technique of mine was to run as fast as I could and dive through a small opening in the bushes at the back of our yard. Once through the opening, to the expansive space in Bob's yard was more than an acre. Unless the kid chasing you was lucky enough to fly through the same open-ing, you were in the clear to find another hiding place. Bob's yard was larger than ours and had fewer trees but was wide open and you usually had an opportunity to outrun the chaser. If you were lucky or fast enough to catch your opponent you would put him in jail. The jail was our picnic table at the side of the house. The game rules allowed for you to be released from jail, but only if one of your teammates could somehow sneak up and tag you while you sat on the table.

One of the yards we would almost never venture into was Mr. Hester's for fear that we might not get out alive if he caught us. He was our neighbor to the south and was an old cranky German that my father did not care for very much. His yard was always meticulously manicured as he was retired and spent countless hours working in the yard. He had what appeared to be a handmade fence constructed out of mostly mismatched pieces of wire and round wooden fence posts. He was clearly from the old county and had immigrated to America after the war and never wasted anything including the wire he had built his fence with. He had a strong guttural German accent, so whenever he spoke, he scared the heck out of me and my friends.

Mr. Hester's last name, closely resembled that of Hitler's, and as a young boy, I didn't want to mess with him. Even at nine years old, the Hitler name was familiar to me because of all the war movies I had watched on TV. Mr. Hester never really spoke much, but when he did it was usually because he was mad and you could barely understand a word he was saying. If he did catch us in his yard, we were usually running away and diving over a section of his fence that was lower where he had apparently run out of wire. If we got cornered and were unable to escape, we were forced to listen to him reprimand us. His broken English sounded more like grunting as his head shook side to side as he got more animated by the minute. Not understanding a word he was saying, we would just start laughing and he would just yell louder with what must have been German cuss words.

Mrs. Hester was just the opposite of her husband, a rather kind and gentle soul. I think she liked children and would often invite us into their house for milk and homemade cookies. Mr. Hester would never be present while we were in the house. He had a massive garden that took up nearly his entire yard that he tended to on a daily basis. He would unleash one of his many tirades on us if one of our balls or Frisbees went over his wire fence. Sometimes the ball rolled and crushed his precious rhubarb or lettuce patch. He hated my rabbits, as they would sometimes escape from their cages and head straight for his yard and eat his lettuce and anything else they could nibble on. There were a couple of times when a few of them would get loose and mysteriously disappear. I never confronted him, but secretly thought he may have eaten them.

My mother, a German herself, would talk about Hasenpfeffer, a kind of German stew where the main ingredient was rabbit cut into small stew size pieces and the sauce, as my mother would explain was, "thickened with the animal's blood." The whole discussion and thought made me sick to my stomach whenever she would mention it as I couldn't imagine my little white bunnies cut up into stew meat. My mother's eyes would light up when she spoke of the dish, because she had experienced the delicacy as a child growing up in Evergreen Park, a predominately German town in Illinois.

We would play all of our games including baseball, football and chase games in our yards. Our chase games would last well into the evening hours. As darkness set in, it presented us with an added advantage for hiding and was my favorite time of the day. After playing and riding our bikes all day, we would stop just to eat dinner and be right back outside playing another game. There simply wasn't enough time in the day to watch TV, while I was growing up. Video games didn't exist until 1972. When I did watch TV, my favorites were shows like the Andy Griffith Show, Mr. Ed, Lassie, and Bozo the Clown.

My best friends, Scott and Billy were both great athletes, but Scott was exceptionally gifted, and had an athletic prowess that I always admired. He excelled in almost every sport we played. He was very competitive and took all of our games very seriously. He was the only kid to actually wear a pair of metal cleats that I think must have been an old pair of his fathers. I have a nasty scar on my leg from his rambunctious hard play. One of his metal cleats tore into my lower leg, as I went to tackle him during a football game. We had put together teams with kids from the neighborhood and we usually wore full gear, including helmets and shoulder pads.

Scott was a few years older than me. He was a tough, physically strong kid that played to win, no matter what. I think the ferocity for which he played was partially the result of pent up anger that seemed to fester within him from not having a father in his life. I always suspected that he harbored a secret level of animosity toward me, that as a young boy, he was unable to control. I did not realize it at the time, but he was helping me to prepare for what would be a grueling almost 1,400-mile bike trip with the Boy Scouts some years later.

ELEVEN

O UR BICYCLES were a big part of our lives growing up in Wood Dale. We lived in a two-pedal world, where our bikes were our only mode of transportation, and we rode them nearly every day. My mother never drove us anywhere and didn't even have a car until my father bought her a little import with a funny name. The Italian auto maker, Fiat, had been exporting cars to the US since 1908, my father told us, but they never took off since most people were buying Fords and Chevys.

As my mother watched in excitement, my father and uncle Jack tried in vain to get that little heap of metal that sat four people to run. They even rigged the ignition with a screwdriver, but she would never drive it. My uncle proclaimed it to be a firetrap as gasoline was dripping onto the engine from some unknown area. My mother was still without wheels and did most of her grocery shopping with my red wagon and three young kids in tow. Most mothers didn't drive their kids anywhere, especially not to baseball games, as we always rode our bikes.

One of the most memorable Christmas gifts I received was an Erector Set. Since my father was so handy, he wanted me to learn how to properly use tools. My new Erector Set was perfect for that purpose. The set was constructed of all metal parts, and the little electric motor that was included was restricted by a short electrical cord. We built robots with wheels and all sorts of trucks and crazy looking cars, but were always limited in the distance they could move across the floor because of that darn cord. We devised an elaborate set of extension cords connected together, so the robots and cars could travel further across the floor. It was a perfect gift for a nine-year-old boy who was already pretty handy with most tools.

The summer of 1967 was a year to remember, as I broke out of the single digits and turned 10 years old on August 6. I was finally able to join Little League and the Webelos. I loved the game of baseball and played nonstop during the summer with all of my friends in the neighborhood. My buddy, Frankie Lullo, had a perfect yard for baseball and that's where we played most of our games. Frankie was a few years younger than me, but as was the case in our neighborhood, that didn't seem to matter as we all played together. If you could run we wanted you on our team. Frankie was small, but very fast. He was a nice kid too and always had a big smile on his face.

Frankie and I palled around quite a bit. It was a sunny day sometime in September and we were on one of our many trips walking to our corner candy store. As we neared a vacant wooded lot in the middle of Harvey Avenue we could hear some rustling of the bushes. The next thing we saw was a snarling vicious dog charging out of the woods headed straight for Frankie. The dog was small, but its nearly 40 pounds was all muscle and razor sharp teeth. I soon recognized it as a neighbor's dog with its distinct orange and black stripes. This vicious dog looked and sounded like a miniature tiger as it darted out of the woods and began charging straight toward us, snarling and teeth drawn like small knifes. The dog's owners had named him Tiger, for what were apparently obvious reasons as Frankie and I were soon to find out.

The dog must have been stalking us for some time because we never saw him until he bolted out of the thick woods and attacked us. As Tiger got closer, we both yelled and waved our arms at him trying to scare him away. Just as he seemed to be turning away, his large box shaped head turned and his dark black eyes became fixed on Frankie. He charged straight for him. Frankie turned in self-defense and tried to protect himself, but nothing was going to stop Tiger's attack as he leaped forward and savagely began biting Frankie's legs, pulling him to the ground. Frankie was screaming and rolling around in the middle of the street trying to save himself as Tiger proceeded to bite the hell out of his legs and lower back. I tried in vain to get Tiger off of him beating the beast with a large stick, but nothing was going to stop his vicious attack. Finally after several minutes, Tony Peters, the dog's owner called Tiger and he immediately stopped his assault on Frankie. But it was too late, and Frankie was bleeding badly from all the dog's bites. The brutal attack would leave a large scare on Frankie's back. He remained terrified of dogs for many years afterwards.

Several months later, Tiger would strike again. This time his unsuspecting victim would be a little girl riding her bike down Harvey; close to where Frankie had been attacked. An alert neighbor, upon hearing the girl's screams, ran to her rescue, kicking Tiger hard in the ribs. The dog released his fangs from the girl's lower right leg and just plopped himself down in the middle of the street, as if he was guarding his prey.

The little girl was losing a lot of blood, but the neighbor was able to stop the bleeding by applying pressure to the wound with his shirt. Two Wood Dale cops who were driving down Harvey saw all the commotion and rushed over to help. The first cop out of the squad car made several attempts to catch Tiger in a noose before shooting him in the head, killing him instantly. The neighborhood was finally safe from this monster. The Peter's family, although showing some concern over the little girls injuries, seemed more upset at the cop for shooting Tiger. They felt the cops had used "excessive force." The Peters family was an odd lot that owned a plumbing company, and lived in one of the largest and most unkempt houses on the block, littered with plumbing supplies.

Frankie's yard was massive and where the trees and bushes stopped, it opened up to a large open field. Where his yard ended another neighbor's backyard began, so we had several acres of open playing field. His yard also sported what was the best feature of his field; a massive outdoor fireplace that we used as a backstop. It was constructed of reddish brick with a white brick cross imbedded in the middle that proved to a great pitching target. A good backstop was particularly important to me because I loved to pitch.

On the day of Little League sign up, I rode my bike up to the baseball field next to Sievers Pharmacy in Wood Dale and signed myself up. Sievers was the only pharmacy in the area and everyone knew the Pharmacist by his first name, and he knew you too. It was a pretty good secondary source for candy and was strategically located next to one of the town's baseball fields.

My baseball team was the Owls and our uniforms were dark blue and grey. My friend, Randy Kiss, was on my team and his father, who was a mailman in town, volunteered to coach us. Randy was a great athlete who had a lot of pent up, sometimes nervous energy. He was a fierce competitor who had a great eye for the ball. We would often butt heads and compete against each other on and off the baseball field. His father was a good coach and for the most part was able to control Randy and the rest of us with our rambunctious tendencies. The Owls were a pretty talented team and would compete in several championship games. The first year I was on the team, I was terrible and played right field most of the year. However, during my second year there was a complete transformation, and my abilities as a player were enhanced. I became a pretty good baseball player and loved to pitch, but really excelled at third base.

Our earliest bikes were a hodgepodge of several bicycles we managed to piece together to resemble real bikes. We built many of them from scratch, tore them apart and built them again always interchanging parts from one bike with the other. I was very mechanically inclined having been taught how to use tools by my father. If I wanted to ride a bike, he would say, I had to maintain it.

It wouldn't be until I was 13 years old that my brother and I would get new bikes as a reward for helping my parents in the yard all summer. The bikes were a gold mustard color with a silver and gold fleck similar to the popular Schwinn stingrays. They were equipped with a 3-speed plastic control handle and a silver flecked banana seat and stingray handlebars with matching colored hand grips. A genuine Schwinn would have been out of the question due to its high cost. The tires were a bit thinner than I had been used to and I wondered if I could jump over dirt piles without popping them. It was a great surprise and reward for all the hard work we had done that summer. I felt odd riding my new bike and missed being able to jump and crash it like my old bike.

The bikes we built from scratch were the ones we had the most fun on. We build them to last figuring we weren't getting new ones; almost nobody did in those days. We were pretty hard on our bikes and road them everywhere sometimes riding long distances on our ventures throughout Wood Dale and the nearby towns. We raced each other on our bikes through the neighborhoods often on a figure eight track that was comprised of two of our neighbor's circular driveways across the street from each other. Our bike races were great events that Scott, Billy and I had devised, until the neighbors who owned the driveways called our parents putting a stop to it. Bicycle helmets were never worn because they didn't exist. We would jump over huge piles of dirt crashing our bikes into the hard ground sometimes injuring ourselves in the process. We were always able to repair any damage to our bikes. We spent most of our daytime hours on our bikes until our mothers would eventually call us in for the night.

We never told our parents that we were bored, because we weren't. We were always too busy playing outside to even contemplate what the word meant. Life was pretty straight forward and simple where baseball, Scouts and riding our bikes dominated our lives. We rarely if ever came in the house during the day and never wanted to either. We were too busy playing. My mother would often make sandwiches for us and we would eat them on our picnic table.

It was a great time to grow up and we had a real value system established by our parents that acted as a guide throughout our childhood. There were fewer constraints and pressures on kids at that time. My father was a natural teacher and had passed on his many lessons and morals he had been taught as a Boy Scout and member of the Order of the Arrow. He had barely completed a year of college, but drilled into each of his kid's heads that education was the key to success in life. This intense belief and desire that his children attend college was coming from a person for whom was mostly self-educated. He would eventually become a partner in a very successful business that he helped to build.

My father was a nature lover and self-proclaimed environmentalist well before the terminology ever became popular. He was an expert in American Indian culture and his love for nature and the protection of it was intensely evident throughout his life. Because of his work schedule he didn't get personally involved in Scouting with me until I was 10 years old and able to join the Webelos. It was the next level of Scouting past Cub Scouts where you could camp and do some of the outdoor things the Boy Scouts were allowed to do.

He took us on a few camping trips, to Starved Rock State Park in central Illinois, where we played a great game of flashlight tag. Another memorable trip was to the Wilmington Strip Mines in Wilmington Illinois where my father had camped with the Boy Scouts and later as a young man with his brothers. We collected fossils and later cooked up a huge pot of tacos in our basement. Ironically, this was the meal I would later prepare as a Boy Scout for my Scout Master, Jerry Risting to achieve my Cooking merit badge. My tacos must have been pretty good as all of my fellow Scouts demolished all the leftovers. I always loved to cook out while camping and had been taught at an early age the art of camp cookery and I would often make pretty extravagant meals on my camping trips.

I struggled in school during my early years due to what my mother called a wandering mind until reaching the fifth grade. There I was elected class president and became interested in science with a particular curiosity toward fossils. My parents in their wisdom of the times did something that was quite common back in the 1960's. They decided to hold me back in the third grade. In an attempt to cover up what really occurred, all traces of my third grade report cards mysteriously vanished from my scrapbook my mother had meticulously maintained.

My parents called me into their bedroom after a family vacation we had taken out West and said that I would not be advancing to the fourth grade. The teachers they said, "had decided to hold me back a year." In that instant, I was sentenced to repeat third grade and immediately began to think about what my friends would think, "Here's this dumb kid that can't even pass the third grade." My life as I saw it was not progressing all that well and I felt an instant sense of failure. I knew I was a little wild but how could I have flunked the third grade? My grades weren't all that bad, certainly no worse than Billy's. I was pretty devastated but powerless and had no voice in the matter.

I guess I was too rambunctious and not able to focus or some other cockamamie story that they had made up at the time. They blamed their decision on my teacher so as to somewhat appease me and not appear to be culpable for my early downfall in school. Later as an adult, I would finally be told the truth about the big cover-up. My mother said that I had actually passed the third grade but it was suggested that I be held back and the final decision was ultimately my parents.

I repeated the third grade but frankly don't remember doing it. The school administrators must have known what they were doing as the pain of that event was lessened. Somehow my parent's and teacher's wisdom paid off in terms of my new and vitalized school career, as I was soon playing quarterback for our schoolyard football games and was considered a natural leader in my fourth and fifth grades.

When my family wasn't camping on the weekends, my parents would treat us to an outdoor movie. Drive-ins were a pretty popular pastime during the 1960's. We would make a huge amount of popcorn and put tons of real butter on it, salt the heck out of it, and put it into a large brown paper bag that we all shared. It was another great time spent together as a family. The kids would always sit in the back seat of our Ford Station Wagon and be allowed to watch the first movie. The later movie was usually more suited for adults, but I always watched while pretending to be asleep and listening to my mother gasp at the content.

TWELVE

BILLY AND I loved the outdoors and liked to camp together and in general, just pal around. Even before we had
joined the Webelos, Billy and I would camp together in our
backyards and occasionally with my family. We met in first
grade at Westview Elementary and remained friends for many
years. He was a pretty stocky strong kid, a little shorter than
me with dark brown hair that was always uncombed. He had
some freckles on his face like his sister Kathy.

Billy's family was of Irish decent and he could be very bull-
headed at times, always wanting his way. When we would get
in to a skirmish, my Italian and German heritage mixed with
his Irish temperament, would erupt in to some intense arguments. We fought like brothers and often tortured each other. I
once tied him to a tree in my backyard and started a fire
around him. I was trying to simulate what the Indians used to
do to their prisoners, burning them at the stake. We would always make-up after our arguments, without actually saying
"we were sorry." After a fight, one of us would come over to
the other's house to borrow something. It was usually Billy
that would give in, since I was bit more stubborn. I always said
yes to whatever he wanted to borrow and that ended our feud.
We would just start playing together again as if nothing had
happened.

My friendship with Billy would last several years, well into
our days as Boy Scouts and our young adulthood. It was kind
of convenient that my best friend and future girlfriend lived in
the same house. I spent a lot of time there, but felt uncomfortable since Billy's father was a bad alcoholic. When the old man
got drunk, he became abusive toward his family. I often felt

sorry for Billy, as it always seemed that he was in some kind of physical and mental pain.

Later, sometime after high school, he joined the army in a desperate attempt to better himself and escape the harsh memories of his childhood. He was involved in a brutal attack overseas and was severely injured in a knife fight. He had apparently pissed someone off with one of his smartass remarks. They ambushed him in an ally somewhere in Germany, leaving him for dead in a large pool of his own blood. His left arm was nearly severed from a cut under his armpit, ending at the bone near his shoulder blade. Knowing Billy, I'm sure he fought them off with everything he had and it may have saved his arm and even his life. He suffered permanent damage as a result of the brutal attack and was discharged from the army.

While on a break from college, I would catch up with him several years after the attack in Germany and was shocked by his overall harsh demeanor. He was a much different person from the one I knew as a boy. He seemed even more cynical after having suffered through the circumstances of the army. His attitude about life had been hardened from years of being poor and the abuse he suffered as a young boy. He never said it, but you could sense that he was resentful of my family's lifestyle, although we were not rich by any means.

Billy was very handy with tools and a great fort builder. Forts were something we built anywhere we could find a hiding place. I was out scouting for a site to build a new fort with Scott and Billy when we discovered what would become our best location. Maher Lumber Company along Irving Park Road was a family owned lumberyard and was always a great source for scrap lumber to build our forts. It was convenient, since all we had to do was cross Irving Park Road from the end of Harvey.

Behind the lumberyard were two sets of railroad tracks and a small creek, only about three feet wide and a large stand of small trees, two-three inches in diameter. The forest of small trees seemed to sprout up from nowhere and there were literally hundreds of them all about the same size. It was common for the lumberyard to receive deliveries of wood and hardware from the trains that would pull into the back of the property along dedicated tracks. The train tracks in Wood Dale ran east and west going through the heart of the town crossing over Wood Dale Road, and paralleling Irving Park Road. It was a busy railway and it seemed as if there were trains always rolling through town.

We knew the instant we saw the spot near the creek that we had found the next site for our new fort. We had an abundance of scrap wood that the lumber company had thrown away in the field adjacent to the new location. We chose to build the fort into the stand of small trees, initially clearing an area about eight feet wide by eleven feet long with our axes. The floor of the fort would be dirt, we decided, and we used all the small trees we cut down to construct the sides and walls and parts of the roof of the fort. It took on mammoth-sized proportions as my brother and all our friends helped to build this great fort. It grew well beyond our original design and resembled a real log cabin.

It all started with just a few pennies that Scott and Billy put on the tracks. After our fascination with flattened pennies ended, we started placing much larger metal objects on the tracks. When the train would come barreling down toward us, we would run as fast as we could to our fort diving through the door and covering our ears. We could hear loud screeching sounds followed by the noise of metal being crushed under the weight of the train. One of the engineers in a desperate attempt to stop his train caught a glimpse of me as I turned to run to the safety of our fort. It wasn't too long afterwards that the police came and hauled three of us to the police station. Our mothers had to come and pick us up. Scott and Billy had escaped and ran home avoiding the wrath the rest of us had to endure from the cop who apprehended us. It would surely be followed by beatings we would receive from our fathers.

Wood Dale is where I had my first experience with a girlfriend. I first met Kathy while playing with her brother Billy in their backyard. I saw his sister often since he and I spent so much time together, but it wouldn't be until I was about 11 years old that I started to really take notice. She was a cute, simple looking girl who always had a smile on her face. Her medium length hair was a curly reddish blonde and her face was heavily freckled. With her slight but strong athletic body, she was fast, and gave all the boys a real run for their money while trying to catch her during our chase games. Kathy was a real sweetheart with a great disposition and a heart of gold. To the best of my recollection, we were in love. We never had sex, but we kissed a lot. In fact my first kiss was with her while playing a game of spin the bottle in her backyard. That was only the beginning because whenever we were together, we kissed and must have really liked it, because we did it all the time.

My first introduction to sexuality came at an early age when Billy and I would watch in amazement as one of my male rabbits mounted a female, biting down on the back of her neck. The male would then proceed as only rabbits can, and screw the crap out of her. The practice of placing the male rabbits in a cage with the female would prove to be the reason why I had so many rabbits. Billy and his sister, Kathy would feed them while I was on vacation with my family. It was Billy and his curious mind that would put the males in the same cage with the unsuspecting females. Within four weeks of my return from vacation, I would be witnessing the birth of several bunnies.

My father was worried that Kathy and I might be venturing toward some level of sexual contact as our relationship progressed over the years. He had a big talk with us one afternoon as we accompanied him to the grocery store. It was a frank discussion about the birds and the bees. Kathy and I giggled a lot as he talked to us, never thinking for a minute about sex. We just loved being together, hanging out and kissing.

January 24, 1967 was an unusual day. I was outside with all of my neighborhood buddies playing our chase game. It was 65°F in the middle of the winter and had set a new record temperature. We loved it since it was usually well below freezing during this time of year. We stayed out late that night and my father built a huge bonfire in our backyard and we cooked hotdogs and told ghost stories. A few days later, the temperature began heading back to normal and a small snowfall of about four inches or so was predicted.

It started snowing at 5:02 a.m. on Thursday January 26, and it didn't stop snowing until Friday morning. An astounding 23 inches of snow had fallen in a short time, and Wood Dale and the entire Chicago area was crippled. It marked the largest single snowfall in the city's history. Unable to move either by foot, train, plane or car, nearly everyone was snowed in. My father was working in the city of Chicago with my uncle Jack at the time and was stranded. They were trapped and forced to stay at a factory. With little heat or food, countless thousands were stranded at offices and schools throughout the Chicago area.

The great Chicago blizzard of 1967 had hit hard with an unsuspecting fury and a blanket of heavy white snow covered the city and suburbs, stranding thousands in their vehicles. O'Hare Airport even closed down as the plows couldn't keep up with the storm's intensity. Irving Park Road in Wood Dale was completely closed down with hundreds of cars stranded in the middle of the road. It was a quiet and eerie sight as there were no planes flying overhead and all you could see were the tops of cars lined up and down the street.

Since there was only four to five inches of snow expected, my mother found no reason to stock up on food and other supplies. When it became evident we weren't going anywhere by car, we decided to venture out to the only grocery store in the area. It would be nearly a two mile walk from our house. With my mother and I at the reins, we trenched through several feet of snow heading north on Harvey Avenue toward Irving Park Road. With no one to watch my younger brother and sister, we pulled them on our large wooden toboggan.

A cold wind was blowing out of the west, whipping snow into our faces nearly blinding us. By the time we made it to the Jewel Food Store, the shelves were almost completely wiped out. My mother snatched the last gallon of milk and was lucky to get a loaf of bread and a few other supplies. In other parts of the Chicago area, the snowfall had caused more serious problems, including the death of a 10 year old girl caught in the crossfire of police attempting to stop looters.

As kids, the snow was a welcome relief, since all the schools were closed for several days. We had a great time building snowmen and igloos and playing in the massive snow drifts in our backyard. When my father was finally able to make it home, he didn't share the same enthusiasm for the snow as I did, and threatened to move to Florida.

THIRTEEN

WHEN BILLY and I both turned 11 years old, it marked a great time in our lives since we could finally join the Boy Scouts. We would be able to proudly wear the coveted khaki green uniform, a symbol that you were a Scout. We had been waiting for what seemed an eternity, biding our time as we struggled through the Cub Scouts and the Webelos. We were ready for the big time that the Boy Scouts promised and we eagerly wanted to join as soon as we were eligible. It marked a time that we could finally start to do some serious camping and all the other things that the Boy Scouts offered. As with everything else that we were involved in, we rode our bikes up the sidewalks along Irving Park Road, heading east about a mile. It was a trip that we had taken many times before, but this time our destination would be the Holy Ghost Church.

As a Webelo, I had observed the Boy Scouts in their uniforms at Sievers Pharmacy on Friday nights, gulping down their soda before heading into their meeting. I visualized myself as a Scout wearing the uniform. Billy and I joined Troop 65 ourselves, as this was just the way things were done back then. We had been raised by our parents to be very independent and make decisions on our own. Many things back then were done on a handshake, and I don't recall my parents even needing to sign anything when I joined the Scouts.

The Scout meetings were always held on Friday nights between 7:00 p.m. and 9:00 p.m. When Billy and I entered the church basement through the large white steel doors, I was instantly in awe of my surroundings. The main room was much larger than I had remembered from our Pine Wood Derby races. The tile floor was a pale green color and there were several metal posts supporting the main level of the church above where Father Thompson gave his weekly sermons. The ceiling was low and the other boy's voices echoed as the chatter was loud and intimidating. Billy and I barely spoke, as we watched, not really knowing what to do yet.

All of the Scouts were dressed in their sharp freshly pressed olive green uniforms and shiny dress shoes that were mostly black. I wondered how anyone could get such a shine on their shoes. I would soon find out. The uniforms that I had always admired from afar were a medium khaki green color. Most of the Scouts wore shirts with collars, although I noticed a few shirts without them. The Scout's pants were held up by an olive green cotton belt with a shiny brass buckle. Everyone wore a bright red neckerchief held together by various types of slides made of plastic or metal. The Boy Scouts were proud of their fleur-de-lis symbol and used it everywhere they saw an opportunity, including on most of the Scout badges signifying rank.

Baden Powell had adopted the ancient symbol that dated back to the Egyptian empire as a badge for the Boy Scouts. He often referred to it as the "Arrowhead," where the three points of the Scout badge would serve as a reminder to the Scout of the three points of the Scout Oath, where he promises to (1) do his duty to God and country, (2) help others, and (3) keep himself physically strong and morally straight.

Some of the Scouts wore more badges and medals than others signifying their rank and stature in the troop. Billy and I were pretty intimidated as we observed the Scouts scurrying about, some talking in small groups while others met with their leaders preparing for the meeting. It appeared that the older more decorated Scouts were running the show while a few of the adult leaders looked on.

I could hear a deep and commanding voice off in the distance directing a few of the older Scouts. He would soon introduce himself to Billy and me as Jerry Risting, our Scoutmaster. He was a younger, slender built man in excellent physical condition that I figured to be about 5'9''tall. Billy and I were pretty nervous, but Jerry's smile and warm voice had an instant calming effect. His smile and gentle laughter kept our attention. He spoke to us for quite a while standing with both arms crossed, only breaking eye contact to adjust his wire rim glasses. It appeared that he was a well-organized and disciplined man. His movements were calculated and planned and he seemed to always be aware of the time, stopping occasionally to check his wristwatch. His simple uniform was without a wrinkle and he was well groomed. His short light brown hair was something that I associated with military men and admired.

He preferred to be called Jerry, and that's what all the other Scouts called him at the meeting. From that day forward, Billy and I would also address him by his first name. It was somewhat unusual for the times as we would never call an adult by his or her first name. It was just the way Jerry preferred it. It was apparent that he had complete control of the troop and all of the leaders under him. All the Scouts responded to him in a very positive and reverent way. It was obvious that Jerry was a very dedicated and gentle man. He loved Scouting; I am sure as much as he loved life.

We were part of the Du Page Area Council and all of the Scout troops in our area wore the same red, yellow and green arch shaped patch on their left shoulder. Below were red patches with white letters clearly identifying who we were, signifying the name of our town, troop number and the state.

There were several other patches the boys wore on their uniforms too, but I didn't know what they meant.

Jerry was not one to wear a lot of badges and his uniform compared to some of the older Scouts was very simple. As an adult leader he always wore a short sleeve shirt without a collar, because he liked wearing the traditional red scout neckerchief. The only patch that I could see sewn onto his uniform was one signifying that he was a Scoutmaster. He also wore two gold colored leadership pins and three small square knot pins. I recognized a small red and white Order of the Arrow ribbon with a small arrow and two bars that signified brotherhood. It was similar to what my father's Scout uniform looked like. Jerry was heavily involved in the Order of the Arrow as a young Scout and later as an adult leader.

The troop's dues were collected in an orderly fashion by one of the older more decorated Scouts, which amounted to 10 cents per week. Billy and I were exempt from having to pay since we were only observers at this point, but it was made clear that the dues were an important part of being a Scout and paying your way. All the dimes that were collected were stored in an old brown leather case that looked like it had been around from the beginning of time. Most troops back then were charging 25 cents per week. Jerry felt that he had an obligation to our troop to be savvy and fiscally responsible. He didn't want to charge a lot for the privilege of being a Scout. The dues were treated as more of an obligation and a way to teach the Scouts the sense of value and how to be thrifty.

The American flag or "colors" as they were called stood proudly in the corner supported by a dark stained wooden pole in a metal stand in the corner of the church basement. The Scout meeting started promptly at 7:00 p.m. with Jerry bellowing out in an authoritative manner, "Fall in!" All the Scouts immediately stopped what they were doing and formed several lines in front of him. The most decorated of the Scouts made up the front of the line. His first command was followed by his second, "Tench- Hut!" and all the Scouts were instantly "at attention." "At attention" was the most rigorous of the Scout postures as you were required to stand upright with your chin up and your shoulders pushed slightly back. Your arms were required to be fixed at your side, along the seam of your trousers, with your thumbs parallel to your pants, eyes looking straight forward and heels together. No movement or talking was allowed during this posture.

The Color Guard marched in to present the colors and we then all addressed the flag and recited the Pledge of Allegiance. After a moment, Jerry gave another command, this one not as forceful but it was still a firm command, "At ease," he said. At this point, everyone placed their hands behind their backs, hands crossed with their legs shoulder width apart. The Scouts, while in this position, were permitted some movement, but their right foot could not leave the ground and they were not allowed to talk. Talking while in this stance was never tolerated as important business was about to commence.

Jerry was a former military man having served in the army while stationed in Germany during the Vietnam War. His command of Scouting unit Troop 65 was evident. All eyes were fixed on him at the front of the room and no one spoke out of turn. It was important to "keep order," as Jerry would say from time to time. Billy and I sat on the cold tile floor as we had been instructed to do so. We were amazed at what was happening around us. We never uttered a single word and watched carefully. Ever since I was a young boy playing on top of the dirt hills in Oak Forest, I had always dreamed of being in the army.

After order was established and all the Scouts were at ease, what would follow was another call to "attention" and all the Scouts would immediately jump in to a more rigid stance, and the weekly uniform inspection of all the Scouts would commence. Jerry would start from his right with the most decorated Scouts and make his way through each of the lines. This appeared to be serious business. If you had forgotten your belt or your hat was not properly placed wrapped around your belt, you were given a warning. If the same thing happened at the next meeting, you were sent home. Everything about your uniform and your personal grooming was inspected from how well your uniform was pressed, to the degree of shine on your shoes. Even your haircut and personal hygiene was scrutinized.

Discipline was always from its inception an important aspect of Troop 65 and Scouting as a whole. Jerry at times had to be a tough leader with some protocol as there were some serious situations that he had to deal with from time to time. He however realized as a leader he had to earn the Scout's respect and be able to get along with them.

After the uniform inspection, more military style discipline was displayed in what seemed to be a sort of game to test the Scout's abilities. "Fall in, fall out, right face, left face," were orders that were barked out by one of the other senior leaders. The basic training Jerry had obtained while in the army was something he wanted to teach and share with the boys. He called them "close order drills." They were a way to easily communicate with the Scouts and in some cases it was essential for their safety. The drills made things happen in an orderly manner and we would practice them in a repetitive fashion. "O'Grady Says," was a drill and a game to keep the Scouts in order and to see how they reacted to a series of change in orders.

We often participated in parades around the county and the close order drills helped in those situations so we could march in unison. Many people who observed our level of discipline could see that we responded quickly to orders, and saw that the boys were well behaved and worked well together as a unit. There was a definite chain of command with Jerry clearly at the helm, but we were relaxed and just a group of kids marching in a parade. It was often said that we were one big happy family that clicked.

FOURTEEN

JERRY WAS BORN in 1941 on the North West side of Chicago where he started his education in Chicago's harsh public school system. He would later attend St. Pascal School and Parish at North Melvina in Chicago near West Irving Park Road for sixth and seventh grade. It was a stone cold school, both in its appearance and how its students were treated. Jerry dreamed of returning to his old school. The parish building was ominous, constructed of grayish brown brick and a red tiled roof. The steeple towered over everything else in the area with a large bell in the middle at its peak. A massive gray cross made of stone adorned its pinnacle.

The school was iconic in its stature having served the community since 1914. Jerry's mother Marie, a staunch Catholic insisted that her children be educated in the more rigid ways of the Catholic school system. His experience at St. Pascal and the lessons he learned would follow him throughout his life. It was a very structured form of discipline, where nuns observed and dictated your every move.

In 1953, his family would move to the small town of Wood Dale, some 11 miles directly west. The population of the town at the time was only about 850 people. As a young boy, Jerry was surprised by the differences in culture and size of the two towns. It would become his new home for the next 26 years. When he and his family first drove into town, he noticed the Francis Farm on the north side, where several horses grazed. He and his younger brother Bob would attend Holy Ghost school, a little country church and school where Jerry would start the eighth grade.

The one story school was constructed of a faded orange brownish brick where many of the classrooms opened up to the outside. Jerry thought that was pretty neat, since he had come from such a different environment in Chicago. He was quickly becoming used to the country way of life and loved being able to run around outside his house without being supervised.

Despite his new seemingly serene and quiet surroundings in Wood Dale, he was reminded of the harsh reality of war, something he and his other classmates were forced to consider on a regular basis. The Soviet Union had exploded its first atomic bomb in 1949, and as a result the American public was nervous. They were aware of the destruction that atomic bombs did to the Japanese cities of Hiroshima and Nagasaki. The new bombs the Soviets were setting off were the much more powerful and destructive H-Bombs. Air raid drills were conducted on a regular basis at many of the schools across the country, including Holy Ghost.

There were times when an ominous sounding bell would go off without any warning and everyone in the class had to run into the hallway and put their hands over their heads and try to protect themselves. If a bomb were to be dropped, the students were told not to look at the flash or they would go blind. This was really scary stuff Jerry thought, and wondered if covering his head would make any difference if a bomb were ever to be dropped on his school. There were times the nuns would suddenly yell, "Drop!" The horrified students would immediately kneel down under their desks with their hands clutched tightly around their heads hoping that it was only a drill.

Father Wagner was the Priest at Holy Ghost at that time and was a big animal lover. It was common to see his Cocker Spaniels and cats in attendance at the services. Even the nuns at Holy Ghost were different; although still pretty strict, they weren't nearly as tough on Jerry as the hardened Chicago nuns had been. His family had moved to a place where there was an abundance of trees and wildlife. It was common to see horses grazing on tall grass in the pastures near his home. His new environment was a stark comparison to Chicago's traffic jams and the cold uninviting stone buildings that lined the city's narrow streets.

Jerry would soon find out that he still needed to behave or he would surely get in to trouble, as discipline was a large part of the culture at Holy Ghost. His father worked for Sterten Werner in Chicago, where he ran large industrial screw machines manufacturing grease fittings for the automotive industry. His father was a hard worker and would typically leave their house at 4:00 a.m. to make the long commute into Chicago. The grueling schedule took a mental and physical toll, and his father sadly passed away at the early age of 53.

Jerry's family lived at the far north end of Wood Dale near Highland School on Hawthorn Lane. Their small two story Cape Cod house was pale green with white trim and a cedar roof. The knotty pine rec room in the back of the house was where the Risting family would often gather to watch their only black and white TV. The large rectangular shaped wooden table, where Scout meetings would often be held, was in the center of the room.

Father Cook was a new priest at the time at Holy Ghost who had just been ordained. He was a rather plump, happy-go-lucky man who had a smile on his face no matter what was going on. He told Father Cook that he hoped that he wouldn't have a problem with him serving mass for the first time because he really didn't know what he was doing. Father Cook said, "Well I hope you don't have a problem with me either, because I was just ordained and am a bit unsure of what I'm doing as well." Jerry thought that was pretty cool and they would soon become friends and get along just fine.

Holy Ghost had three school buses that Jerry, at 12 years old, would help move to pick up the other kids. In addition to his duties as a priest, Father Cook also drove a school bus. One day he asked Jerry and some of his friends, "Are you guys in the Scouts?" Jerry and his friends snickered at the thought, thinking that the Scouts were a bunch of pansies. He and his friends had no plans of ever becoming Boy Scouts. Father Cook persisted and reminded Jerry that the Scouts were meeting at 7:00 p.m. that night and that they should come by to the church basement. The boys never showed up to the meetings, but Father Cook persisted. Jerry would just say, "Yeah ok, we'll come," never having any intension of going to a Scout meeting.

It was about 6:45 p.m. one evening and out of the corner of his eye, Jerry could see Father Cook's car pull up into his family's driveway. Nervous and thinking that he might be in trouble, he hid in a back bedroom. To his surprise, Father Cook came up to the front door and told Jerry's parents that he was there to take him and the other boys over to the Boy Scout meeting. His parents thought it was a good idea that Jerry should be involved with such an upstanding organization. Without questioning their decision, off Jerry went that evening to his first Scout meeting at Holy Ghost Church.

Troop 65 was founded and first chartered by Mel Brockman and Tony Langfeld in 1951. When Jerry first joined the troop, it was a relatively new organization and Tony would become Jerry's first Scoutmaster. To his surprise, joining the Scouts turned out to be a heck of a lot of fun. As a Tenderfoot Scout, he loved all of the crazy things like snipe hunting and gooney bird chasing. His first camping trip went too quickly, and he was hooked on Scouting for many years to come He would remain actively involved in the organization until 1979.

As a young Scout, Jerry, would soon find out that Mr. Langfeld, who worked for the White Rock Bottle Company, could be a pretty stern leader. The young Scouts never questioned his discipline. Mr. Langfeld was a seasoned military man having served his country as a tough drill sergeant while in the army. The kids would often comment that he was like a general, and when he said something, he meant it! When given an order, you would not question his authority, you would just do it. Mr. Langfeld was admired by his young Scouts and considered a great leader by his peers, but there was no horsing around.

As Jerry got older and started to help more with running the troop, Mr. Langfeld became more approachable. However, the two men had their differences and their philosophies on Scouting sometimes clashed. They both wanted to keep Scouting going during the summer months as attendance would often drop off because of baseball and other activities. Mr. Langfeld believed that if the kids didn't make the Scout meetings that they shouldn't be allowed to go on the campouts. Jerry was clearly against this policy saying that he understood that they could not make every meeting and was happy to see them occasionally. They would eventually come to an agreement on many things regarding the troop and learned to respect each other.

"He was good boss and Mr. Langfeld counted on you to help with the troop and you did so without question," Jerry would say. It wasn't until later in the troop's history that the Salk District Council asked Mr. Langfeld to be their commissioner. Although it was a difficult decision since he enjoyed being with the Scouts, he agreed to their proposal and Ed Kosic then became the troop's Scoutmaster. However, because of his love for

Scouting, Mr. Langfeld continued to be involved in the troop's activities and also became its committee chairman. Scouting was an important part of his life and he was always there for Troop 65.

By the time Jerry had joined the Boy Scouts, he was already familiar with a strict level of discipline he would encounter there. Discipline was a way of life during this time. A value system along with a set of rules had been introduced to him by his parents at an early age. His parents would guide him with common sense rules where there was an emphasis on good manners. Being polite and offering courtesies such as "please" and "thank you," were stressed. He was taught to address all adults with a title of Mr. and Mrs. Honesty among all things was emphasized in the Risting household along with being helpful to others. It would prove to be a combination of discipline and lessons that Jerry had been taught while at home, school and the Scouts that would mold the future leader of Troop 65.

When Jerry first joined the troop his early lessons in discipline and courtesy toward others would continue to be enhanced by the Scout Law and Scout Oath. The Oath says that a Scout will do his best and obey the Scout Law. He will help other people at all times, and keep oneself physically strong, mentally awake, and morally straight. It would prove to be a pretty heavy task for a young boy and Jerry wondered if he could live up to the expectations of what the Scouts expected of him. The Oath is very explicit in what it expects from its new recruits. It doesn't say, "I will try to do my best," but rather it says, "I will do my best."

It was a rather difficult concept for a young boy to grasp at times while growing up, especially when his mind was focused on fishing in Salt Creek and riding his bike. As he got older and more involved in the Scouts, Jerry began to equate the Twelve Scout Laws of being Trustworthy, Loyal, Helpful, Friendly, Courteous, Kind, Obedient, Cheerful, Thrifty, Brave, Clean and Reverent to the Bible's Ten Commandments. As an older Scout, it became clearer to him that over time he would be able to mold his life around the principles of the Scout Law and Oath as well as the Ten Commandments. However, as a young boy it was at times a very rigid path to follow. It would later prove to be his guiding light as he pursued his life in Scouting.

Troop 65 in its early history was steeped in Catholicism, and Father Wagner of Holy Ghost was a traditionalist and strict Catholic. He closed the troop to kids of other faiths. Troop 60 in Wood Dale was a public troop and anyone could join. Father Wagner was eventually transferred, and replaced by the more liberal minded, Father Ryan, who was a real humanitarian and strongly supported the Scouting movement.

As Jerry took on more of a leadership role, he would eventually speak with Father Ryan about getting other kids into the troop that weren't Catholic. Father Ryan was outraged by Wagner's policies and said that it was a lot of baloney. He felt strongly that any kid no matter what his religious beliefs were should be able to join the Scouts. Father Ryan was an advertising man before becoming a priest and was not particularly an outdoors type of person. He would go out to see the Scouts while they were camping, but would not stay the night. As much as he supported Troop 65, Father Ryan had an aversion to sleeping on the ground. His decision to allow all boys despite their faiths to join Troop 65, proved to be a real boon. It really filled up after he gave the okay. There was no doubt though that the troop was influenced by the Catholic Church. Jerry had attended both the church and its school as a young boy, and their lasting impact on him was evident at our Scout meetings. A Scout would always close our meetings with a prayer.

Scouting was a big deal in Wood Dale when Jerry was growing up and was roundly promoted by several influential people in the little town, including the Mayor, Herb Gilbury. He wholeheartedly supported the movement and arranged to have the Boy Scout Handbook sold at the gift shop at the train station. Wood Dale was a very close-knit town and in those days the police department consisted of only two cops. Police Chief Adolf was also a big supporter of the Scouts. The Boy Scout Handbook at that time was the same one my father had used while growing up depicting an Indian on its cover. I used to love reading it as a boy and dreamed of someday being able to join the Boy Scouts.

During Jerry's early days as a Scout there were no real modern conveniences and even things like a portable radio were real clunkers. Scouting back then was more focused on camping and woodcraft and the principles of doing a good deed. The Order of the Arrow had been spawned by the great naturalist and Indian expert, Ernest Thomson Seton. His deep love and reverence toward the Indians and their culture was evident throughout Scouting. Scouting in its early days had an enchanting Indian-like way about it. The culture was centered on the idea of spirits and reverence toward a supreme being. The land was their life blood and a source of food and shelter, and they had a great deal of respect for it.

Jerry loved the outdoors and camping. It was a big part of his life and the reason he stayed so active in the Scouts. Region 7 Canoe Base was a wilderness Scout camp established in 1943 in northern Wisconsin on White Sand Lake. It was originally established as a Civilian Conservation Corps camp with the closest town being Boulder Junction some five miles to the north. It was a majestic place with hundreds of serene lakes and rivers with lush pine and oak forests. It was a favorite destination for Jerry and his fellow Scouts and he looked forward to his trip with anticipation of camping like the Indians in the wilderness. It was quite an adventure from the beginning as the Scouts would take a one track train up to the camp. They would spend the next six days traversing White Sand Lake and several other connecting lakes and rivers.

Equipped with topographical maps and their camping gear, the Scouts were having a ball in the serene and dense pine forests of northern Wisconsin. In an effort to set up a fire pit for cooking, they used five large iron pipes they had brought with them. Jerry had never seen so many stars in his life that night as the fire roared and ghost stories were being told. He and a buddy who were intrigued by the blackness of the night sky and the bright stars, quietly slipped away from the group to smoke cigars and talk about the next day's adventures.

As they prepared to leave their base camp the next morning and canoe further into the wilderness, something seemed strangely off and the Scout's sense of direction became quickly skewed. They would later discover that the iron they had ingeniously used as a fire pit was distorting their compass readings. Not fully realizing that their compasses were off, they ended up confused and went into a big area south of White Sand Lake, ironically known as Lost Canoe Lake. With their compass readings off, they had no clue as to their whereabouts. After a grueling portage to another lake hoping that they were on the right track, tempers began to flare. Some of the boys began to panic. The older Scouts calmed everyone down assuring them that they would be ok and after a while calmer heads prevailed. Finally, after many hours of paddling and another portage, the tired Scouts found their way back to their base camp along White Sand Lake. As Scouts, they were disturbed by the fact that they had been lost and made a pledge to be better prepared and decided to use something other than iron for a fire pit.

Throughout high school, Jerry stayed very active in the Scouts and when his Scoutmaster, Tony Langfeld became the commissioner, Ed Kosik would try to run Troop 65. Jerry was only 16 years old at the time and had two brothers in the troop. Although he had good intentions, Ed ran the troop as though it was a business venture. He was a dedicated and sharp guy with two sons in the troop. He was doing what he thought was right for the troop, but it wasn't working as well as he wanted it to and enrollment began to slack off.

FIFTEEN

JERRY WAS ONLY 18 YEARS OLD and an Explorer Scout when Ed Kosik left the troop. For the first time in its history, Troop 65 was without a Scoutmaster. Bob Bender, who was the troop's committee chairman realized the urgency of the situation and began to look in earnest for a new Scoutmaster. "Someone needed to lead the troop" was the general sentiment. Despite the efforts of the committee to recruit a new Scoutmaster, no one was willing to take on such a large responsibility.

According to official Scout rules, a Scoutmaster needs to be at least 21years old. Bob Bender realized that he had to resolve the situation quickly and assumed an interim role as Scoutmaster. Realizing that the troop would be doomed if they didn't secure a leader soon, he stepped up and signed the charter so that Jerry, who was only 18, would be Troop 65's new Scoutmaster.

It was 1959 when Jerry would take over at the helm and become the youngest Scoutmaster in Troop 65's history. Father Ryan, was a staunch supporter of Jerry's new assignment. He provided him with a great deal of encouragement during this tumultuous time in the troop's history. Under Jerry's leadership and the support of Father Ryan and others in his community, the troop flourished, and enrollment really took off.

A few years later, Jerry and his younger brother, Bob were on vacation hiking in the Black Hills of South Dakota when they got the news that Jerry had been drafted into the army. The war in Vietnam was raging and Jerry was still in college at the time. He thought about fighting the draft, since he was in school, but with the way the war was going, it was anybody's guess when it might end. After talking it over with his family, he decided to serve his country, a duty for which he felt a strong sense of conviction.

John Smith was the assistant Scoutmaster at the time Jerry would have to report into the army. He was a man of enormous stature who was good hearted and easy going. The boys seemed to respect him as they responded well to his command. John agreed to take the reins of the troop in Jerry's absence. His last meeting before reporting to the service was an emotional event for him. In a special ceremony, the Scouts awarded him a trophy in an effort to show their appreciation for his service and dedication to the troop. He assured all the boys at the meeting that he would come back to lead the troop once again.

He would do his basic training at the massive army base in Fort Knox, Kentucky. On his second day, military life became a reality as all his gear was handed out. He was immediately subjected to a series of shots for potential diseases he might come in contact with while overseas. The military barbers, not known for their compassion, completely shaved his hair. When he finally finished his basic training, his official orders were posted indicating that he would be reporting to Germany. Others would be headed for Vietnam, which was quickly escalating into a major war.

He and his family were thankful that he would be stationed in a small village in Germany away from any major conflict. His tour of duty would last two years. There he would take advanced courses in aviation and worked as a mechanic. He had the responsibility of maintaining 18 of the army's massive Sikorsky CH-37 Mojave Helicopters. The CH-37's were deployed in Vietnam in early 1963 to assist in the recovery of downed U.S. aircraft. With its two massive Pratt & Whitney R-

2800's, the heavy-lift helicopters were enormous and a key workhorse for the army. Spanning over 64 feet in length with its huge clamshell doors, the aircraft could carry 26 troops and equipment including jeeps and artillery pieces. Jerry would soon be in charge of his group due to his keen troubleshooting and management skills.

While not working on the CH-37's, Jerry made the best of his time while stationed in Germany. It was the army's practice to pay its troops once a month, but you had to have your hair cut during that period of time. Haircuts back then were about 50 cents. Jerry bought a set of clippers and would cut hair for the rest of his crew at a reduced rate. In addition to his talents as a barber, he was also a master of using photo oils to turn black and white photos into colored pictures.

It was Friday, November 22, 1963 and Jerry was winding down his time in the service with his two-year tour nearly complete. The base commanders made the announcement that President Kennedy had been assassinated. He had always been a Kennedy supporter and was deeply saddened by the tragic news. Everyone on the base was tense and were put on high alert as they waited in anticipation for what might be new orders.

Sometime after the crisis, Jerry would be honorably discharged from the army and head home to Wood Dale where he would try to resume his life. However, there were some in the community that had other plans for him. He had been back in the states only a few weeks when he received a phone call from Bob Steffki, a former Cub Scout leader. He and John Zweifler, had been helping to run Troop 65 in Jerry's absence. Bob wanted to get back to running Cub Scout Pack 34. John, who owned GEM Plastics, did not have the time to dedicate his full attention to the troop. They wanted Jerry to resume his duties as the troop's leader and asked him if he would consider coming back. He was still officially Troop 65's acting Scoutmaster, as he had not fully resigned his duties while away in Germany. Jerry was exhausted from his army service and needed a rest. However, his young Scouts and their interim leaders persisted.

It was a crisp December evening when Bob asked Jerry to come to Holy Ghost for a meeting in the church basement to discuss the future of Troop 65. The boys, dressed in full uniform, were lined up at attention. They stood quietly in the dark basement of the church waiting for Jerry to arrive. Having no idea what was about to happen, the basement's fluorescent lights flickered on as he entered through the basement doors. The boys still "at attention," gave him a rousing applause. "We knew you would come back!" they shouted out. "You are coming back, aren't you?" they asked. "Sure I am," Jerry responded, still surprised. At that moment, he felt an intense sense of loyalty and conviction to the boys. The Scouts had kept their surprise a secret but more importantly, their leader had kept his word to come back as their Scoutmaster.

In 1963 after having served his country for two years, Jerry came back home to his kids of Troop 65. Although he was happy to be home with his family, he realized all along that he had an obligation to his Scouts for whom he viewed as his other family. He would never have a son of his own in the Scouts. When asked about his family life and not having any kids in the troop, he would often comment, "Oh but I do, I have 65 of them!" He would, with honor and commitment, assume the duties as Troop 65's Scoutmaster for the next 16 years.

Jerry was soon approached by Adolph, the manager of Wood Dale's new water filtration plant, asking him to work in the laboratory. His knowledge of the plant was limited and he was reluctant to take the position. After further discussion, Jerry decided to take the job so he could be closer to home as his father had been taken ill. A number of years later, he would be promoted to manage the city's public works department.

SIXTEEN

WHEN BILLY AND I left our first Boy Scout meeting that night it was sometime after 9:00 p.m. It was dark and the moon was only a sliver of itself and nearly nonexistent. We didn't talk much as we jumped on our bikes for the trip home along Irving Park Road. As we concentrated on our ride and traversed across several driveways dodging curbs along the way, all I could think about was my next Scout meeting. It would mark my first opportunity to wear my new Boy Scout uniform.

I think Billy and I were both in shock, not realizing how much was involved in being a Boy Scout. The meeting had been unlike anything we were accustomed to in the Cub Scouts. I was a bit intimidated and scared but anxious to get started at becoming a real Scout. When we finally reached Harvey Avenue and were about to head in our separate directions, we stopped for a brief moment and I asked Billy, "Do you think we can do it?"

"Yes we can do this, we have been camping since we were kids," Billy replied. That was all I needed to hear, and we both took off, heading in different directions until we would meet up again next Friday at the corner store. This time we would be in full uniform and proud to be a Scout.

As a young boy having just joined the Scouts, most of my attention was on all the campouts and hikes we would soon take. However, it was also a time in our country's history that was fraught with anxiety over the raging Vietnam War. The American involvement in the war peaked in 1968, just as Billy and I had joined the Scouts. Each night as my family huddled around our TV set, we watched in horror as a streaming message was displayed across the bottom of the screen listing the hundreds of dead US and Viet Cong soldiers killed that day.

The atrocities of the war would become even more evident when our favorite babysitter, a young man who lived down the block, was killed on a combat mission in Vietnam only a few months after his deployment. Before his death, I would often overhear his mother speaking with mine sharing her anguish and fear that her son might be killed. It was a terrible tragedy and one that would be felt throughout our small community.

War and the thought of joining the army someday had taken on a new meaning for me after our babysitter died that summer. It was no longer a game that I loved to play as a child, but rather a question of life and death. The end of the 60's was marked by a war that would never be won and a protest that would be heard by many at Woodstock in 1969. It was a tumultuous time in our country's history and what many believed to be the last of the innocent generation.

The Boy Scouts were a big part of my life. It was an organization that I had wanted to become part of ever since my father and my uncle Jack had started telling us stories of their camping adventures. Troop 65 was a very active troop and we camped and went on many more excursions than most other troops in the area. It was known as a high adventure troop due to its activity and focus on thrilling trips. The troop took its first trip to the Grand Canyon in 1967, followed by a trip to Glacier National Park in 1969. We were blessed with a great and dedicated leader, as Jerry took the time away from his family and his job to support the troop.

Jerry truly cared about all of us as Scouts. He not only taught us how to camp and survive in the wilderness, but he also shared with us his knowledge about life and how to get along with others. He took the whole matter of training his

PAUL REGA

young leadership staff seriously, with an emphasis on working together. When a weekend campout would be approaching, he got very excited about the trip. "Are you excited?" he asked them.

"About what?" they said.

"The trip!" Jerry replied. His level of enthusiasm for all our trips was contagious, and eventually everyone would be excited about our upcoming adventures.

We were "Jerry's Scouts," and for all intents and purposes, I think we were his kids too. On one of the Grand Canyon trips, the Scouts were wearing their summer uniforms and needed to wash them at the Laundromat in town. For a short time, they weren't wearing their uniforms. While they were waiting for their laundry, they went to a little ice cream stand and Jerry bought each of the half dozen or so Scouts an ice cream cone. When they were getting ready to leave, a little boy who had been watching the Scouts saw that Jerry had bought cones for all of the boys, and whispered to his mother, "Are all those his kids?"

"I think they are," she said. Jerry was very proud of all his kids and marveled over their display of good manners wherever they would go. He always enjoyed having the Scouts for several days at a time while on their trips away from home. He had the opportunity to work and teach them things while experiencing their companionship. There was always a good deal of chemistry, friendship, and camaraderie that was developed during those trips.

Fellow Scout, Jeff Anderson once said to Jerry, "You always speak to us in parables, like the time you told us to always stick together as a group, so you can never be pulled apart." Jerry lived and taught us the morals of Scouting, emphasizing a strong set of values that he had learned as a young Scout.

There was a focus on the principles of the Scout Law and Oath, and he spoke to us often about the Scout Slogan, "Do a good turn daily."

It wouldn't be until many years later that I would personally learn to appreciate Jerry's wisdom of Scouting. My family owned a house on Lake Michigan in Indiana. Sometime in the early 1990's, my father had started to paddle out to his boat in a small dingy, when he got caught in a strong rip current. He was powerless to try to paddle out of it and was stuck in place swirling around like a cork bobbing up and down. Seeing that he was in distress, I swam out to him and climbed into his small craft.

For the next hour as we floated in place, not moving any closer to his boat, we talked about everything from issues with kids to business. It was a chance to catch up on all that we had missed over the past several years. When we did occasionally talk, he would always ask me, "How's your business?" The subject of our talk would always then turn to business since we were both business owners. I voiced my concerns about a project that I had been working on and was disappointed in the outcome. He asked me, "Did you do your best?"

"Yes," I said, without hesitation.

"Well, that's all you can do then," he replied. His comment whether he knew it or not at the time, was straight out of the Scout Oath.

Our troop always seemed to be involved in some type of community service project whether it was the recycling efforts of our paper drives or helping homeowners to shore up the banks of Salt Creek. Jerry wanted us to become an integral part of our community and make it a better place to live. He instilled in us a sense of community spirit. It became a part of our value system, and what it meant to be a Boy Scout and a good citizen of Wood Dale. Our paper and scrap metal drives were major fundraisers for our troop's activities, providing us with a means to purchase more equipment.

Our paper drives were a great event and the entire town of Wood Dale would get involved. They began early in the morning and lasted well into the night. It seemed like everyone in town knew we were coming. Homeowners would tie a white rag on their mailbox and we would pick up their scrap newspapers from their house. We had teams of Scouts pick up the newspapers in trucks, vans, cars and any other vehicle that could haul newspapers over to a massive boxcar. We would stack the papers from the floor to the ceiling, completely filling the boxcar.

Scouting had a rich history of recycling, dating back to World War I, where the Scouts were called in to action to support the war effort by collecting everything from newspaper and scrap metal to milkweed floss that was needed as a substitute for kapok in lifejackets. The entire experience taught us the value of working for something we wanted.

One of my favorite events was helping at the Lamb's Farm in Libertyville, Illinois during their yearly picnic. Thousands of people would come from Chicago and the suburbs. Lamb's Farm was an organization that had been founded by Bob Terese in 1965. Bob's only son, Mike Terese was our troop's assistant Scoutmaster. Mike's father had started a small pet store on Chicago's State Street in 1961, where he employed individuals with developmental disabilities. His vision was to purchase a farm and have mentally challenged adults work in the pet store and on the farm so that they might lead productive lives. His dream would come to fruition when noted philanthropist W. Clement Stone purchased the land and ultimately donated it to the Lambs Farm organization.

As Scouts on a mission, we would make our yearly trek up to the farm to help the residents run their picnic.

We always camped near a lake on the Lambs Farm property, so we could be close to the swimming area. We watched in awe as fast ski boats wielded their skiers around the lake pulling them over a large wooden ramp, hurdling them skyward. The skiers were amazing to watch. I can't remember anyone crashing, but always thought they might since they had to make a tight turn after their jump to avoid running into the banks.

A few hours before the festivities at the farm were scheduled to start, I was sitting around a campfire with my buddy Danny Zoubek finishing my breakfast, when I heard a loud scream and cry for help. It was coming from the lake area and Danny and I jumped into action. We both ran toward the lake to help whoever might be in distress. When we got there, I saw one of our fellow Scouts apparently drowning as he was bobbing up and down in the water, occasionally dipping out of sight. He had slipped away from the rest of the troop and was swimming alone, which was against our buddy system.

A few of the other Scouts who had arrived on the scene before Danny and me were preparing to throw an air mattress they found to him. In their haste, they had grabbed Mike Terese's mattress from his tent as well as his prized down sleeping bag to treat the victim for shock. We had all been taught that when attempting a water rescue to first try to reach the victim, and if that was impossible, to throw a rope or a flotation device. As a last resort, you would swim to rescue the drowning person. We all thought that throwing an air mattress to the drowning Scout was our safest bet.

Jerry's planned water rescue demonstration had its drawbacks, in this case. What amounted to the ransacking of Mike Terese's tent due to our quick response to "save" our fellow

Scout, had not made Mike very happy. His personal belongings had been trashed and completely covered in sand. Mike was our assistant Scoutmaster and an Eagle Scout. He was a very meticulous, organized guy as was evident by the way he dressed and kept himself groomed. He didn't like it when someone messed with his belongings, especially his new sleeping bag. Mike was pretty mad that day and he let the Scouts know it. "I don't care what you do to me, but don't touch my equipment," he said. Everybody respected Mike and often would turn to him for help as he had a compassionate ear and seemed to understand how to deal with things in a helpful and discreet way.

Mike started in the Scouts when he was just 11 years old and at 18 would become the Troop's first junior assistant Scout Master. His father was very committed to his mission at the Lamb's Farm and as a result, Mike gravitated toward the Scouts. When he first joined Troop 65, he was a rather small kid sporting a short crew cut his father insisted on. The other kids would often overpower him due to his size. Despite his small stature, Mike was tough minded. He quickly progressed in the Scouts by doing whatever was necessary to move forward and advance his rank. After a while, Mike matured as a Scout, and by the time he was 12 years old had realized his direction and just seemed to do everything right. Jerry would soon begin to lean more on him to help with all the record keeping that was required. "He was a mature young leader, that made things happen," proclaimed Jerry. Troop 65 was an organically grown troop where nearly all the leaders were raised from within.

SEVENTEEN

THE DUPAGE AREA COUNCIL would often refer to Troop 65 as a renegade troop behind Jerry's back. With many of their newly adopted policies, Jerry thought that the Council was beginning to take the true meaning of Scouting away. It was becoming less and less of a youth run organization. The adult leaders were instructed to take on more of a decision-making role. This went against Jerry's philosophy of Scouting. He persisted with his style of leadership and felt that through his teaching and methods of allowing the boy's freedom to do what they wanted was working. As a result, the kids were sticking with Scouting.

Jerry definitely had his own way of doing things. He was a meticulous guy and his exercises were always well thought out. He wanted his boys to experience real life things so that if they ever needed to act, they would do so without hesitation. They would be prepared. He involved us in many mature types of activities such as traffic control around town, riding on a fire truck and being part of a rescue team that involved our troop's water rescue boat. Danny Zoubek was heavily involved in several water rescue exercises and a part of the Troop's elite civil defense team. Our troop owned a rescue boat and an emergency service trailer that was sponsored by the Fire Department.

It was a fall day in late October and the weather was starting to turn colder. Our small group of Scouts were camped in the woods out near the Wood Dale Junior High School where we used to play capture the flag. As the day wore on, it started to get colder and we needed more wood for the campfire to stay warm. We each pulled out our axes from our backpacks and removed their protective sheaths. We had been instructed to always take care of our ax to protect the blade. "A sharp ax was an effective and safe ax," Jerry would say. Just as we started to chop up the wood, I noticed a car pull up into the school parking lot. I recognized a few of the men as members of the Scout Council. They were walking fast, heading our way apparently to observe what we were doing. I heard one of the older men say something to Jerry about lighting a lantern. The Council, a few months before, had banned the Scouts from lighting one citing safety concerns.

They were appalled by what they saw as several of us had axes in our hands and were in the process of doing some serious wood chopping. One of the Council members who had graying hair and was dressed in a suit said, "What happens if they cut off their foot?"

"The boys have been well trained and we've never had any incident or problems," Jerry replied. "You need to trust the kids and let them know that there are limits. It's the only way they are going to learn how to do some of this stuff." The Councilmen rolled their eyes and seemed a bit put off by Jerry's comments and left soon afterwards mumbling something as they headed back to their car.

It was about a month or so after our encounter with the Scout Council that 16 of us were out on a hike during a weekend camping trip to Danada Woods in Wheaton, Illinois. The winter had arrived early that year and it was bitterly cold so we were out gathering some kindling to start a fire. We had set up our 16 x 16 army tents, so each of the openings faced each other in an effort to keep us warmer during the night. The sides of the tents were designed to roll up so we could easily crawl in and out.

We had just walked past one of the lakes in the park when we heard someone cry out for help near our campsite. We all rushed back to find Bert Bell, one of our fellow Scouts lying on the ground screaming in agony. His eyes seemed to roll back in their sockets each time he would let out a yell for help. There was a hand ax next to his side covered in fresh blood. Horrified at what we all saw, several of us jumped into action and began to administer first aid. Danny Zoubek, who was only 11 years old at the time, looked as though he might pass out. Blood was gushing from Bert's wound and he lay on the ground wrenching in pain. There was an exposed jagged piece of bone and bloody tissue sticking out through his pants. It was clear that he had just cut deeply into his leg with an ax, severing an artery.

The incident scared the hell out of me despite all the first aid training I had received from my father and Scoutmaster. I was pretty well versed in first aid and knew exactly how to treat my fellow Scout and had jumped into action. We immediately applied pressure to the wound in an attempt to stop the massive amount of bleeding. Some of the Scouts started to treat Bert for shock. We had been instructed by our Scoutmaster that if untreated, shock can kill you just as easily as the injury itself. So, we covered our victim with a blanket from one of our tents and put another sleeping bag under his feet. We had been well trained from the beginning, as first aid was emphasized as a way to always be prepared for the unexpected.

I was a young Scout at the time and unaware that this was another one of Jerry's planned first aid training exercises. The older Scouts watched as we tried to treat our buddy who had appeared to have cut off part of his leg. They played it out and instructed us on how to treat Bert, as if he had really cut into his leg with his ax. It sure looked real, and the lessons I learned that day would be something I would never forget.

Jerry and the older Scouts would help to plan the first aid training exercise and when you least expected it, some sort of accident would occur. That was the point of it all; you never really knew when it would happen, so you had to be prepared. They used a chicken bone and wound filler made from mortician's wax and mixed dark rouge and blue food coloring to create just the right effect. Jerry would buy the wound filler from Mr. Geils who owned the local funeral home.

Our troop was all about reality training and we were involved in many real life exercises. I camped almost every weekend during the summer with my family or the Scouts. Because our troop liked to challenge ourselves, we were involved in several winter campouts too. The DuPage Area Council had very specific guidelines in order to achieve a patch they called the Polar Bear Camp. It was one of the niftier looking patches that featured a Polar Bear standing on top of a snow-covered mountain. The Council rules stated that we had to camp outside for two consecutive nights where the temperature had to be below 32°F.

It was bitter cold on the second night out and Billy and I who usually camped together were not as prepared for the extreme cold as I thought we were. We all huddled around the campfire trying to stay warm until a few of us snuck away to smoke cigars. Later that night, as we all retired to our tents, Billy and I both lay in our sleeping bags shivering unable to sleep. Somebody with a thermometer said it was five below zero. I was pretty lean back then, at about 120 pounds, so I had very little fat on my bones and I couldn't stop shaking from the cold.

In desperation and fearing that hypothermia might set in, I came up with an idea to keep us warm. I would use my cooking Sterno. Since it contained alcohol, it never froze and made a perfect cooking fuel in cold weather. The only smart thing we did that night was vent the fumes out through the screened part of the tent. Beyond that act of brilliance, having what amounted to a lit stove in a flammable nylon tent, was extremely dangerous. We were lucky we didn't kill ourselves.

The next morning, it was clear that most of us had not slept all that well. Many of us emerged out of our frost-covered tents with blankets wrapped around our still frozen bodies. We were getting ready to start a fire when one of my buddies spotted Jerry emerging from his International Scout looking pretty rested, carrying his sleeping bag and pillow. We all teased him for a while afterwards about sleeping in his truck, but also realized that he was human and had a few faults just like us.

As a requirement for our Second Class rank, we had to take a five-mile hike and demonstrate a proficient use of a map and compass. It was an early December morning in the dead of winter and the temperature had dropped well below zero. All of the young Scouts on this hike earned their badge that day as winds in excess of 35 miles per hour turned a cold day in to one that was unbearable. All of our gear was stashed in our small packs, including emergency cold weather supplies and provisions. When we got past the Junior High School, the winds really started to kick up, blowing snow everywhere. It created a dangerous situation where there was almost zero visibility.

We all huddled together, covering ourselves with all of our available blankets in an effort to stay warm. The winds eventually died down, and with our visibility restored, we were able to get a bearing on our position. When we finally emerged from the woods, we looked like a group of soldiers from the Revolutionary War, still bundled up in our blankets. We had survived, because we had stuck together and didn't panic. As a troop of high adventure, we never shied away from the cold, but rather used it to learn survival skills. Jerry was experienced in survival techniques he had learned while in the Scouts and the army. He would push us in to situations where we learned something about survival, and often something about ourselves.

The first summer survival campouts we attempted were a lot of fun. We had chosen an area near the Vermilion River, which my father had suggested to Jerry. It was as remote an area as you could get in Illinois and there was an abundance of plants and animals we would need to survive on. Gooseberries were my favorite and recognizable as the berries when ripe are a deep maroon color and had somewhat of a tart but sweet taste. They grew everywhere in the dense forest near the river. No one was allowed to bring any sort of food. This was a true test of survival that would last two days and nights. All you could bring was one pound of gear. To be sure no one violated the rules; the adult leaders told us to turn all of our pockets inside out.

We were instructed to gather our own food during the night when the crawdads were active and sleep during the day. We constructed a large shelter using massive leaves from some sort of tree whose leaves looked more like those found in the jungle of Brazil. All of the Scouts were innovative when it came to locating food on our survival trips. However, fellow Scout, Ed Lasara, was among the most creative and made a soup out of grasshoppers. You could see the parts of the grasshoppers in the soup and he asked Jerry to try it. Reluctantly, he did, and thought it was good.

Camporees were held in the spring and fall and were a big deal when several Scout troops from the DuPage Council and Sauk District would all converge into one campground. The troops would hold competitions amongst themselves on things like fire building, knot tying, and first aid. It gave all of us a chance to see what the other troops were doing and a real opportunity to learn some new skills. The first camporee I attended was in 1969, followed by others in 1970 and 1971. Jerry believed in introducing us to other ways of thinking and methods of doing things. Our troop was well known for our realistic first aid displays.

EIGHTEEN

J ERRY LIKED TO DO "nifty neat things," as you would often hear him say. He wanted to do some 'he-man' long-term trips, too. As a result, the troop planned trips to the Grand Canyon and Glacier National Park, eventually culminating in our bicycle trip to Florida. Jerry wanted to use the money we made from our paper drives to help promote and make our troop better. We bought our own canoes from the proceeds of the paper drives. There was a company in Addison, Illinois that manufactured plastic type canoes. Every once in a while there was a reject where some part of the mold might not make the perfect canoe, so it would be priced for only $50.00. Jerry wanted to buy more of the rejects, figuring that with the money we had earned from the paper drives, we could afford to buy 24 canoes. When the guy realized that Jerry wanted to buy that many, he offered to sell new ones to him at the reject price. "Well at that price we can afford to buy 32 brand new ca-noes," Jerry said. The owner was ecstatic with our large pur-chase and it was a big boost to his business.

Lou Giannini was one of the boy's fathers who would be-come one of our adult leaders. He was a very handy guy and a good welder and was able to build the Scouts three nice canoe trailers. We were well equipped with watercraft, as we now owned our own canoes and trailers and an emergency service trailer. Troop 65 was becoming very popular with many of the kids in town, as they all wanted to go camping. When they saw us heading out of town on a weekend trip with our trailers filled with canoes, they thought "Wow, that is pretty neat" and wanted to join the Scouts.

The Scouts were canoeing down the Current River one year, when they noticed a guy on a little raft with a kerosene lantern. He was apparently selling watermelons to anyone who wanted to buy them. Jerry paddled over to him during the evening guided by his little kerosene light and purchased some watermelons. On his way back to camp, he looked out over his Scout troop camped along the rocky banks of the Current River. His attention was drawn to all the little tents and young boys skirmishing about in the woods. He thought about the great responsibility that he had for all the lives entrusted to him, and marveled over what an honor it was to be with the kids. "That's what it's all about for me," he thought.

The boys were intrigued by the man paddling around at night with just a lantern to guide him and said, "Let's do a night canoe trip sometime." That fall, we did a night canoe trip along the Fox River just north of the low head dam near Carpentersville, Illinois. What was supposed to be an important training exercise turned in to a rather disastrous and nearly fatal trip. The sky was pitch black that night and it was pouring rain. My canoeing partner was barely visible in his green poncho. I could hear the river below us begin to hit the canoe harder as the water began to move faster pulling us further down the river. All of our attempts to use our flashlights failed, as they must have shorted out because of the heavy rain. The only light we had that night came from a few candles that were quickly extinguished from the deluge.

After that incident, Jerry was determined to find a solution to our problem of needing a light source that would work in all inclement conditions. We were, after all, an adventure troop and weren't going to let something like a little rain deter us from our excursions. Jerry was very innovative and devised what we would all simply call, "candle lanterns." I can remember him showing us how to build them using a Mason jar where we incorporated a heat shield using part of a venetian blind. It would act as a spring and easily bend into place protecting the candle from the rain. Surprisingly they really gave off a lot of light and soon all the Scouts were required as part of their training to build one. Some of lanterns we built had innovative designs, many with wire handles and multiple candles. The lanterns were relatively safe, too, and the candles would always extinguish themselves if the lantern fell over. We never had an accidental fire using them.

We were on one of our camporells with several Scout troops outside of our district, when one of the council members noticed everyone in our troop had candle lanterns. Disgusted with what he saw, this big shot came over to our campsite and told all of us to put our lanterns out, citing safety issues. We stopped going to the camporells as a result. Our candle lanterns always hung outside of our tents and never posed a fire hazard.

Jerry's involvement in Scouting extended well beyond our meetings and the time he spent together with us camping. The Scouts knew that if they needed help, even with something as simple as a school science project, they would get it. Most families had more than one kid and the dads were working hard and did not make a lot of money. When some of the boys would get in trouble at school, Jerry would get a call from the principal saying that they needed to talk with him. He would always phone the parents first to make sure it was ok to go to the school and they always said yes. Most of the time the parents wouldn't even go to the meetings, saying they were too busy and seemed not to care as much, figuring that Jerry might be better equipped to handle the situation.

A fellow Scout by the name of Curt Unzer was about 12 years old and was given the assignment of delivering flyers for an upcoming event. Like all of us, he had to deliver them to a certain number of houses in town. He was instructed to place the folded flyers on all the mailbox flags. Well, it wasn't too soon after Curt returned to the church that there were a number of telephone calls to Jerry indicating that someone had broken several flags off their mailboxes. Curt became the obvious culprit, since Jerry knew that the damaged mailboxes were in his designated delivery area.

Expressing his disgust with the issue, Jerry took Curt over to Maher Lumber and purchased a piece of Masonite. He and Curt then started the arduous task of tracing out the shape of what amounted to several broken flags. They carefully cut out each one and hand drilled, and painted each flag. They then went to all of the houses where Curt had vandalized the mailboxes and replaced the broken flags. It was like a scene out of one of the episodes of The Andy Griffith Show and a tribute to Jerry and his method of teaching. It was a life lesson that I am sure to this day Curt still remembers.

In a more serious instance, Jerry got a call from the Addison Police Department to come down to the police station. It was late on a Friday afternoon when he got the call and he was just starting to close up shop, but left immediately to try and help a fellow Scout. Apparently, one of his lads was caught stealing something from a store. Jerry arrived at the police station where they knew of him and all of his work with Troop 65. As he sat in on the interrogation, they read this kid the riot act, "How could you do this, you are a Scout!" they said.

Afterwards they all talked amongst themselves to try to work something out, as the young Scout sat quietly, listening in angst at what might become his fate. Due to Jerry's urgings, and his pledge to keep an eye on the boy, the police eventually released him into his custody. The young Scout had learned his lesson and promised everyone that he would never steal again. Ironically, he would get a job with the same company some years later. Jerry trusted his Scouts, and this was just another one of life's lessons that he had taught to a boy that veered off the path.

I can't remember Jerry ever being called to the school on my behalf, but I do know he had been there for others as I would frequently see him at the Junior High School. He didn't look his typical cheerful self as he left the building on his way back to work at the city's water filtration plant. His dedication to his boys in the troop was unquestioned and it ran very deep in the community. We were all very grateful for his help but as young boys you don't realize the sacrifices that are made on your behalf until you are much older.

Our troop was always seeking new challenges and our annual ski trips up north near Fox Lake were the highlight of our winter excursions. Jerry had first learned how to ski in Switzerland while in the service and he wanted the Scouts to experience the sport. He bought his first set of black, Head 360 skis, and when polished, they glowed. They were always in perfect condition until a few of the Scouts unintentionally skied across them.

Jerry always took care of his stuff and passed that lesson down to us saying, "If you take care of your things you will always have them when you need them." It was at times, a painfully simple lesson to put in to practice but was also one my father had taught me. We were instructed to always take care of our stuff. We had to work hard for what we got back then and consequently had more respect for our things. We were never given something just because we wanted it, except maybe on our birthdays, Christmas, or some other special occasion. We appreciated what we were given, never expecting or asking for more. We knew we wouldn't get it, so we never asked. The words "instant gratification" was not part of our makeup as kids back then.

One of my jobs as a young boy was to insulate the back porch of our house. It was something my father because of his sheer size could never do himself, so he employed me. It was a terrible job. I had to lie on my back on a cold spider infested brick floor with plastic safety glasses to protect my eyes from the fiberglass insulation. I stapled all 250 square feet of it into place under the rafters of the porch. My reward was a set of Cubco bindings that cost about $25.00. I loved those bindings, and it served as a good lesson for what hard work could buy.

I first learned how to ski at 11 years old with the Scouts while on an annual trip we would take up North. We would always stay at the Beau Rivage Motel in Cary, Illinois. It was a great trip and something I really looked forward to each year. It was a long weekend. We would stay Friday and Saturday night, and then leave on Sunday morning after breakfast at the Four Horseman Lounge next to the motel.

The Four Horsemen restaurant was an octagon-shaped building that looked more like a huge spaceship than a restaurant and sat high on a hill overlooking the motel. A set of concrete steps led up to the restaurant from the motel below that had 24 units on several wooded acres. The new restaurant was the third location in a chain, and featured jukebox dancing, live entertainment and a basement dining room used for banquets and meetings.

The old jukebox was really neat and there was always music playing. Elvis had just released his new hit, "If I Can Dream" during his 1968 NBC Come Back Special, and it seemed to play continuously as we all ate our breakfast anxious to get on the slopes.

I was equipped with my new Cubco bindings that my father and I had mounted the night before to a set of wooden skis I got for Christmas. I was anxious to try out my new Colfax leather ski boots I had received as a Christmas gift from my uncle Bob. I can remember the excitement and anticipation of the trip and all the packing and preparation that went in to it. We had been instructed to bring a second pair of warm socks and extra clothing as it was likely that we were going to get wet since most of us were new to the sport.

Jerry had found the Fox Trails ski resort in Cary Illinois but we needed a place to stay that would be willing to house nearly 32 Scouts for two nights. Our assistant Scoutmaster, Jack Froehling, and Jerry went to the motel and told the owner that we wanted to rent several of his rooms. Some of the kids had restaurant experience so he told the owner that we would help with our meals. There was some initial resistance from Bill, the owner but he finally gave in after Jerry expressed our willingness to help.

We would get there late Friday night and sleep eight kids to a room with some of us sleeping on the floor in sleeping bags to keep our costs down. The owner of the hotel got a kick out of us helping prepare and serve the meals to the Scouts and some of his customers. We always got the restaurant cleaned up after we ate breakfast and then headed for the slopes. We gave Bill a certificate showing him our appreciation for his hospitality and he seemed to really like it.

The Fox Trails ski resort, a former farm, first opened in 1962, and was the brainchild of two local business men. The resort was situated in a wooded area with rolling hills and featured a Swiss-style chalet built on top of the main slope. It had glass across the entire back of the building so you could watch the skiers from the restaurant. There was also a ski school built next to what had been the farm's horse barn. The remodeled barn housed the ski rental area, ski patrol and a first aid station.

There were 30 acres that featured seven trails and nine tow ropes with the longest hill being two thousand feet. The steepest slope was called "Nosedive." It also had the largest stand of oak and evergreen trees of any other run. Because of its vertical drop and natural obstacles, it was my favorite, but it was also the most challenging and potentially dangerous. We had all received a basic ski lesson earlier that day, but because most of us were novice skiers, we didn't venture up to the higher slopes for the first hour or so.

Danny Conoboy, who was always a lot of fun to be around was also a little crazy, and skied with a bit of reckless abandon. He was thrill seeker and loved speed and was usually covered in snow from all the falls he had taken. Several of my friends including Billy Lonergan and Arlin Barton, who in his own right was a little nuts himself, were skiing behind Danny when he just took off down "Nosedive," yelling, "Race you to the bottom!"

We all took off flying down the hill at breakneck speed. Danny had gotten a lead on us since he had jumped off the rope tow sooner than all of us and just blew down the hill. He never stopped until he collided head on with one of the biggest trees on the slope. As a last ditch effort to avoid hitting the tree, his legs opened up at the last minute as he desperately tried to avoid hitting it. When his body hit, there was a loud thud as the flesh from the inside of his legs met the tree bark followed by his head smashing into the tree trunk. It was a violent crash that thrust Danny forward in a whiplash like fashion. Several low-lying branches that he hit first seemed to somewhat cushion the blow.

There was an almost eerie silence after the crash and his body went limp. As we all rushed to Danny's side, we thought he might be dead. We all knew from our first aid training not to try and move him as that could cause more injury. He was breathing but the shock from hitting his head on the tree had knocked him out cold. Hitting the low-lying evergreen branches before the tree's trunk may have cushioned the blow and saved his life. A nearby ski patrol had witnessed the accident and rushed to his side and immediately started to render first aid. As Danny came to, it was evident that he had sustained a head injury. He was incoherent and was babbling something about our race.

Three ski patrol guys dressed in orange jackets took him off the hill on a stretcher they pulled behind themselves. We were only two hours into skiing when the accident occurred. As Danny recovered from his accident in the ski patrol office up in the old horse barn, all the Scouts were immediately called off the slopes for a meeting. We debated whether we should continue with the ski trip or go home because we were getting too crazy. We all agreed to stay but had to make a pledge to be more careful on the slopes. Our days of racing down "Nose-dive" were over, at least for this trip.

NINETEEN

BILLY AND I continued to advance in the Scouts over the next few years and would both be awarded the rank of Tenderfoot at our first Christmas court of honor in December 1968. It had been about five months since we had joined the troop and we were excited to be receiving our first rank. It was a big deal as many of our parents and others from the community would be in attendance. Our parents had a lot to do with the success of the troop and Jerry made a point to recognize them for their contributions.

Rank advancement took on a high level of seriousness and Jerry did not believe that it should come too easily. He was a stickler for detail and you really needed to know your stuff. It was not uncommon for the Scouts to go longer than six months between ranks where other troops in the area seemed to more rapidly advance their young Scouts, Jerry was more interested in developing the Scout's skills. He wanted to make sure they were ready for the next level of rank rather than focusing on the rank itself.

The court of honor was an awards ceremony Troop 65 held twice a year around Christmas and in the summer. The Christmas court of honor was a grand ceremony held in the basement of the Holy Ghost Church. It would be my first court of honor and I was very anxious, as the new inductees were required to recite the Scout Oath and Law. It all started when the lights would flicker on and off and the Color Guard marched in from the back room to present the flags. We would all stand to address the American flag and begin to recite the Pledge of Allegiance.

The senior patrol leader would light the first candle on the rack and all the lights would go off signifying the beginning of the ceremony. There were twelve candles in all representing the twelve points of the Scout Law. Three of the candles were in the center of the rack and represented the three parts of the Scout Oath. A faint almost shadowy white light was positioned behind the badge illuminating it against a glowing red background. It had a mystical almost spiritual appearance and represented my first level of advancement in the Boy Scouts. The Tenderfoot badge was then awarded to us followed by the coveted red Scout neckerchief. I had finally been inducted into the Boy Scouts of America and I could not hold back a big smile as I caught the proud look of my father in the audience.

The rank of Second Class focused on outdoor survival and camping skills. It also signified my first opportunity to earn merit badges. When I completed the requirements and was awarded the rank of Second Class at the December court of honor in 1970, I was hooked. The badge is the first Boy Scout patch that says, "Be Prepared." It's followed by the ranks of First Class, Star, Life and finally Eagle.

I wanted to continue in the Scouts and do the best I could and learn as much as possible. I dreamed of someday becoming an Eagle Scout. It was a lofty goal but one I had set my sights on ever since joining the troop. An Eagle Scout was the culmination of everything that Scouting stood for. The Scouts were a lot of fun and because of Jerry's dedication to the troop it was challenging, too. I was a very dedicated Scout and loved being involved in everything that our troop had to offer. The friendships and camaraderie I would develop would last many years and well into my adulthood.

From the moment Billy and I had stepped into the Holy Ghost church basement for our first Scout meeting, Jerry had introduced us to a way of life, governed by the "Scout Spirit." We were taught how to be role models to our peers and to live by the principles of the Scout Law and Oath. Scouting in Troop 65 was never about how many events or camping trips you attended, but rather how you helped to bring out the best in others.

"I hoped that the individual would relinquish themselves to believe in and abide by the Oath and the Law, and use it as a guidepost and as a way to get through life," Jerry said. "It was important to do things together acting as a cohesive group, guided by the Scout Law, but most importantly, to value your fellow Scouts. It was seen as an accomplishment for all of us to do things together and have fun doing it," he concluded.

Scouting for Jerry and all of our fellow Scouts was a matter of getting together each week and enjoying the companionship. We did nearly everything as a unit, and at times were blinded by our spirits and always stuck it out no matter what the challenges were. I can still her Jerry saying, "Stick it out boys, we can do it!" It would be that exact rallying call a few years later, that would enable all 32 of us to make our way from Wood Dale, Illinois to Jacksonville Florida, on our nearly 1,400 mile bike hike. Without the Scout spirit that had been infused into us at an early age, I am certain we would not have been successful in our quest for adventure in the summer of 1972.

The summer court of honor events was considerably different than the Christmas ceremonies. They were held outside under the stars where we all sat on lawn chairs around a massive bonfire. It was a beautiful clear night in June 1971 and there seemed to be a much larger crowd of people than what we had expected. As we scurried to locate more folding chairs from the church basement, the event got started on schedule with the Color Guard marching in and posting the colors. It was during this court of honor that I would be awarded the rank of First Class, a rank that signified my skills in cooking, nature lore, camping, and mapping.

I was working hard at being a good Scout and was awarded the rank of Star at the Christmas court of honor on December 20, 1971. Soon afterwards, I was elected to become a patrol leader. The rank of Star was a huge accomplishment for me. I realized that I was in the Scouts for the long haul and was anxious to start working toward the rank of Life Scout. This was an even loftier goal as it required that I earn a total of 10 merit badges.

In 1972, the Boy Scouts of America raised the number of merit badges required to achieve the rank of Eagle from 21 to 24. It was a requirement that had stood since 1911 when the BSA was first formed. I was a bit discouraged but forged on and was awarded the rank of Life Scout on June 12, 1972. Life would be the highest rank I would achieve during my six years as a Boy Scout. Having obtained the rank of Life was a major accomplishment for me. My father recognized all my hard work and dedication by purchasing a mummy style sleeping bag for me that cost $100.00. It was a quite a sum of money to have spent on a sleeping bag back then and was a fantastic addition to my camping gear. It was piece of equipment that I would cherish for many years.

The concept of earning merit badges was as old as the BSA itself. It was designed to become a sort of roadmap to a Scout's life as he progressed through his ranks and could eventually lead to his life's work. The merit badges I had first started to earn as a Second Class Scout were ones that I had personally chosen. I had earned 10 merit badges that became a model for my life and represented the person I would eventually become as an adult.

The only other award besides the rank of Eagle that generated as much interest and was the most sought after in our troop, was for "Scout of the Year." After all the other awards were given out at the court of honor, the "Scout of the Year" medal was awarded. There were two bronze, one silver and only one gold medal that would be awarded. After a lot of hard work and dedication, I was fortunate enough to have achieved the Bronze Scout of the Year award in the summer of 1972.

TWENTY

I T WAS THE SUMMER OF 1969 and the structure of our small family unit would change significantly. My grandmother Rega had just moved into our basement. All of a sudden, I had three parents instead of two. For me that was a problem since I loved to explore and didn't want another set of watchful eyes on me. Billy and I did some crazy stuff as young boys. My grandmother had raised four of her own boys and knew what we were all about. She was much more curious about my whereabouts than my own mother had ever been and I found myself trying to avoid her. It would prove to be a difficult transition for my family but an experience and relationship that would forever change our lives.

Her old neighborhood had started to turn bad and a crime wave had begun to sweep through the section of Chicago where I had lived as a young boy. Several homes along her street of Hermitage had recently been broken into. She was getting pretty scared as a few of the home invasions involved armed robbery. There seemed to be a racial element at work as many of the Italian families that had originated in the neighborhood were beginning to move out in droves.

Even though I had just turned 12 years old that summer, she still insisted on calling me "Pauly." She was a strict disciplinarian and I could clearly see where my father got his tendencies toward discipline. She was a spanker too. Still in all, I was her oldest grandson and had been named after my father and late grandfather and she seemed to have somewhat of a soft spot for me. If I got out of line however, she was still quick for her age and would chase me through the house yelling, "Come back here you little son-of-a-bitch!" I of course ran like hell, so she wouldn't crack me with the black plastic ironing cord she was wielding in her hand.

My mother having seen my grandmother disciplining me soon adopted the ironing cord method of beating her kids. I think she must have carried the cord on her somehow because when she came after me I don't recall her stopping to unplug the cord from the iron. I just felt its sharp sting across my head when she connected. I had to be careful with my mother too since she had been a track star in high school and was pretty darn quick.

Despite my grandmother's watchful eye, she was a big supporter of the Scouts since her best friend Ann Walters was my father's first den mother. She would often say, "Be a good Scout Pauly, and run down to the corner store and get me a sack of flour," or whatever it was that she needed that day. She advanced me five dollars on several occasions during the winter months on my promise that I would wash her car come the summer. I never forgot my pledge to her, as she was more than generous. Her "tips" allowed me enough money to buy a lift ticket at the local ski resort.

It was shortly after my grandmother moved in with us that we would take one of our many family vacations to Florida. July 20, 1969 was marked by one of the most historic events in our country's nearly 200 year existence when Neil Armstrong, an Eagle Scout, and Buzz Aldrin landed their Lunar Module dubbed the "Eagle in the Sea of Tranquility."

When the astronauts of Apollo 11 were preparing to land on the moon we were already in Florida driving down a lonely stretch of highway when our car radio started to lose its reception. My father jerked our station wagon off to the side of the road and jumped out grumbling some explicative while desperately trying to extend the antenna. The radio came back on eventually although the signal was still weak with a lot of static. As we drove further down the road, the signal seemed to get stronger and we were able to listen to a somewhat more audible Walter Cronkite. He described in detail how the astronauts had to fly past their original landing spot since it was riddled with boulders larger than our car.

With only seconds of fuel left, Armstrong, an experienced naval aviator was able to visually locate a more suitable landing site for the Lunar Module. The two astronauts would soon touch down safely on the moon's surface at 4:18 p.m. EDT and Armstrong reported, "Houston, Tranquility Base here. The Eagle has landed." Armstrong would be the first man to set foot on the moon and voice his now legendary words, "That's one small step for man, one giant leap for mankind." My father was a big supporter of the space program and we would visit the Kennedy Space Center that summer.

That same summer Jerry and a few of my fellow Scouts had taken a long bike trip out to one of their familiar destinations. The Verona Father's Retreat was some 80 miles of biking each way and was located southwest of Wood Dale. It was an unusually hot Sunday afternoon and the small group of Boy Scouts including Steve Mahoney, Jeff Anderson, and Ray Bender had stopped for a break after having bicycled several miles. They were fairly close to home and it was a scorching hot day with a thunderstorm looming in the distance. They needed a break from the sun that had been beating down on them for the past several hours. Just as they were passing a small white farmhouse where an older woman was tending to her garden, it started to pour.

The woman seeing that Jerry and the boys might be in trouble called them over to her garage where she had taken refuge from the sudden storm. As they waited for the rain to subside, one of the boys said, "I think we should all go someplace farther on our bikes."

"Well, where do you think we should go?" Jerry asked.

"Let's go to Florida!" Jeff Anderson blurted out. The other two boys got really excited by the idea of riding their bikes to Florida. That hot summer afternoon in 1969 would mark the day our incredible bicycle journey from Wood Dale, Illinois to Jacksonville, Florida would first be hatched by a few visionary Scouts. Without their spirit and quest for adventure, the trip would have never taken place. There were a number of other big trips already planned, including one later that summer to Glacier National Park and two others that would follow. The boys realized that there would be some delay in their quest to head to Florida and understood that a trip of that magnitude would require a great deal of planning. They all agreed that the only time they could go would be in the summer of 1972.

A week or so later Jerry was attending one of the mother's group meetings when one of ladies said, "So I hear you're going to Florida?" It was quickly followed by what seemed to be a barrage of other questions about a trip that would not take place for almost three more years. The buzz quickly became more of a mantra in the weeks that would follow and the message became clear, "We were going to Florida, on bicycles." Jerry would usually say, "If the kids said we were going, we went." After all, he believed strongly in a youth-run organization where the boys would help to plan their trips and make the tough decisions.

His philosophy and strict adherence to the principle of a youth-run organization had been something he had been taught in the Order of the Arrow. It became an inherent part of the way he ran Troop 65. His methods of training his young Scouts were another way of ensuring that the troop's leaders would come from within the troop itself. As a result, Troop 65 became a very close-knit group of Scouts that relied on and trusted each other's judgment. Many of us including myself and my friend, Danny Zoubek were being groomed as future leaders of our troop and would soon become patrol leaders. So, when a few of our fellow Scouts said, let's ride our bikes to Florida, without really thinking twice that it was well over a 1,000 miles away, Jerry in his wisdom went along with the idea, realizing that we could do it.

The mom's club or the "HHY" as they called it was an acronym for the Historical Horizons for Youth. The influential group was the brainchild of Scoutmaster, Tony Langfeld who helped to organize the mother's group with the purpose of supporting the Scouts. Jerry's mother, Marie and Betty Rohl, fellow Scout Mike Rohl's mother were good friends and together with Tony's wife, Dorothy, and Mrs. Froehling formed the nucleus of the group. The HHY often helped to organize the troop's transportation to various places around the country. They helped to raise money for the purchase of an old school bus the Scouts would affectionately call, the "Blue Flash."

Jeff Anderson, Ray Bender and Steve Mahoney were like the "Three Musketeers" Jerry said. It wasn't unusual that they had been on the Verona Fathers bike trip together that summer as they seemed to always be doing something together. When we would eventually take off on our bicycles on July 22, 1972, our adventure to Florida would mark the longest organized bike hike in the history of the Boy Scouts of America. Sadly, the Three Musketeers were unable to go on the trip that they had envisioned due to their work schedules.

In the summers that would pass before the trip to Florida, my family would take vacations and my father wanted me to be with him and our family. Consequently, I would not go on any of the long summer trips with the Scouts to the Grand Canyon or Glacier National Park. However, the bicycle trip to Florida somehow was different, and my father allowed me to go. He indicated to Jerry that he understood the magnitude and importance of the trip. Many of our family vacations would bring us to Florida as my father's business enabled us to stay at the Lago Mar Resort, a renowned ocean front hotel in Fort Lauderdale.

When I wasn't vacationing or camping with my family, I was very active in the Scouts during the years before our bicycle trip to Florida. Billy was in my patrol and was a big help in organizing our camping trips and other activities. His camping skills were pretty advanced compared to most others, as he had been camping since he was a young boy. He continued to advance in rank, although not as fast as I had, and would achieve the rank of First Class. Reaching a certain rank in the Scouts was just not very important to Billy.

The spring of 1971 seemed to be much wetter than normal as rainstorm after storm pummeled our small community and Salt Creek was once again flooding. Danny Zoubek's house was located on Grove Street along the creek just north of the railroad tracks that ran through town. Although their house sat up pretty high, the creek was only about 400 feet away from the back of his house. When the creek would rage over its banks, his basement would sometimes flood.

Forest View was the next street just east of Harvey Avenue and the creek was just a short distance east of that. The large creek had been formed some 15,000 years before Billy and I encountered it from the melt waters of the Wisconsin glaciers. Starting at its marshy birthplace in Inverness, Illinois, it runs some 40 miles before draining into the Des Plaines River.

When the Potawatomi Indians first lived along its banks, the now muddy sewage filled creek was a sparkling clean stream with a stone bottom. It was home to a large game fish population including bass and walleye. Over the years, Salt Creek had succumbed to the onslaught of modern society and its resulting pollution.

The mighty creek that was once a living, thriving entity seemed angry that year. In an effort to fight back, it unleashed its fury and flooded homes and businesses along its route, causing millions of dollars in damage. Some had said that the creek was just doing its job as it was created by nature to flood. Where soil had once existed, concrete now replaced it and the flooding waters simply had nowhere to go, except into all the manmade structures along its crowded banks.

Billy and I spent a lot of time exploring the creek and when we saw one, would catch a ride on one of the huge oil drums used to store heating oil for homes back in those days. They would somehow find themselves in the creek, as people would sometimes use it as a dumping ground for things like that. As Scouts, it drove us nuts, as we were constantly on clean up duty to try and rid the banks of what seemed to be an endless amount of trash.

Shortly after a rainstorm, Billy and I had ventured out and were hiking through a neighbor's yard on the far eastern side of Forrest View that boarded the creek. The water had come all the way up to their back door and was threatening to flood their house. As Billy and I stood watching in amazement at the creek which had turned into a raging river, we spotted an oil drum lodged in-between two small trees. It was impossible to tell exactly how deep the water was but be had a pretty good idea based on how high the creek had risen on the tree trunks. The oil drum wasn't that far from the back of the house, so we both looked at each other and made a decision to try to jump on it. Sightings of the drums had become rarer as people began switching to natural gas to heat their homes.

We both grabbed a large stick so we would have something to use to help navigate our oil drum through the torrent of Salt Creek. By the time we reached the drum, it was starting to work itself out of the trees as the creek continued to rise. As we boarded our small rusted craft and started to push our way closer to the main part of the creek, I took a glance back toward the house. The brown murky water had now breached the neighbor's back door. As Scouts, we had helped homeowners and businesses to make hundreds of sand bags piling them near large sections of the creek that often flooded.

As we inched our way closer to the main part of the creek, I caught a glimpse of Billy's face. He had that crazed look in his eyes that I had become familiar with over the years. We were both strong kids and our balance was excellent. We decided to stay outside of the creek's center where we could see the water moving at a fast pace. The brown water churned in a ferocious manner as it carried tons of debris including parts of houses, and anything else it could suck up and carry away. Despite steering clear of the main torrent, we were moving along at a good clip bobbing up and down trying to keep ourselves upright. The sticks we had grabbed proved to be a lifesaver, as they helped to stabilize our drum.

The creek takes a sharp turn to the west, cutting past Harvey Avenue just as it begins to flow through the Salt Creek County Forest Preserve. Up to this point, we had done a good job of navigating our small craft, keeping it out of the center of the creek. As we began to make a turn back to the east, the creek had its own ideas as to where we were going and pushed us squarely into its center. We began to pick up a lot of speed as we were catapulted out of the loop and were now heading dead east. Trying to stay calm, we both knew we were in trouble and were at certain risk of drowning as the creek was now in complete control of our oil drum.

The creek takes another sharp turn to the south heading deeper into the forest preserve. As we bobbed up and down, like a fishing bobber, it started to rain again and our visibility was severely hampered. We decided to sit down on the drum as any attempt to try to steer or propel ourselves to the banks was futile. If we failed to get our drum out of the creek, or at least to the banks, the next destination would be Oak Meadows County Forest Preserve where the creek straightens out.

There's an access road that runs east and west through the entire length of the park with a one lane wooden bridge over the creek. Our visibility had now been reduced to no more than three feet in all directions. It was pouring so hard that I couldn't make out where we were in reference to the banks of the creek. I was completely disoriented. Our drum began to spin wildly around, caught in some sort of whirlpool in the middle of the creek. I saw terror on Billy's face as we twisted and turned out of control. It felt as if we were on a Tilt-A-Whirl at an amusement park. Just as quickly as it started, we got pushed farther down the creek and were heading straight for what I thought was the bridge.

Billy saw it, too, and we both stood up with our sticks to help stabilize ourselves on our rain soaked steel drum. "It's the bridge!" I yelled out. The water had all but covered the bridge except for a slight bit of wood planking that was barely visible. We had been down Salt Creek a few times on the same type of oil drum but had always gone under the bridge. This time would be different as huge logs and other debris had started to collect around the front and top of the bridge.

As we got closer I knew we would have to act fast and I yelled out to Billy, "When the drum hits, we have to jump to the bridge!" He nodded and the oil drum crashed violently into the side of the bridge. We both jumped landing on top of the water soaked bridge. We ran across the wooden planks as quickly as we could to the safety of the shoreline. Exhausted from the terror we had just experienced, we watched in awe as the old drum worked itself up onto the top of the bridge. A few minutes later, it was washed further downstream. The creek was still rising and more dangerous than we had ever seen it.

Billy and I had both turned 13 years old the summer before and were only a few months away from being 14. Despite the obvious danger, we each had an adventurous spirit and a keen sense of invincibility running through our blood. It would be one of our last great adventures together. We would never again take an oil drum down the mighty Salt Creek, knowing that our lives had somehow been spared that day.

TWENTY-ONE

TROOP 65 WAS WELL KNOWN for high adventure and had successfully completed several trips that required a lot of planning and preparation. Most of the parents were confident in our leaders and their ability to pull off such daring trips. They knew that the troop had extensive experience with long trips and were able to manage the kids during such excursions. However, the bicycle hike to Florida was unlike other trips the troop had tackled in the past. The distance seemed to be a factor for many of the parents and they voiced their apprehension at times during the early planning stages.

For the most part, Jerry was able to calm most of the parent's initial fears. My father was a voice of reason as he realized that this was a noteworthy experience and felt strongly that the troop should go on the trip. The sheer distance from Illinois to Florida and our chosen mode of transportation was a problem for some of the parents. They would ask, "Are you really going that far on a bicycle?" As time went on and the number of our training sessions increased, our parent's attitudes toward the trip began to change. They seemed to be more at ease with the idea as they just figured we were going. Jerry had always maintained an open level of communication with the parents and they knew that he and his assistant leaders would take care of the kids.

Despite Jerry's confidence in his Scouts and his enthusiasm for the trip, he was well aware of the potential risks and pitfalls that such an adventure posed. It was by far one of the most challenging trips to prepare for and would require him to marshal all of his organizational skills and experience. The complex trip that would require a great deal of logistics was solidly on the shoulders of a man, who was just 31 years old. The "Three Musketeers" had set this trip in motion and Jerry was just acting as the agent whose job now was to maintain order and bring life to their dream.

He was always fighting with Committee members trying to convince them that the kids could take these types of trips. He was very cognizant of the fact that some of the Scouts may not be ready for a trip of this magnitude. There were several issues regarding the boy's maturity that had to be taken into consideration. Some were rather embarrassing, such as bed-wetting. "It was a process," Jerry said. "It took about a year to see what made a kid tick," he said. He wanted to see whether they would sleep walk or what possible mental hang-ups they might have before they could go on such a long trip.

Bed-wetting in particular was a problem for some kids. Jerry would often stay up late while on campouts and make the boys go to the bathroom hoping to alleviate any problems in the morning. As a younger boy sometime before my Scouting days, I too, had an issue with bed-wetting. I don't recall ever having had an accident while camping with the Scouts. I suppose it's possible though as I was pretty adept at the art of bed-wetting. It was a glorious feeling and was usually a dream where I had gotten out of bed to pee and then would just let it go. It was a warm and somewhat comforting feeling. Then, the shock came! I would wake up and to my horror be immersed in what was now a cold puddle of my own piss. It was a terrible and potentially embarrassing situation. I had to quickly get up and try to hide the evidence. It was certainly harder to do while camping with a bunch of other boys. Jerry made an effort to try to prevent any embarrassment that was sure to follow such an accident.

Despite the early rumblings by some of our parents about our bike trip, it was now pretty much a reality that we were in fact going. The official announcement wasn't made until the early fall of 1971. Jerry realized that if the trip were to be a success, he would need to focus all of his attention on managing the logistics of such an operation. His former military training would come in handy as he began the task of organizing his young staff.

It wasn't until early September of 1971, that we began the actual planning of the Florida bike trip. We decided that our initial planning session would be held at Jerry's house on Hawthorn Lane. The Risting house had not changed much over the years with the exception of a new color TV having replaced their old black and white model. The knotty pine rec room where the family often gathered still had the rectangular shaped wooden table where many previous Scout meetings had taken place.

I had turned 14 years old in August, and would be a junior leader on the trip and helped in the early planning phase. Having demonstrated leadership qualities and a high level of self-confidence in my abilities, I never backed down from a challenge and was always enthusiastic about being involved in a project. I had reached the rank of First Class and would soon achieve the rank of Star later that year at our Christmas court of honor. I was a serious Scout on a fast track and was working hard at becoming the best Scout I could be. On July 12, 1972, with less than two weeks before we would depart on our great odyssey, I would be awarded the rank of Life. I would soon begin to set my sights on what my Eagle project might be. I dreamt of a major cleanup of Salt Creek.

Most of our Scout meetings at Jerry's house were held in the evenings since he and the other adult leaders, including Lou

Giannini and Bob Sample, had to work. The rest of us were still in school. We all gathered around the table in Jerry's rec room for our first planning session. He had already purchased the maps we needed to plot our route. Only a few of us had actually been to Florida. The furthest anyone had ridden their bikes was to the Verona Fathers Retreat some 80 miles away.

Our first line of business was to decide exactly where in Florida we were going. Everyone agreed that it was important to determine our destination before we could start to map our route. The only computers back then were the megalith IBM machines owned by large companies and government agencies. All the planning and mapping had to be done by hand using several maps for each state we would decide to travel through.

Bob Sample, who was a Wood Dale cop, was able to program the route we had chosen into their police headquarters computer. The print out, or "trip ticket" as it was officially dubbed by Jerry, helped to organize the route. It listed all of the roads and directions we needed to travel in order to get to our destination. All the cities and towns we would pass through, including their populations, were listed on the trip ticket. Also included was the total number of miles traveled and the distance between each destination. A number of parks and campgrounds were also listed and what facilities were available at each location. Knowing where we might be able to shower and get a hot meal were extremely important aspects of the trip. We would be on the road, camping wherever we could find a large enough strip of grass to sleep 32 people.

Some of us wanted to go to Disney World, which would soon open its doors on October 1, 1971. After some lively debate, the elders in the group thought it would be wise to do something more patriotic in nature and provide an educational experience for the boys. After further discussion, we all decided that we would leave Wood Dale the morning of July 22, 1972. We would travel an estimated 1,400 miles on our bicycles ending with our final destination in Jacksonville, Florida. Upon our arrival, we would take a 147-mile bus ride south along the Florida coast to the Kennedy Space Center. Since I had already been to the space center in 1969, I wasn't as excited about our choice, but still thought it would be neat to see the rockets again.

As we spread open, the first map onto the table there was a certain amount of anxiety that seemed to fill the air as we started plotting our route. Although Jerry had never been to Florida, he still had traveled extensively throughout the United States and abroad while in the service. He realized that planning and logistics of such a trip were very important elements if he was going to move such a large group of people and equipment across several states. This trip would prove to be much different than any other that he had previously embarked on. There were many unknown factors, which were associated with such an adventure. After all, the mode of transportation was a bicycle. All of the little roads had to be mapped out, as bikes are not allowed on any of the interstates. That simple fact would make the mapping of our trip very challenging. There were several opinions voiced that night as to what the best destination and route should be.

I knew that we had a lot of planning ahead of us when Jerry opened and spread out the first map onto the table. It would be followed by nine other maps; one for each state that we had planned on passing through. The first map was quite large and showed all of the states comprising the eastern half of the US. At first, we thought it was best to focus on one map in an effort to get some perspective of where we were going. Jerry then proceeded to draw a straight line on the map from Wood

Dale to Jacksonville, Florida. We were planning to travel through nine states including, Illinois, Indiana, Kentucky, Virginia, Tennessee, North Carolina, South Carolina, Georgia, and finally into Florida.

Mr. Giannini or Mr. "G", as we fondly called him, had traveled extensively across the US vacationing with his family. He opened the Illinois map first, spreading it out on the table, and tried to transpose the line Jerry had drawn on the larger East Coast map. He continued the process with the other state maps. It was a good theory, but, unfortunately, it didn't work as we had originally planned. As we looked at each map, it was nearly impossible to decipher what roads were there. We tried to stay along the original line from the larger map as much as we could, but it proved to be impossible. The state maps were more detailed and had many more roads than the larger East Coast map depicted.

What we had originally thought to be a simple task had turned in to an arduous lesson in mapping. As Scouts, we lived for the map and compass. After our first attempt at developing our route failed, it seemed to turn into a challenge. As Jerry and some of the other adult leaders proceeded to map out the route, it appeared that there were dozens of little roads that we would need to take to reach our destination. It seemed that everyone had a slightly different opinion on exactly what the route should be. Disagreements and discussions like that were typical though, as Jerry had trained all of his young leaders to voice their opinions. We always seemed to work it out and in the process learned something valuable. Whatever problem or issue we were dealing with it was always a combination of ideas that brought us to a solution. The debate continued well into the night.

Bob Sample possessed a pretty forthright and confident demeanor and was usually the most outspoken amongst us. Mike Terese and Jack Froehling usually spoke their minds, too, when it came to things regarding the troop, but were more diplomatic in their approach. Mike was always the more introspective one in his response where his answers were thought out and calculated. Jack was more spontaneous and freely shared his opinion. Neither approach was good or bad, just different. As a young leader, I observed their way of solving problems that might arise for us in the future.

Mike Rohl, the youngest of the adult leaders, was our junior assistant Scoutmaster and had joined the troop when he was just 11 years old. He was only a few years older than I was at the time of the trip. He had a stout build for his age and his pitch-black hair was always parted to the right side. His thick black rimmed glasses were always securely attached to his head with an elastic band. Mike was a very meticulous and organized guy. His black dress shoes always had a high gloss shine, the kind that if you were standing next to him, you could see your own reflection. He seemed to be obsessed with time and always wore a silver Timex watch he had received as a gift from his father.

Mike was close to his dad who had a love for nature and was quite an accomplished outdoorsman. He taught him some real commonsense outdoor woodsman skills. Mike's father was a good-natured guy with a funny sense of humor. He would often accompany us on campouts and was always telling jokes and stories around the campfire, clutching a cup of coffee. He loved his coffee and whenever you saw him, he seemed to have a cup in his hand or was devising some ingenious way to make a pot of the stuff.

There were very few fathers, like Mike's that actually camped with us but when they did, the kids got a real kick out of it. It was often some of the dads that made the troop what it was. Mike's father, Frank, was special and "a real Camperoo," Jerry would say. He was a real tall guy and at times was kind of hard to understand as he spoke with a strong southern drawl. Many of Mike's outdoor skills came from his father's early teachings and his love and dedication to Scouting was evident. He achieved the rank of Eagle at an early age and demanded a certain amount of respect despite being much quieter than most of the other leaders.

Mike didn't talk much, but when he did, you had better listen to him as it always seemed to be something important. He often struggled in his ability to communicate with the younger Scouts. His voice wasn't always heard, and at times the younger boys had trouble listening and taking direction from him. Over time though, Mike would begin to speak his mind and develop into a stronger leader under Jerry's tutelage. He became very helpful to the other Scouts and was a good organizer. His input into the planning of the Florida bike trip was invaluable. It would become evident while on our month long trip, that Mike had developed into a good teacher and a strong leader of his fellow Scouts.

Jack's personality was just the opposite of Mike's. He was outgoing and personable and a real screwball at heart. When his family first came to Wood Dale, Jack was a wirily 11-year-old, exceptionally strong for his age and full of energy. His father thought the Scouts would be a good place for him to expend some of his youthful vigor.

Jack's family was building a house that had heating elements installed in the floor that caused a fire just before they had planned to move in. Jerry was on the fire department at the time and his volunteer crew was able to quickly extinguish the fire. The fire had delayed the Froehling's move but shortly after they settled in, Jack joined Troop 65. While in the Scouts, he loved to clown around and was always pulling some sort of practical joke. Despite his antics, he developed into a very responsible Scout leader that Jerry could count on. He would often take half the troop and Jerry would take the other half and meet somewhere in the middle. He was that trustworthy.

No matter what might happen along our long trip to Florida, Jack could be counted on for his resourcefulness and to maintain morale amongst the Scouts. He always had an outgoing personality and effervescence that followed him wherever he went and was known by everyone in the troop as "good-natured Jack." I always looked up to him as a strong leader despite the fact that he was only a few years older than I was.

As the night wore on and we continued our painstaking efforts to map out our trip, it became clear that there were certain parts of the route that we began to focus on. As Scouts we were drawn to the Great Smoky Mountains National Park, because of the natural beauty and abundant wildlife. The Smokies are among some of the oldest mountains on Earth and are located in the Appalachian mountains of North Carolina and Tennessee. The park encompasses over a half million acres making it one of the largest protected areas in the eastern part of the United States. Many of the Scouts had never traveled outside of Illinois. This single trip would take us through nine states all in one summer. It was an opportunity for all of us to explore new parts of the country as we shared a boyish curiosity and quest for outdoor adventure. We were after all, Boy Scouts on a mission.

Jerry had visited the Great Smoky Mountains National Park some years earlier while on a family vacation and wanted to share some of his experiences with the Scouts. One of his most vivid memories included the famed outdoor play called "Unto These Hills." The play depicts the early history and eventual plight of the Cherokee Indian. As he described the play that takes place on a stage cut into the side of a mountain where Indians dance through hoops of fire, my mind began to wander. I found myself thinking about the stories my father used to tell me about himself and my uncle Jack and the dance team they had formed while in the Order of the Arrow.

The route that we had begun to map out, would take us right through the heart of the park on Newfound Gap Road, where we would have to climb to an elevation of some 5,048 five. The Smoky Mountains became one of the main focal points of the trip, and would prove to be one of the troop's greatest challenges on our journey to Florida.

My family had traveled to Florida many times and I had been through the great mountain pass in our car. We had camped and hiked throughout the park. Much of it is heavily wooded with over a hundred species of trees and old growth forests. Miles of rocky streams meander throughout the park filled with many species of game fish. A few years earlier my father had taught me how to fish for brook trout, a native fish in that part of the country. It's an unusual looking fish and one I had never seen before that's mostly brown in color with distinctive yellow and red markings across its body. It was the first time I would see someone fly fish, as they stood out in the middle of the rapids tossing their line attached with a small fly. Although I didn't see anyone catch a trout using this method of fishing it looked like a lot of fun.

The Park is home to thousands of plant and animal species including a rather large population of Black Bears. I had always been taught to be cautious around bears ever since our family's excursion around Lake Michigan in Michigan's Upper Peninsula. The Black Bears in that part of the country were more aggressive than the ones we would encounter in the Smoky Mountains. "A bear is a bear, and is no match for a man," my father would often say. I would be sure to heed his words of caution, as we would be traveling through the mountains on bicycles.

TWENTY-TWO

AS JERRY AND THE OTHER LEADERS continued to talk about our route through the Smoky Mountains, I wondered what it would be like to ride our bikes through the park with all its steep narrow roads. From an early age, I had ridden my bike throughout most of Wood Dale and many of the surrounding towns. This trip would be quite different since we weren't just talking about a few hundred-mile jaunt to another Illinois town. We would have to first navigate our way over the foothills and then make our ascent over the Great Smokies. In order to safely accomplish this monumental task, we would need to be equipped with a more advanced type of bike called a "10-speed." Certainly, no one that I knew of owned one or had even seen one, except maybe on TV. The closest thing to a multiple speed bike in town was my Stingray.

The 10-speed was originally used by European cyclists to climb mountains during the 1940s. It wasn't until the early 1970s when the United States became more environmentally conscious due to a looming oil crisis, that the 10-speed would become popular. What resulted was known as the American bike boom of the 1970s. It was proclaimed as "the bicycle's biggest wave of popularity in its 154 year history" according to a Time Magazine article in 1971. Schwinn, the largest bike manufacturer at the time had sold all its planned production for that year.

Mastering the new style of bike would prove to be a real challenge for all of us. It would take several weeks of training and lots of stripped gears before we could even think of taking them on our cross country jaunt to Florida. I was pretty confident in my riding abilities despite the new bikes and anxious to get the initial planning stages over with. I wanted to start what would be months of training exercises on our new 10-speeds. Actual training however would not start until the following spring, as there were still a lot of specifics to work out, including what brand of bike we would purchase. The two brands initially mentioned were Raleigh and Schwinn, as they were the most popular.

We would also have to devise a lightweight but sturdy means to carry all of our gear on our bikes. The idea of a lightweight tent was brought up since nylon was becoming a more widely used material and the cost was beginning to come down. Keeping the weight on all of our gear to a minimum was something we put a lot of thought into; since we knew climbing the mountains would be difficult.

Over the next several months, we would meet in Jerry's rec room on a regular basis and continue to hash out all the details that were essential to the trip's success. As time went on and we got more involved in the planning of the trip, it was clear that this venture would require help from many people in our community. Bike riding until the big boom was considered an activity reserved mostly for kids in the US. Certainly, anything resembling a cross-country trip was unheard of, especially for a group of kids, some who would be as young as 11 years old.

In order to more accurately determine the cost of the trip, we would need to investigate the price associated with our bikes. Jerry was very cost conscious and conservative with everything associated with the Scouts. Our trip to Florida would be no exception. He rarely, splurged on anything for himself or the troop, and felt it was essential to show the boys by example the importance of a thrifty lifestyle. He knew early on that the costs would be considerably higher than those of other trips they had taken. The next several weeks would be spent discussing ways to keep our costs down in order to sell the trip to our parents.

A number of families, including mine, were tight on money back then. I used to cut my neighbors grass to make some spending money. Although gasoline was only about 55 cents per gallon, the average income in those days was barely $12,000. Most mothers stayed at home and tended to their families and the dad's worked hard, but didn't make a lot of money. Jerry knew that some families would have trouble paying for the trip despite his efforts to keep the expenses as low as possible.

There were times when Jerry would quietly help to pay out of his own pocket for a kid to go on a trip. Because so many Scouts had expressed an interest in going on this trip, it posed a more difficult challenge to raise money for everyone that wanted to go, but couldn't afford it. As a junior leader, I was aware of some of Jerry's generosity and it would prove to be another lesson in, "what goes around comes around," something my father had taught me.

Jerry was always trying to figure out new and innovative ways to raise money for the troop in addition to our paper drives. The mother's group was instrumental in fund raising and through their efforts helped to pay for some of our transportation costs for our trips. The idea of obtaining company sponsorships was first discussed at one of our planning meetings. It appeared to be a possible answer to raise the funds for some of my buddies who wanted to go on the Florida trip. It was determined that at least nine kids would need some type of financial assistance, and Jerry would privately seek out several potential corporate sponsors. All of the boys who needed help were active in the Scouts and really wanted to go on the trip. Our Scoutmaster was not going to let a financial hardship get in the way of letting them go.

Jerry had made a pledge to the Scouts that he would do whatever he could to help them, and he followed through on his promise. It wasn't surprising that he was successful in his fund raising efforts. He was able to secure pledges from several companies in each of the boy's names. Shortly after the bike trip, he and the Scouts, dressed in full uniform, would meet each of their corporate sponsors, and present them with a special plaque. It was a great lesson in teaching us the importance of goodwill.

Since the Raleigh and Schwinn bike companies were among the most well-known, it made sense that Jerry had decided to speak with them first. He indicated to each company that we needed upwards of 30 bikes of the same model, so the parts would be interchangeable. It quickly became evident that neither company could guarantee delivery of that many bikes, stating that they had too many other orders.

After several weeks of research, Jerry was starting to think about other options for the bikes we needed. It was then when John McClure from Sears first approached him. He had heard about our bike trip from a fellow employee and said, "I think we can help you guys." Sears had just started selling a new model of a 10-speed bike under their Free Spirit logo. They were anxious to sell as many as possible. It appeared to be a win-win situation for both Sears and Troop 65.

John realized the predicament we were in and the urgency that was required in placing such a large order for the bikes we needed. He suggested that he should come out to the Scout meeting that evening and observe the Scouts. It was important for him to understand what we needed since there was such a wide range of ages between the boys. Some of the youngest

Scouts were only 11 years old. I was almost 15 and one of the older Scouts. The bikes we needed would have to accommodate all of the Scouts, including our five adult leaders.

It wasn't too long after John arrived at our meeting and had an opportunity to meet some of the boys when he said to Jerry, "I have some bad news. Some of the kids won't fit on a 27-Inch bike."

"Can we use blocks or something attached to the pedals and lower the handlebars so the younger kids will fit on the bikes?" Jerry responded.

"No, it would be a very unsafe," John said. He realized that it was important that we have the same model bike and said that he would put a lot of thought into our problem and get back to us with an answer as soon as possible.

Early the following week Jerry got a phone call from an excited John McClure. "I think I may have solved the problem," he said. John went on to explain that he felt that a workable solution would be to equip all of the older boys and adults with their new 27-Inch bike they touted as their 10-Speed Free Spirit Racer. The new Racers were equipped with dual position hand brake levers and a 10-speed derailleur system that featured a 38 to 100 gear ratio range. John explained that the new bike's mechanicals would enable us to climb the nearly 6,000 feet of elevation in the Smoky Mountains. Jerry would later try to explain all of this to us at our next brainstorming session. Since the bikes were so new and akin to some exotic beast, no one really understood the significance of the bike's gearing system. We just knew that it would be a vitally important feature on the bike that would get us safely up and through the great mountain pass.

The most significant aspect of John's solution to our problem was that the younger boys, as he explained it, would be provided with their new 24-Inch bike. The smaller bike was being manufactured for Sears by Murray Bikes. The 27-Inch bikes were being produced by the Austrian Puch company. The larger bike was a hodgepodge of components manufactured by a number of different companies. The steel frame was sturdy and lightweight compared to the Schwinn Varsity we had looked at. It was painted a pearl shiny white color with two red, white, and blue decals.

The smaller 24-Inch bike was Sears's answer into a more mountain style bike, which they saw as an emerging market. The smaller bikes had a wider knobbier tire than the 27-Inch models. They were also equipped with a 10-speed derailleur system, although the gear ratio was lower at 29 to 86. What it really meant was that the younger Scout's bikes were equipped with smaller front and rear sprockets and would have to complete several more rotations of their crank. They would essentially have to pedal more than the boys did on the larger bikes, just to keep up the same speed.

John said that the smaller bikes would however have a slight advantage while climbing the mountains. Jerry thought that was a reasonable tradeoff for their safety since the younger boys would not fit on the 27-Inch bikes. Any sort of rigging to allow the boys to ride the larger bikes was considered an unsafe option. All the parts on the smaller bikes were interchangeable with each other. The same was true with all the larger bikes, should there be a breakdown. Seven of the 32 bikes that we would eventually purchase from Sears were of the smaller size and were painted red, white, and blue.

Sears was anxious to get their new Free Spirit Racers out into the market and they were willing to work with us. The idea to use two different size bikes seemed to be a solution to our problem and was also an opportunity for Sears to promote their new bikes. The Free Spirit name was symbolic for us too. Jerry and the rest of us thought that the name closely matched the troop's level of enthusiasm to take on such a big challenge. After all, we were definitely a bunch of free spirited boys and men anxious to get on the road and test our skills on our new bikes.

We were always willing to pay for the bikes, but John McClure wanted to help us and said that he wasn't able to give us the bikes due to his company policy. However, he could sell them to us at their cost, which amounted to $40.00 per bike. That was a great deal for us since the cheapest Schwinn 10-speed was well over $100.00. The Free Spirit had a list price of $81.99, so John helped us out quite a bit, enabling us to keep our trip costs down.

Sears offered a neat coupon that you could send in to receive a "Free Spirit" patch for your jacket with each purchase of a Free Spirit bike. Danny Zoubek was a very innovative guy that was always thinking. He was determined to get one of those patches for his red Scout jacket. Sometime after we had secured the bikes from Sears, Danny was shopping with his mother at the Sears near the Woodfield Mall and noticed the ad for the patch. He received it before we left on the trip and his mother, who was a much better seamstress than mine, sewed it on his red poplin Scout jacket.

When Danny started in the Scouts about a year after I had joined, he was 11 years old and was just one of the kids at that point. Jerry never thought he would do much in the Scouts, but little did he know that Dan was just getting his feet on the ground. When he was 12 years old, he was elected as a patrol leader. At the Green Bar Meetings where we planned our campouts, Danny had some great ideas. He had a knack for knowing how Scouts do things and often expressed his views. His advice and vision was well respected. He really excelled as a patrol leader. He knew his stuff and stuck to it. Danny was proud of his troop and the fact that he was a Scout. Jerry was always impressed with Danny as being a true believer in the system.

Sears was similar to the Wal-Mart of today, although the quality of the products in its stores was of a higher quality. It was well known for its sports equipment and their great toy department with yards of Lionel train track winding its way throughout the toy section of the store. One of my first base-ball mitts was a Sears's brand and I loved it, never giving a thought to the fact that it had the "Sears" name embroidered on it. The company and its products were part of our American culture and everyone had a Sears catalog.

All of the Scouts really appreciated our new Sears Free Spirit bicycles. There wasn't a lot of peer pressure back then where you had to have the best stuff. We never thought that way, and it certainly never crossed our minds that if we didn't have a Schwinn, you didn't have a bike. It just wasn't like that when I was growing up as a boy in small town America. In early May, 1972 when we would eventually take delivery of 32 Free Spirit bikes from Sears, most of us were awe struck with the new 10-speed contraption, and were anxious to test our riding skills on them.

TWENTY-THREE

THE FLORIDA BRAINSTORMING meeting on April 10 was a bit different, as we would all be fitted for our bikes that evening. John McClure from Sears would be there to help us determine what size bike each Scout needed. It was quickly decided that we would need seven of the smaller red, white, and blue 24-Inch bikes and twenty-five of the 27-Inch bikes. Since the bikes would not be delivered until sometime in early May, we started our training sessions using our own bikes.

After weeks of discussion, we had finally worked up an estimate of what the total cost of the trip per Scout would be. There was a lot pressure from our parents to keep our costs down. We decided to make some of the items we needed for the trip. The amount of $270.00 was slightly rounded up to give us a cushion should we run into any unexpected expenses. Everything had to be considered, including the cost to fly the bikes back from Florida on a separate airplane. The mothers of the HHY vowed to help us raise some money through various fundraisers.

The length of time that we would be away from home, and the cost of our equipment, including our bicycles, made it the most expensive trip to date. The money each Scout would need to raise was used to cover our bikes, meals, plane fare, clothing, saddlebags, and all the other miscellaneous items we might need. We would be on the road for 30 days. Also planned, were a number of activities that would require admission fees such as our trip to the Kennedy Space Center. Our budget allowed each Scout to bring a total of $30.00 for spending money. Jerry would give us each a $1.00 a day over the 30 days that we were on the road. He knew that if he had given us all of our money up front, that we would have spent it in a few days. At that time, you could buy a candy bar and a pop with a dollar and still have money left over. To ease the burden a bit, the money needed for the trip was collected in increments. The first deposit was due on April 14, at our Scout meeting.

On Saturday, April 15, when we first assembled our group of 32 Scouts and leaders at the Holy Ghost parking lot, it was a cold day and snow was in the air. I was excited about finally being able to start our training sessions. Billy had made a decision not to go on the trip despite my constant urging. It was a pride thing with him as money was always an issue with his family. After he spoke with Jerry about a sponsor, he felt that it was something he just wasn't comfortable with.

I was able to work something out with my father where I paid for some of the trip with the money I had earned from cutting grass, and he paid the rest. We were usually able to work out some sort of a deal, especially if he thought it was something worthwhile. If it wasn't, I was usually on my own. I would surely miss Billy's companionship and maybe even some of his guidance, as we were used to camping together. That was just how Billy was though, and I had to respect his decision.

The spring and summer of 1972, right before the trip, would be very busy as we continued to have our weekly planning and brainstorming sessions at Jerry's house. The mother's group was hard at work coming up with new ideas to raise money for the trip, and had planned an art fair in early June to help pay for some of our expenses. My mother was an artist and had initially suggested the idea and the rest of the group loved it. There seemed to be an endless amount of preparation needed for this trip, and since so many Scouts had decided to go, it made things more complicated. The entire town of Wood Dale was getting into it, and many people and businesses were helping us by donating things we needed, or by organizing fund raising events.

When we all arrived at the church lot at 10:00 a.m. to start our first training session, we looked like a rag tag bunch of young boys on old bikes. Most of our bikes resembled a Frankenstein type contraption where several parts of other bikes had been pieced together to make one bike. Nearly everyone's bike was like that since most of us could not afford new ones. Many of us were handy and had pieced together the best parts to make one bike. Some of us road bikes with banana seats and chopper style handlebars and some were equipped with 3-speeds. Other bikes the Scouts rode were old and looked like they had been handed down from their parents. We stopped many times during our training sessions just to repair all the old bikes.

Our first training session was an ambitious one that was scheduled for the entire day beginning in the morning and ending at 7:00 p.m. It was supposed to be a bicycle-conditioning hike as the schedule had indicated, but it soon turned in to a bicycle repair clinic. No one knew how bad it was until we all showed up. Shocked at what he saw, Jerry left abruptly and soon returned in his truck with his tools, an air pump and a few oil cans. We did the best we could as kids trying to fix our own bikes, but we had many breakdowns in our early training sessions since most of the bikes were so old.

Most of us could fix a flat tire without taking it off the rim and could repair almost everything on our bikes that went wrong. Many of the Scouts were handy, like Danny Zoubek and his older brother Steve, since our fathers had taken the time to show us how to use tools. Not all the boys were mechanically inclined though and you could tell by the way their bikes were maintained. A few of the younger boys showed up on bikes with chains that were rusting and nearly falling off. Their tires were so low on air; I wondered how they managed to even make it to the church. We quickly realized that a bike inspection prior to each training session was needed prior to any riding on the streets.

Jerry had planned on putting our group through a rigorous training program to prepare us for the long journey to Florida. The first two practice sessions were scheduled for April. The initial conditioning hikes amounted to just riding through several industrial parks in Wood Dale. Those would be followed by several more throughout May, June, and July. One hike would take us into Elgin, some 20 miles away from Wood Dale. An even further four-day excursion to the Mississippi Palisades State Park, near Savanna, Illinois was planned. Most of our bike hikes were scheduled every other day where we would pedal to nearby towns. It was important for us to condition our bodies for our long trip even though many of us were already in good shape having spent most of our time outdoors running around.

Getting in shape was critical, but the level of discipline that was needed to enable us to make such a long trip possible, was equally important. We needed to function as a unit that would work in unison since there would be 32 bikes on the road. It was important for all of us to be in tune with each other and aware of what each person ahead and behind us was doing at all times. A crash on the highway could result in a serious injury or even death.

Most of us were raised in a strict environment where excess was rare, and abiding by our parent's rules was paramount. Discipline was an essential element of our upbringing. It was a thought process that our parents instilled in us at a very early age. Our ability to follow rules was now being reinforced by our Scout leaders and was an important element in the success of our trip. We had been taught how to be self-sufficient at a young age and were not given very much. When we did get something, it was usually in the form of a hand-me-down and needed to be repaired. Consequently, many of us were taught how to use tools to fix things and we really appreciated everything we got.

Our Scout leaders made it clear, that when we did get our new 10-speed bikes it was important to maintain them and keep the bike in the best mechanical condition possible. Our bikes would be our sole mode of transportation for almost a month. If your chain wasn't properly lubricated, or your spokes were loose, it could cause some real problems. If your dad had not taught you how to fix your own bike by then, you were soon going to get a crash course in bicycle repair. Bike safety was something we were starting to hear a lot about from Jerry at our Friday Scout meetings.

Our next conditioning hike was much less ambitious and was scheduled for the evening of Thursday, April 27 from 6:30 p.m. to 9:00 p.m. Due to the adult leaders work schedule, we often road in the dark during many of our training sessions. No one except Jerry had a light on their bikes much less any reflectors. Up until the bike boom, there was not a lot of safety equipment available for bicycles since they were regarded as children's toys. We didn't wear helmets back then, because they didn't exist. Before the mid-1970s, the only type of bike helmet that was available was made of leather and was used by racing cyclists. It provided a minimal amount of protection against impact. The first commercially available bike helmet wasn't sold to the public until 1975 and was manufactured by Bell Sports, a maker of auto racing and motorcycle helmets.

There was never any mention of wearing bike helmets for the trip. Even safety in cars seemed to be lacking in those days as no one I knew, including my parents, ever wore seatbelts. They were usually found stuffed under the seats coated in spilled pop and melted candy and were more of a nuisance than anything. Seatbelts weren't legally required equipment on new cars built in the US until 1968. Even then most people didn't start wearing them, until the government finally amassed enough data to prove that wearing the new safety devices saved thousands of lives.

Since our new bikes hadn't arrived yet we were forced to continue training our own bikes. Some of the younger boys had small bikes with banana seats and had to travel twice as far as some of the boys that had larger 27-Inch bikes. The adult leaders decided that we should stay relatively close to home in case of a breakdown. During one of our jaunts around town, Jerry announced that our first bike rules of the road class would be held at our next Scout meeting. A lot of us chuckled at the idea, and I can remember saying to a few of my buddies, "rules of the road; for bikes?"

Boys at that age weren't very interested in bicycle safety, much less having to take a bike rules of the road course. As we would soon find out, it was going to be mandatory if you wanted to go on the trip. Wood Dale's Chief of Police, Ray Woods, had worked for the State of Illinois, and wanted us to become familiar with the rules of the road for bikes. A safety program that had been established by the Bicycle Institute of America, an organization based out of New York City, was a model for Illinois and several other states. Our first bike rules of the road session took place on April 28. As we all sat, fidgeting about trying to concentrate of something most of us weren't interested in, Jerry tried to keep our attention. He told us that we would be tested on the bikes and there would also be a written test. If we passed both tests, we would be issued a Safe Driver License. Safety was now becoming a regular theme at all of our meetings.

There would be five road instruction classes. It was becoming clear that the Scout leaders were serious about all this safety business and I realized there was a lot to learn about the rules of the road. The police chief explained that the bike rules of the road were similar to those we would learn in our high school driver's education class. That seemed to quell a lot of our annoyance with taking the classes, as we were all anxious to drive. As we got more involved with the safety classes, it was apparent that it was something we all needed to learn. The classes covered everything from traffic regulations, like stopping at stoplights, giving the right of way to pedestrians, and the proper maintenance of our bikes. It was just another part of our training that would prove to be invaluable, and help us to ensure our safety while on the road.

As we anxiously anticipated the delivery of our new 10-speeds, our training sessions continued using our own bikes. We were still having some problems with breakdowns, but Jerry would just say that it was good training should we need to fix our new bikes. Our bike training sessions usually lasted about two and half hours and sometimes longer if we had problems with the bikes. We were still in school so we couldn't ride too far, but we often pushed it, and wouldn't get home until quite late.

Most of us were in relatively good shape and were used to riding our bikes for extended periods of time. We had all ridden our bikes on the streets of Wood Dale at night, so we were accustomed to riding in the evening hours and familiar with the roads in the area. As it got darker, we tried to stick to the local, less busy streets like Deerpath Road in town to reduce the chances of any accidents. When we would eventually get our new 10-speeds, we started to venture out onto busier streets like Irving Park Road, and biked through other areas near O'Hare Airport. Jerry thought it was important for us to practice riding in all types of conditions and on many different streets.

On May 8, a big Florida meeting had been planned for all the parents and the boys. It was announced that our new bikes were scheduled to be delivered on Wednesday May10, and they would have to be assembled. Jerry was looking for volunteers because he knew that it would take a lot of time to put 32 bikes together. We were instructed that the new bikes were to be used strictly for our training, although we would be allowed to ride them home.

When the bikes finally arrived in Wood Dale, they were shipped in a semi to Mr. Giannini's house where we began the assembly process with teams that we had set up. When I first arrived at Mr. "G's" house that night to help put together the bikes, I was shocked to see all the cardboard boxes lined up two abreast in his front yard. All 32 of the rectangular shaped boxes were stamped in several places with the Sears Roebuck and Co. name and a large colored picture of the new 10-speed bike. Under the bicycle's picture were the words, "When you have a Free Spirit, you'll always have somewhere to go."

When we finally opened the first cardboard container and emptied its contents onto the grass, I was shocked to see so many plastic bags filled with bike parts, most of which I had never seen before. Each bike would take well over an hour to put together and several more minutes would be spent making adjustments. Once assembled, each bike had to be taken on a test run to check all of its components. It was a real process and we set up an assembly line with teams assigned to certain tasks. After we got the first couple of bikes assembled, the rest went together more easily. We were all anxious to start using our new bikes. Jerry and the other leaders were getting fed up with all the breakdowns with our older bikes.

Once each bike was assembled and thoroughly tested, Jerry would take the serial numbers off the bottom of the crank and kept a record. Each bike would be assigned to a Scout, and since they were alike, it would be the only way to identify whose bike was whose. Jerry had a system for everything, and it proved to be a critical element in the success of our trip.

Ron Herff had just gotten out of a full body cast and was still limping around as the result of a car accident he had been in with his father over the winter. Despite his severe injury, he insisted on helping to put the bikes together. He was definitely one of the more dedicated Scouts in Troop 65. Nearly all hopes of going on the trip had vanished in a single moment that winter. His father had started to pull out onto the main road when their truck was struck on the passenger side. The thrust of the accident was so strong that the truck's door was driven into Ron's pelvis, breaking both of his legs and smashing the upper part of his hipbone. The crash was so violent that glass from the shattered windshield left lacerations on his face and several of his teeth were knocked out when his face hit the dashboard. After surgery which required several screws to reassemble his hip, Ron was placed into a full body cast from his neck to his toes. He would lay immobilized in a bed in his living room for several months while he recuperated.

Despite his noticeable limp, Ron was a real trooper and dedicated Scout. Despite not being able to go with us to Florida, he still wanted to help. He was a stocky athletic guy and being laid up in a bed for so long drove him nuts. He was determined to get better and his condition was improving by the week. He realized any hope of going on the trip had been erased as the result of his accident. He had been in the Scouts for quite some time now and would have been one of the older boys on the trip.

Ron's younger brother, Nick, was stocky too and a big kid for his age. He had been assigned one of the larger bikes despite being one of the younger boys. He was a blond haired kid and usually good-natured but like his brother, had a serious side, too. He was smart and always clever enough to be able to figure things out and was a good Scout. Ron was always pretty serious in his demeanor, especially after the accident, and didn't like the idea of his younger brother going it alone. He still wanted to go to Florida with us, but realized his body might not hold up over the long grueling ride that would last almost a month.

As was the case with everything we did in preparing for our trip, it was no accident that the bikes were delivered to Mr. Giannini's house. He was the handiest among us and had a bigger front yard than Jerry. Mr. "G" worked as a tool and die maker for a company in Chicago called Gottlieb, who manufactured pinball machines and he could build and repair just about anything.

Mr. Giannini was considerably older than the other adult leaders, and at 51 years old, Jerry questioned whether he would be able to manage the practice trips. He would become further alarmed when Mr. "G" had to miss a few of the training sessions due to his busy work schedule. He made a pledge to the Scouts and himself that despite some of the constraints surrounding his job, he would do everything necessary to get into shape for the trip. He trained on his own many times late in the evening and was making a real effort to be prepared for the trip. True to his word, after several weeks of riding with us and on his own, Mr. "G" was able to lose quite a bit of weight and get into shape for the trip.

Mr. Giannini really enjoyed being with the Scouts and was the only dad on the trip. His youngest boy, Jeff, would be his only son to accompany him on the trip. Jeff would ride one of the seven smaller 10-speeds. Mr. "G" was very active with the troop and went on many of our campouts. Nothing ever seemed to rattle him and he had a kid-like quality and was always smiling. You could talk to him just about anything. He was one of the most loyal adult leaders in Troop 65's history. He was always there for you, freely sharing his knowledge or lending a hand.

Louie was just a "nifty guy, and someone fun to be around," Jerry would often say. His overall demeanor was enhanced by his warm smile and the twinkle of his dark brown eyes when he laughed. His caring ways were evident in his rather soft-spoken voice and gentle manner. He was a like a big teddy bear, and his rather large stature when he began the trip would be significantly reduced in size by the time we would return from Florida.

His courage to even embark on such a trip was a story about how the human spirit can overcome nearly all adversity. Some suggested to him that to attempt such a feat at his advanced age and physical condition was dangerous, even life threatening. He persisted though, and I always admired his courage and his ability to overcome hardship. Mr. "G" became a model for all of us while on the trip to Florida, encouraging us through personal example. He would often say to the younger Scouts, "If I can do it, I know you can." You never heard him complain as he led our large group of 32 Scouts. He was always pushing us forward despite the challenges and physical difficulties we experienced during the trip. He was a model Boy Scout leader who not only shared his values with us, but also shared his time.

TWENTY-FOUR

S INCE WE WOULD BE CAMPING along the entire route, we needed an efficient and lightweight method to transport all our gear. Saddlebags seemed to be the simple solution but buying them proved too costly. As was the case with many projects our troop took on, we decided to make them ourselves. It would be a big project since we needed 32 of them and someone would have to design and then sew all of them. Mr. Giannini was a man who understood precision after having spent several years as a tool and die maker. He knew that whatever design we chose it would have to be durable. It wasn't any surprise that Jerry assigned him as our research engineer to determine what the best design was and what materials to use. Weight and water resistance were two important factors that would determine the final design of the saddlebags.

We needed a sturdy metal carrier to hold the weight of the saddlebags and their contents. Mr. "G" looked at several different racks and eventually found one that fit our bikes and was able to support the weight of the bags. After researching many different types of materials, he drafted a design for the new saddlebags. The canvas material he had chosen was thick and difficult to sew. Mr. "G" was not one to give up and after several failed attempts, he developed an ingenious way to sew the bags and was able to make a prototype.

The carriers were made of a new lightweight metal that had a dull finish and two supports on each side that attached to the rear frame of the bike. Mr. "G" explained that the carriers were made of a new alloy that had been developed for the space program. The brown prototype saddlebags were constructed of a heavy grade vinyl coated canvas. They consisted of two semi-box-shaped storage compartments with flip-over tops that hung over each side of the rear tire of the bike. One piece of canvas joined the two bags together that would be slung over the rack and attached to each side with an ingenious tether strap.

Mr. Giannini and his wife had done an excellent job of designing and sewing the first saddlebags. With only few modifications, it would become the model for the bags that we would use for our trip. When we first tested the bags on our new bikes, we realized that each bag had to be packed with the same amount of weight, or it would cause some instability. It would become a daily exercise in packing, as it was critical that each bag was properly packed or you risked serious injury if your bike was unstable.

From the beginning, we were concerned that a motorist might run into us from behind. We were like a slow moving train winding our way down the road, and knew that we had to do something to prevent a rear end collision. The new bikes came equipped with amber colored reflectors embedded in the sides of both pedals, but that was it as far as reflectors were concerned. We had to devise our own system to ensure everyone's safety. John Zweifler, who had acted as a Scout leader when Jerry was in Germany, owned a small plastics company called GEM Plastics. He realized that it was important for the bikes to be visible on the road and developed special reflectors that attached to the spokes he called, "Spokeroos." The bikes were equipped with two amber colored reflectors for the front wheel and two red colored reflectors for the back. Since most of our early training sessions were during the evening hours, it was important that the motorists could see us on the road.

When we would eventually leave for Florida, riding at night was nothing new to us. We always got up very early in the morning and rode several miles before eating breakfast. Most of the time the sun hadn't fully risen and there weren't very many cars on the road. I think Jerry wanted to take advantage of our energy in the morning with the promise of breakfast if we logged in some good miles. There were many times we road at dusk and into the early evening hours until we could find a suitable campsite. Since only a few of the adult leaders had lights on their bikes, all the reflectors we had, including the Spokeroos, was the added safety measure we needed.

Our new saddlebags provided us with one more place to become reflectorized. We each had two large round red reflectors that were housed in a rectangular shaped piece of plastic and sewn onto the back of each saddlebag. The triangular shaped reflectors were designed for slow moving vehicles like a tractor and we adapted them for our own use. There was also a round red reflector attached to the back of the bikes metal carrier. "We are pretty reflectorized," Jerry told a group of concerned parents. He was concerned that someone might hit him from behind, as he would always take up the rear of our group.

At our May 12, Scout meeting, Jerry told us that our new Free Spirit bikes were nearly completely assembled. He had brought his own bike down to the meeting so that we could all see what they looked like. Many of the boys who had never seen a 10-speed before were intrigued by the bike's nifty gadgets. When we completed our scheduled bike rules of the road instruction, Jerry would give us a demonstration on what this new contraption could do. It was amazing to see this bike in action, and I couldn't wait to get my hands on mine and ride it. Since our bikes wouldn't be ready until the 15th of the month, our next training session schedule for the 13th would be the last time we would need to use our own bikes.

The 1972 June board of review was fast approaching and I was busy trying to wrap up all the requirements for five of the ten merit badges I would need to receive the rank of Life. I had already completed most of the requirements for my swimming, lifesaving, personal fitness, and safety badges but needed one more to reach the magic number of ten merit badges. For whatever reason, I had chosen "Metalwork" and was having a lot of trouble finishing my project. I was in danger of not being promoted before the trip. I was trying to build an elaborate candle lantern and my father kept saying, "You can do better than this Pauly."

When we finally took possession of our new bikes on Tuesday, the evening of May 16, there was a feeling of excitement in the air and we all just wanted to jump on our bikes and start riding. That of course wasn't going to happen. We had scheduled a conditioning hike for that night but it would be cut short since we needed to make a lot of adjustments to the bikes. We had already been instructed on how to use the gears and the braking system. The Free Spirits came equipped with many new features that we had never used before including shift levers and duel hand brakes for the front and rear. The 10-speeds were new to everyone and it was evident that we would need a lot of practice before we could even think about taking them out onto the open road.

One of the Scout's uncles was a bike trainer who had raced bikes for many years and came to talk to us one evening. When he saw how the pedals of the bike were set up, he suggested that we use what he called a "Rat Trap" that attached on top of the pedal. With a foot in one of the pedals, you could pull the other pedal up and it would make it easier for everyone to pedal their bikes. The Rat Trap would be clamped onto our stock pedals. There was a lot of debate about the idea and

Jerry eventually put the kibosh on the racer's suggestion. He was concerned that the boys might get their feet stuck in the pedals if they were trying to save themselves from a fall. As it turned out, he would be right, as a number of the Scouts had trouble riding their new bikes. Even the handlebars were different than anyone was used to, since they were the turn down type. Then there was the shifting of gears and no one had ever experienced a bike with more than three speeds.

The boy's uncle who made his money on racing bikes was adamant about how each of our bikes should fit us, especially our seats and handlebars. "Each bike should fit you like a shoe," he said. If you were sitting on the seat of your bike and were to push the pedal with the arch of your foot, your leg would need to be straight but when you put the ball of your foot on the pedal; your leg would need to be slightly bent. Our handlebars had to be fit so that when you put your hands on each side of the bars, your back would be at about a 15-degree angle. It was important to our well-being the racer noted, that you had to have a two-finger clearance on the center bar and your crotch, so that when you stopped, you could safely put your feet on the ground. "If there's less space, you're going to hurt yourself at some point when you hop off the seat to stop," he said. All of the bikes needed to be adjusted before we could ride them anywhere. Our first opportunity to test our new Free Spirits was quickly slipping away that night, but Jerry wanted us to be able to ride our bikes home.

When all the bikes were finally adjusted, we started testing them in the church parking lot. Riding the new bikes was like taking a spaceship out for its maiden voyage for all of us. No matter how many times this racer or Jerry, who was turning redder by the minute, would tell us how to shift gears; we all stripped a lot of them that night. Eventually as the night wore

on, we began to get the hang of the bike and all of its equipment. Jerry approved all of us to ride our bikes home after we
made a few short jaunts around town. We must have surprised
him after our shaky start in the parking lot, because when we
took our bikes out on the streets of Wood Dale, we only had to
stop a few times. Our boyish instincts and bicycle riding skills
were kicking in despite the fact that we were now riding a racing bike and not the hand-me-downs most of us had ridden our
entire lives.

As I headed home that night on my new Free Spirit, I had a
big smile on my face and was proud that I was getting the hang
of my bike. I loved the speed I could travel with only a few
pumps of my pedals. Having 10- speeds was incredible and
completely different from my little 3-speed Stingray, which
now felt like a toy. As I raced home, I had to be careful not to
jump the curbs as I was used to doing. The boy's uncle had explained that the tires and rims on our new bikes were more
susceptible to damage than our older bikes and were not meant
for jumping. That would be something me and all my friends
would have to get used to since jumping our bikes was something we did all the time.

When I rounded the block at the corner of Irving Park Road
and Harvey Avenue, it was already dark and I noticed Billy riding his bike down the street. He was getting ready to turn and
take the shortcut to his house through an empty lot. I yelled
out to him and he stopped pedaling. When I caught up to him
he had a big grin on his face and just stared at my bike for
what seemed to be several minutes. "I was just over at your
house, and your mom said that you were getting your new
bike, and you might be late," he said. "I would have waited
around longer but my dad's been on the warpath again, and I
should get going." That's all he said, and took off racing like a

mad man on his bike through the empty field, all the while dust kicking up behind him as he popped wheelies the entire way. I felt bad afterwards and thought that after seeing my bike that he might reconsider going on the trip, but knew that he had already made his decision not to go. He never said it, but I think his father really didn't want him to go, as he relied on Billy to do most of the chores around the house.

Regardless of whose choice it was, that was just Billy's way. When he made a decision, he stuck with it, and I admired him for that quality. Since starting our training sessions, we hadn't played together very much and I think it was starting to wear on both of us. He started to miss more of the Scout meetings, too, but still made most of the campouts. Our annual spring camporee was coming up and he said that he would try to make it, despite an increase in his father's rants. He seemed ashamed of his father's obvious drunken behavior and used the campouts to get away from all of the abuse. I just hoped he would go on this one, as it would be the last major campout before we would leave on our trip on July 22.

I had my doubts though, if he would actually go, as it seemed that the Scouts were becoming less important to him as we were both getting older and the thoughts of high school and girls were on the horizon. To be a Boy Scout in high school was not that cool. Most of the boys dropped out shortly before or sometime after starting high school. I suppose the idea of quitting occurred to me, too, but our upcoming bike trip to Florida seemed to quell most of my thoughts of dropping out. Besides, I had more to accomplish and still had my mind set on achieving the rank of Eagle. Billy, on the other hand, had reached the rank of First Class and seemed content on not advancing any further. My confidence level was growing and my thoughts toward what I felt I could accomplish in the Scouts was high. My father finally broke down and helped me finish my metal lantern project. Now, all of my requirements to be promoted to Life were in the hands of the upcoming board of review.

When we assembled at the church parking lot on Thursday for our next training session, I could tell that this one would be much different. Nearly everyone was riding pretty well and I only witnessed a few instances of gears being stripped. There were usually 27 to 32 bikes during each practice depending on the leader's work schedules. We had been strategically placed within our caravan of bikes for discipline and morale reasons and had assigned places in the lineup. The order seemed to change nearly each training session as we continued to work out all the kinks.

From the beginning, I rode directly behind my buddy, Arlin Barton. Arlin was a bit of a crazy kid with a real wild streak. I suppose that's what I liked about him. We had that in common, although I was a bit more in check. Mischief was his middle name, and if there was someone that was going to get into trouble on the trip, it would be Arlin. He was a big stocky kid, who was tall for his age, and a bit on the heavy side. He didn't like playing baseball or other sports requiring running, except maybe football. He was a real bull on the playground often tackling kids just for the hell of it. If he tackled you, he meant to put a hurt on you. Although he was physically strong, he always seemed to struggle during our training sessions. As time went on, he got into better riding shape and was able to keep up. I was a stronger rider and in better condition, so I was positioned directly behind him and would remain there throughout the entire trip to Florida.

Jerry would be last in line behind Mike Rohl. It was decided that Mr. Giannini would take up the lead because of his navigational skills. Jerry was secretly concerned and did not want him to have a heart attack or something, if we pushed him too hard. His main job was to keep the pace, while Jack Froehling and Mike Terese, were usually in the middle of the pack keeping an eye on all of us.

It was like a large wagon train or a "convoy" as Jerry called it heading down the road, just at a much faster pace. Everything we did had to be timed just right. Mike Rohl, one of only two Eagle Scouts, on the trip felt that he could keep a better eye on everyone from the rear. Jerry had an impressive number of extra reflectors on the rear of his bike. He had selected himself to take up the rear of the pack just in case some nut might hit us from behind. With the added reflectors, Jerry thought that someone would be able to see him first and hopefully not careen into his bike. He didn't like the idea of getting hit, but thought it was his responsibility to protect the troop. It was our "last line of defense," he would say.

As an added bit of protection, Jerry and a few of the other adult leaders were equipped with lights for their bikes. They were large white headlights mounted on the left side of the bike's frame, along with a small red taillight powered by a six volt, three-watt generator. There was no need for batteries as every pedal powered the lights and helped guide us through the dark on several occasions.

As we got closer to the end of May, our bicycle conditioning hikes were scheduled nearly every two days. We still took time out for other activities like our annual survival trip. It would be held on Starvation Island lasting three days from May 19-21. It was an ominous sounding name, that gave some of the parents pause, but the chatter soon died off and they just let us all go. They figured in about a month and a half, we would be riding our bicycles to Florida. The survival trips were always such a great time and although Jerry knew we needed to keep consistent with our bicycle-training schedule, he figured that this was training, too, and it involved other Scouts that were not going on the Florida trip. When we returned from the island, we hit the road again wanting to get a few days of riding in before the Memorial Day Holiday.

The days seemed to be flying by that summer and our spring camporee was getting closer. Billy had promised me a few days earlier that he would be going but now that was in doubt since his father grounded him for dropping garbage in their yard. What had really happened was that raccoons had jumped into one of the open cans and had a field day strewing garbage throughout the Lonergan's front yard. It was doubtful he would be going, as his father seemed to be getting more irrational and nastier each day.

My mother was one of the moms of the HHY who helped to run an art fair during the same weekend, trying to raise more money to help cover some of our travel expenses for our Florida trip. We would all be flying back from Florida on a large jet, but our bikes would need to be flown back separately in the belly on a new wide-bodied plane called a 747. All of the HHY moms were a big help to the troop and stayed actively engaged in nearly all facets of the trip. Jerry was in the early stages of designing a tent needed for the trip that the mothers had agreed to help make, as there would be a lot of sewing involved.

We were close to finalizing our route to Florida but as new information came in, we continued to tweak it all the way up until the first part of July. We established a list of towns along the route with populations of around 1,000 people. The mother's club sent letters to each of the town's mayors and the chamber of commerce letting them know that we would be passing through during the months of July and August. They also enclosed a questioner where the towns were asked to check off items that we made inquiries about including accommodations, restaurants, parks, showers, and laundry facilities. The moms also enclosed a self-addressed stamped envelope. To our surprise, we didn't receive very many responses from the towns.

Jerry was a bit shocked and somewhat concerned as he had never been to Florida before and the lack luster response by the town's officials surprised him. He thought they may have considered our letter to be a joke because who would be crazy enough to travel from Wood Dale, Illinois to Florida on bikes. Despite the poor response, we carried each town's questionnaires with us on the trip whether they had responded to us or not. By some long shot, we thought they might remember our gesture and help us.

BOY SCOUT TROOP 65

Boy Scouts of America

TAKES PLEASURE IN AWARDING THIS

Certificate of Appreciation

TO

Paul Rega

IN RECOGNITION OF

Exceptional preformance in carrying out his assigned duties and providing good
discipline and high moral for the thirty - two scouts and leaders on the most
adventurous expedition in the history of Troop 65 on a bicycle trip from
Wood Dale, Illinois to the State of Florida.

July 22 1972
August 20 1972
DAYS

Michael Rega Sr.

Danny Scott swearing in Billy Mikuls at traffic court.

Clifty Falls State Park, Madison, Indiana (Paul Rega center).

The Milton-Madison Bridge on US 421, crossing over the Ohio River into Milton, Kentucky.

Daniel Boone's Grave, Frankfort Cemetery, Frankfort, Kentucky

Norris Dam, Lake City Tennessee. (Arlin Barton at rear right)

Pitched tents near Sylva North Carolina, just outside of The Great Smoky Mountains National Park.

Paul's postcard to his parents describing the bike hike through the Smoky Mountains.

Scouts of Troop 65 reach the Georgia State Line
on their Free Spirits.

WOOD DALE BOY SCOUT TROOP 65 is enjoying a bicycling trip to Florida. They have enjoyed visiting along the way as Wood Dale's Youth Ambassadors of Good Will. As of press time this week, there had been no major incidents and were due to arrive at O'Hare Field next Sunday.

*Scouts from Troop 65 cross into Florida
after bicycling over 1,200 miles.*

*Troop 65 pedals into Wood Dale from O'Hare International
Airport after having been on the road for nearly a month.*

Final leg of the trip riding on Irving Park Road
(Lou Giannini on left).

Paul

Welcome Home, Troop 65 And Leaders!

Scouts are welcomed home by thousands of Wood Dale citizens.
(left front) Lou Giannini, Steve Sykes and Jeff Bandel. (right
front) Bob Sample, Ron Herff, Jerry Lettenberger, Dave Miller,
Billy Mikuls, Arlin Barton, Paul Rega and Danny Zoubek.

(top left to right) Paul's father, Paul and his brother, Mark.

Paul with his mother, grandmother and sister Robin, (center).

(top left to right) Scoutmaster Jerry Risting, Bob Sample, Mike Terese, Lou Giannini, Jack Froehling, and Mike Rohl receiving awards at the Wood Dale Junior High School welcome home ceremony.

Paul loading his Free Spirit into his dad's car.

```
MILES    CITY           TRAVEL    POPULATION
TRAVELED TOWN           DISTANCE
(LEAVE WORD DALE AND TRAVEL SOUTH ALONG WOOD DALE ROAD
     0    WORD DALE,ILL              9500
     2    ADDISON,ILL     8        16997
     4    VILLA PARK,ILL  2        15967
TURN EAST ON NORTH AVE (ROUTE 64)
     5    ELMHURST,ILL    1        41600
SOUTH ON ROUTE 83
     3    YORKFIELD ILL   2         1800
    11    OAKBROOK  ILL   4         1646
    14    HINSDALE  ILL   3        14738
    17    WILLOWBROOK ILL 3          157
    21    LAMBERT ILL     4       (NOT GIVEN)
    25    (TO JCT ROUTE 45)
TURN SOUTH ON RT 45 AND TRAVEL THROUGH THE FOLLOWING CITIES
    29    PALOS PARK ILL  4         2169
    32    ORLAND PARK ILL 3         4509
    35    ARSURY HILLS ILL 3       NOT GIVEN
    37    (TO JCT RT 30)  3
    43    MATTESON ILL    6         3696
    47    WOODROW WILSON WOODS 4
          (WOODROW WILSON WOODS IS ON RT 30 & RT 1.NO FACILITIES ARE OFFERED)
    51    EAST CHICAGO HTS ILL 4    4295
    57    DYER ILL        6         3993
          CROSS ILL/IND STATE LINE
    60    SCHERVILLE IND  3         3347
TURN SOURTH ON RT 41
    63    ST.JOHN IND     3         1128
    68    COOK IND        2         1128
    77    BELSHAW IND     4        NOT GIVEN
    83    SCHNEIDER IND   6          405
LASALLE STATE FOREST IS LOCATED 1/4 MI SOUTH OF THE KANKAKEE RIVER VIA US 41 IN
SCHNEIDER IND. OFFER LAUNDRY FACILITIES.
    85    LAKE VILLAGE IND 2         300
    88    CONCORD IND     3        NOT GIVEN
    96    ENOS IND        6        NOT GIVEN
    99    MOROCCO IND     5         1341
   112    KENTLAND IND    13        1783
CONTINUE TO INDIANA RT. 52 AND TRAVEL THROUGH THE FOLLOWING CITIES
   113    EARL PARK IND   1          551
```

Trip ticket leaving from Wood Dale, Illinois.

```
(EARL PARK REST AREA IS LOCATED AT RTS 4165 NO FACILITIES OFFERED.
   116    GRAVEL HILL IND  3       NOT GIVEN
   122    SWANINGTON IND   3       NOT GIVEN
   124    ATKINSON IND     2       NOT GIVEN
   128    TEMPLETON IND    2       NOT GIVEN
   131    FORESMON         3       NOT GIVEN
   134    OTTERMON         1          788
   138    MONTMORENCI IND  4          100
   145    LAFAYETTE IND    7        47000
   157    MONROE IND       12         499
   178    LEBANON IND      21        9533
FIESTA LODGE (PRIVATE) IS LOCATED 6MI. EAST OF LEBANON ON HIWY 32. SHOWERS
   189    ROYALTON IND     11         100
   192    TRADERSPOR ND    4       NOT GIVEN
   198    FLACKVILLE IND   6          500
   204    INDIANAPOLIS IND 5       530000
LEAVE INDIANAPOLIS SOUTH ON RT 31 AND TRAVEL THROUGH THE FOLLOWING CITIES
   215    GREENWOOD IND    11        7169
   220    WHITELAND IND    5       NOT GIVEN
   225    FRANKLIN IND     5        11292
   230    AMITY IND        5       NOT GIVEN
   236    EDINBURG IND     6         4543
ATTERBURY STATE PARK 1MI WEST OF EDINBURG ON EDINBURG RDPRT31. NO FACILITIES
   240    DRIFTWOOD CAMP (PRIVATE) IS LOCATED ON RT31&165  SHOWERS.
   240    TAYLORSVILLE IND 4       NOT GIVEN
   248    COLOMBUS IND.    8        34782
WATCH FOR IND RT 7. TURN SOUTH TOWARD SCORPIO,IND.
   262    SCORPIO          IND 14    4307
   269    NORTH VERNON IND 7         4307
   277    DUPONT    IND    8          300
   284    HIRT      IND    7       NOT GIVEN
   290    MADISON   IND    6        10648
CITY OF MADISON CAMPGROUND
CITY OF MADISON CAMPGROUND IS IN CITY. HAS SHOWERS & LAUNDRY.
CLIFTY FALLS STATE PARK IS 1/2 WEST OF MADISON ON US421-HWY56&107 SHOWERS.
          CROSS INDIANA/KENTUCKY STATE LINE
   292    MILTON KEN       2          365
   304    BEDFORD KEN      12         717
   321    CAMBELLSBURG KEN 17        349
```

Trip ticket crossing Indiana-Kentucky State Line

```
325   NEW CASTEL KEN      8        699
335   NORTH PLEASURVILLE  6        466
338   DEFORE KEN          3        NOT GIVEN
350   FRANKFORT KEN       20       25000
      (DANIEL BOONES GRAVE NEAR HERE)
371   LEXINGTON KEN
371   LEXINGTON KEN       21       62801
CLAYS CAMPGROUND (PRIVATE) IS 7MI SO OF LEXINGTON ON I-75 CLAYS FERRY EXIT
TO KENTUCKY RIVER ON US-25.

CHANGE TO KEN RT25 TOWARD CLEAVLAND

393   CLEAVELAND KEN      22       500
397   WHITEHALL 514       4        NOT GIVEN
403   RICHMOND KEN        6        20000
416   RR
416   BEREA KEN           13       4302
420   BOONE KEN           4        NOT GIVEN
423   CONWAY KEN          3        NOT GIVEN
430   RENFOR VALLEY KEN 7          NOT GIVEN
RENFOR VALLEY CAMPGROUND(PRIVATE) IS 2MI NORTH OF MT.VERNON ON US75 & I75 18MI
SOUTH OF BEREA KENTUCKY.
439   LIVINGSTON KEN      9        419
465   PITTSBURG KEN       26       810
467   LONDON KEN          2        4035
471   FARRISTOWN          4        NG
475   LILY KEN            4        400
481   CORBIN KEN          6        1600
GULF STATION PARK (PRIVATE) IS OFF I-75 ON US25W EAST IN SOUTH CITY CORBIN
IT OFFERS SHOWERS AND LAUNDRY.

CHANGE TO 25E AT CORBIN

486   GRAY KEN            5        860
496   BAILEY SWITCH KEN 8          NG
497   HEIDRICK KEN        3        500
50,   FLATLICK KEN        11       NG
515   PINEVILLE KEN       7        600
PINE MOUNTAIN STATE PARK 1MI SOUTH OF PINESVILLE ON US25E HAS SHOWERS
520   CUMBERLAND GAP NAT'L PARK
527   MIDDLESBORO KEN     6        14000
FROM MIDDLESBORO WE LEAVE KENTUCKY,PASS THROUGH VIRGINIA AND MOVE IN TENNESSEE

      CROSS KENTUCKY/TENNESSEE STATE LINE
```

Trip ticket crossing Kentucky-Tennessee State Line

```
530   CUMBERLAND GAP TEN  3        291
544   TAZEWELL TEN        14       1626
567   THORNHILL TEN       23       NG
SOUTHER BOAT DOCK (PRIVATE) IS N72 NE OF RUTLEDGE ON US11W SOUTH 3 1/2 MI.
TO JCT TENN 11W & 25E TURN EAST (LEFT) TO MORRISTOWN TENN.

577   MORRISTOWN TEN      10       21211

FROM MORRISTOWN TURN SOUTH ON RT 66

583   VALLEY HOME TENN    6        NOT GIVEN
595   DANRIDGE TEN        17       1500
DANRIDGE BOAT DOCK (PRIVATE) LOCATED SOUTH ON HWY 92 1/2 MI HAS SHOWERS&LAUNDRY
600   SHADY GROVE TEN     5        100
608   POWDER SPRINGS TEN  8        200
611   CATLETSBURG TEN     3        96
614   SEVIERVILLE TENN    3        3000

TURN SOUTH FROM SEIBERSVILLE ON RT 441&411

61,   PINE GROVE TEN      4        NG
634   GATLINBURG TEN      16       1764
DIXLEY CREEK TRAILER PARK(PRIVATE) IS NORTH OF GATLINBURG ON RT 441 SHOW&LUND

      CROSS TENNESSEE/NORTH CAROLINA STATE LINE

650   NEW FOUND GAP NC    16       NG
662   CHEROKEE INDIAN RES 12       NG
667   WILMONT             5        NG
670   BARKER CROSSING     3        NG
674   DILLSBORO           3        NG
681   GAY                 7        194
694   FRANKLIN            13       2500
DIAMOND KOA (PRIVATE) IS ON HWY441 1 1/2 MI NORTH OF FRANKLIN  SHOWERS&LAUNDRY
TOTEM POLE CAMPGROUN (PRIVATE) IS 6MI NORTH OF FRANKLIN. SHOWERS ARE OFFERED.

FOLLOW RT 28 SOUTH FROM FRANKLIN TOWARD GNESISS

702   GNESISS             5        NG
711   HIGHLAND            9        11000

      CROSS NORTH CAROLINA/GEORGIA STATE LINE
```

Trip ticket crossing Tennessee-North Carolina State Line and
North Carolina into Georgia.

```
715   SATOLAH GEO          4        NG
719   PINE MOUNTAIN GA     4       1000
SUMPTER NAT'L FOREST-GEN.-PICKEN DIVISION

        CROSS GEORGIA&SOUTH CAROLINA STATE LINE.

724   MOUNTAIN REST SC     5        NG
732   WAHALLA SC           8       4000

FROM WAHALLA TURN SOUTH ON RT 183

739   WESTMINISTER SC      7       2413

FROM WESTMINISTER TURN LEFT ON RT 24.

748   OAKWAY SC            9        150
758   TOWNVILLE SC        10        200
766   ANDERSEN SC         10X      JUDUL
6     ANDERSEN SC         10      41316
TAKE RT 28 SOUTH FROM ANDERSEN

785   ANTERVILLE SC       17        NG
800   ABBEVILLE SC        15       5436
SUMPTER NAT'L FOREST-LONG CANE DIVISION
821   MC CORMIC           21       1990
825   PLUM GROVE SC        4        200
828   PARKSVILLE           3        168
835   MODOC                7        100
THERE ARE 3 FREE CAMPSIGHTS ALONG THIS ROUTE AT MODOC,CLARK HILL & MERRINEATHER
840   CLARKS HILL SC       5         25
842   MERRINEATHER         2      19755

        CROSS SOUTH CAROLINA/GEORGIA STATE LINE

856   AUGUSTA GA          14        NG

TRAVEL SOUTH ON RT56FROM AUGUSTA GEORGIA.

872   MC BEAN GA          16        NG

TRAVEL TO RT23 SOUTHBOUND TO SHELL BLUFF

882   SHELL BLUFF         10        NG
892   GIRAD               10        248
```

Trip ticket crossing Georgia-South Carolina State Line and South Carolina-Georgia State Line.

```
898   SARDIS               6        829

ROUTE 24 FROM SARDIS TO HILTONIA

907   HILTONIA             9        353
918   SYLVANIA            11         NG
PINEVILLE TRAILER COURT (PRIVATE) 2 1/2 MI SOUTH OF SYLVANIA ON US 301 HAS
SHOWERS AND LAUNDRY FACILITIES TAKE RT 21 FROM SYLVANIA TO WHITE HILL
924   WHITE HILL           6        409
929   SHEPPARD             5         NG
933   NEWINGTON            4        500
937   KILDARE              4         NG
946   LORENZO              9         NG
652   SPRINGFIELD          6        858
959   RINCON               9       1057
968   PORT WENTWORTH       7       3705
970   GARDEN CITY          3       5451
974   SAVANNAH             5     149245

TRAVEL RT 17 FROM SAVANNAH GA.

992   RICHMOND HILL       18        800
1005  MIDWAY              17         NG
1012  RICEBORO             5        254
1019  SOUTH NEWPORT        7         NG
1028  EULONIA              9        250
1040  DARIEN              12       1569
1045  BROADFIELD           5         NG
1058  BRUNSWICK            5      21703
BLYTH ISLAND NAVAL RES IS IN BRUNSWICK  CHEEROKEE CAMPGROUND(PRIVATE) IS 15 MI
SOUTHEAST OF BRUSWICK OFF US17 VIA GEORGIA CAUSEWAY SO . IT HAS SHOWERS&LUND.
1064  SPRINGBLUFF          6         NG
1071  WAVERLY              7        712
1074  WHITE OAK            3         NG
1081  WOODBINE             5        845
1085  SEALS                4         NG
1092  COLESBURG            4         NG
1100  KINGLAND             8       1536
1110  BECKER              10         NG
1113  YULEE                3         NG

        CROSS GEORGIA/FLORIDA STATE LINE

1136  JACKSONVILLE FLA    23     198000
```

Trip ticket crossing Georgia-Florida State Line.

TWENTY-FIVE

A S WE BEGAN our June conditioning hikes, our bikes as the racer said, were beginning to fit us like a shoe. We were all gaining more confidence on our 10-speeds. We practiced everything from making turns in different directions to normal and fast stops in case of an emergency. We were still used to abusing our old bikes since we raced them, crashed, and jumped them over dirt and gravel piles. We were rough on our old bikes, but what kid wasn't, and if they broke, we just fixed them.

It took time to erase that mindset and treat our 10-speed bikes differently. Some of the kids, when we first got the new bikes, tried jumping curbs in the church parking lot, which was something we all did with our old bikes. That practice was short lived and quickly quelled once Jerry caught wind of what they were doing. After a while, it became more of a mantra as you could hear both Mr. "G" and Jerry saying, "Keep your bikes in good condition boys, they are your only transportation and will need to get you all the way down to Florida."

Our train of 32 bikes practiced many different kinds of maneuvers including both wide and tight turns. It was important that everyone was in sync with each other. It seemed at first that there was no way to manage that many bikes, all with different riders, all with different mind sets. What each one of us should have been doing, was not exactly what each of us was doing. We stopped a lot in the beginning, readjusting the lineup in an effort to make it more efficient. As time went on and we continued practicing, we all got more comfortable with our bikes.

Finally, something just clicked and we were seemingly better able to feel and anticipate each other's actions. We were becoming a well-oiled machine. I even got accustomed to Arlin being in front of me. This despite the fact that I felt as if I were one or two pedals away from a train wreck, that he was inevitably going to cause. It was no accident that Jerry had positioned him in front of me. We were pretty good friends, but I think he wanted me to try and keep an eye on Arlin and maybe even motivate him a bit. Danny Zoubek was directly behind me and being that he was a much more responsible Scout; I had little worries about him running into me.

As we got closer to the end of June and our group had several training sessions now under its belt, we were beginning to act as one unit. We still had a lot to learn though, and our conditioning hikes would last all through July 18 before we shoved off on July 22. A big test of our abilities was scheduled shortly after the July 4th holiday where we would take a four-day excursion with all our gear to the Mississippi Palisades State Park. The park was 130 miles west of Wood Dale. Some thought of it as a "shake out" as we planned to traverse a total distance of 260 miles on Route 64. The leaders would be observing us very carefully on this trip. They expected to encounter the same conditions as we might face while traveling through all nine states on our way to Florida. It was considered a "dry run" of sorts and was designed to challenge our newly learned bicycle riding skills.

Our safety was a principal concern for Jerry, and he felt that it was important for us to know how to act should something unexpected occur. If someone in our convoy was experiencing a problem, we had already trained for that possibility and knew what steps to take. We tried hard to anticipate the conditions that we might encounter on our way to Florida. We prac-

219

ticed simulating a derailment and several other problems such as a flat tire or someone dropping out of line. We devised procedures to handle each occurrence. In the case of a derailment, we were taught how to fall out of line so that we would not cause a chain reaction crash. We practiced passing one another and riding in a straight line, being careful not to pull out of the line or to weave out into traffic.

We trained riding on the side of the road, hugging the white line making sure not to run off onto the soft shoulder. That could be disastrous, since the tires on our bikes were very thin and would sink into the soft gravel of the shoulder potentially causing a crash. Crossing railroad tracks posed another problem and we had to guard against the skinny tires becoming caught between the rails.

Our bike rules of the road instruction had taught us to always ride in the same direction as the cars were traveling. This was contrary to what many of us had been taught as kids. We were told to ride against traffic so the cars could better see you. Over time, that idea had been proven false and was considered more dangerous. Our instructor pointed out that all the traffic signs are positioned with the flow of traffic. We learned that the law was very clear stipulating that bicyclists have all the rights and responsibilities as drivers of automobiles. Our upcoming state test would prove to our leaders what Scouts were listening and which ones were not.

We rode mostly in a single file line and were doing pretty well except for a few minor mishaps, usually because of chain derailments. We tried to introduce something different each time we went out. There were times we would be heading down a side street, and Mr. "G" would signal a turn to the right and then on the same street we would make a left-hand turn.

He wanted us to get the feeling of just how each type of turn affected the long trail of bikes.

When all 32 bikes were on the road in a single file line, we estimated it to be nearly 380 feet of bikes and what was supposed to be a bike length in-between. It was an incredible sight to see that many bikes all heading down the road together. As we traveled through different parts of Wood Dale and the surrounding towns on our training sessions, we seemed to know people wherever we went. They would often encourage us waving and cheering us on. Some of the practice runs were more grueling than others and it was uncanny how Jerry knew where every hill in town seemed to be.

The leaders developed an ingenious system of what we called road guards to help us safely pass through major intersections in busy towns. As we approached an intersection a couple of boys would pull out to block it from oncoming cars as the rest of the crew rode through. It was important to keep the unit together. Our system reduced the chances of anyone getting hit if the light turned before we could all make it safely through the intersection. When we needed to stop for something whether to fix a tire or check our map, we practiced a system that allowed the word to be passed up from Jerry or from Mr. "G" in the lead. As more time passed and our riding abilities improved, we also practiced riding two abreast, a formation we used when we got out onto the open road.

Jerry devised systems for everything we did on the trip so that we could be the most prepared and efficient group possible. He knew that with this many bikes it was essential that we practiced and became proficient at everything we were being taught. I was on one of two tire repair crews. We practiced changing tires in nearly every scenario, including while riding on a busy road. I never knew when we would get the word to pull off the road as the element of surprise was built into Jerry's system. We had to be ready at all times to do our repairs under different conditions including fixing a flat in the rain. Our repair crews became very efficient and we could fix a flat tire within 10 to 15 minutes.

Steve Zoubek, Danny's older brother, was a handy guy and one of the best at changing tires. He was able to fix just about anything that went wrong with our bikes. Danny was assigned to a different repair crew and was handy, too, as their father had taught them both how to use tools at an early age. Steve was a real tall kid whose mechanical ability surfaced at a very early age. Before he was even 16 years old and able to drive, he was already doing a valve job on a car he had bought. Like his brother, Danny, he always came up with the most innovative camp gadgets.

If a tire were to blow, we might be able to fix it without even taking it off the rim as long as we were able to patch it. Since I was one of the crew chiefs, I carried a tire pump. Once the tire was changed instead of using the pump, we would use a CO_2 cartridge to blow the tire up to the required 60 pounds of pressure. It was nearly impossible to blow the tire up to that amount of pressure using a regular bicycle tire pump. We only used the pumps if someone's tire needed a shot of air to keep it to the required pressure.

It was an organized and efficient team, and while one guy would work a wrench on one side of the bike, the other would help stabilize it. We were like a pit crew on a racetrack, when our services were needed, we jumped into action. The back tires were always a bit more difficult to fix since all of the gearing mechanism are located there. In addition to my tire repair crew, different teams were established for other repairs needed on the bikes. None of the boys were allowed to adjust the spokes, Mr. Giannini and Jerry always did that.

I had just returned from swim camp where I completed the requirements for my swimming and lifesaving merit badges. It started out as a typical conditioning hike toward the end of June. The spring rainy season was coming to an end. It had rained almost continuously for two days and was playing havoc on our training sessions. It was getting dark fast as another storm was getting closer. As we neared Wood Dale, the sky just let loose and it began to pour. The rain was so intense that I could hear the cars zipping by us but could barely make out their images. The deluge of water hitting my face was nearly blinding me. The cars were traveling at a high speed along a busy stretch of North Avenue. Every time a car would hit a patch of standing water, we would get drenched with a wave splashing into our faces. We were completely soaked. When we came to a section of the road where we needed to cross, it became apparent that it was going to be almost impossible to get everyone safely across. As each minute passed, our vision was becoming more impaired as the rain intensified. You could feel a certain degree of uneasiness in the group, and everyone was focused on Jerry's voice. He repeated himself several times, saying that we would be crossing together and that no one should cross alone.

The traffic was relentless as one car after another flew past us launching more water in our direction. After several minutes the word was once again passed down that no one was to cross until further orders were given. We all knew it was impossible to cross the street and would most likely have to keep moving until a more suitable place could be found. We were an organized group and had devised several methods for crossing busy roads in all kinds of conditions. If we made a mistake, someone could easily be killed.

One method we routinely used was to stop in a single file line and cross the road all as one bike. Up to this point this approach had always worked. The rain was finally starting to let up somewhat but the traffic was still heavy. Just as we were getting ready to attempt another crossing, a police officer who noticed the predicament we were in, stopped, and turned his lights on, halting traffic in both directions so we could cross. We thanked him and we went safely on our way.

Our next Scout meeting would mark our last bike rules of the road instruction class. We were all anxious to get it over with and dreaded the upcoming test now only a few days away. My grandmother had driven me to the meeting since it was the day all of our Florida clothing had to be turned in for marking. Jerry wanted all of us to be dressed as Scouts so that anyone who might meet us along the way would identify us as Boy Scouts. Since our clothing all looked the same, it was imperative that everything had to be marked or there would be a lot of confusion once we got on the road.

We had a very limited amount of space in our saddlebags to pack all of our gear and knew it was important to keep the weight down. As with everything for the trip, we tested exactly what amount of clothing and other supplies would fit comfortably into each bag.

Equipment and clothing list: (Some of these items will be worn on the day of departure.)

1* = 1 of those items will be worn on the day of departure.
The remaining items will be carried on the bicycle.

3 Boy Scout Tee Shirts 1*

3 Pr. Underwear shorts 1*

1 Pr. Boy Scout Uniform Shorts 1*

2 Pr. Boy Scout Knee Socks 1*

1 Pr. Boy Scout Garters / Green Tassels 1*

2 Pr. White Cotton Socks

1 Pr. Scout Long Pants

1 Boy Scout V Neck, Short Sleeved Uniform Shirt

1Red Neckerchief

1 Scout Field Cap 1*

1 Scout Belt 1*

1 Pr. Light Swim Trunks

2 Handkerchiefs 1*

1 Plastic Rain Suit

1 Towel

1 Toothbrush

Fish line and Hooks

Canteen on belt Setup 1*

Silverware

Cup

1 Pr. Low Quarter Lace Shoes with Heel 1*

1 Red Poplin Uniform Jacket.

OPTIONAL ITEMS
Pocket knife
Camera and film
Sunglasses if normally worn

Our Boy Scout uniform shorts, although durable were not really optimal for a trip where we would be sitting on a small bicycle seat and pedaling nearly 1,400 miles. The leather low cut shoes that were chosen resembled more or a work boot and was a disaster waiting to happen. When it rained, which was often, they filled up with water and no matter how much water proofing material we applied; they became saturated and turned into lead weights. It was a poor choice, but I think we had gotten a special deal to purchase them at cost. They were not the kind of shoe that you would want to effectively pedal your bike across the country, but we had no choice.

The simple fact that we would all carry canteens around our waists was a crazy idea too, but we all did it. Bicycling across the country was a new idea and most people that road their bikes during that time were not covering the distance that we had planned. Special types of clothing and equipment designed for cyclists did not really exist. Even if such clothing had been available, the chances that we might have worn them were slim unless they had the Boy Scout insignia plastered all over them.

We needed several tents for the trip since we had planned to camp the entire way. Jerry was concerned about the weight load and wanted to make sure they were lightweight. He designed the tents out of rip stop nylon so that they would be light but also durable. The bright orange nylon he selected would be coated with vinyl on one side to make them waterproof. They fit three people and had a back wall and small sides about a foot high. The tents had been designed without a door since Jerry felt that the Scouts could determine what direction a storm might be coming, and pitch their tents accordingly. Several of the moms from the mother's group helped to sew all eleven tents.

Although she was not officially a member of the mother's group, my grandmother was an expert seamstress and volunteered to sew a few of the tents on her Singer sewing machine. She looked like a mad woman on that machine, swearing up a storm if she made any mistakes. She worked the machine's pedal with a good deal of precision while her hair that looked more like a wig was flying around in every direction. It was clear from the finished product that she had sewn a few things in her life, including many of my father's clothes as a kid.

TWENTY-SIX

AS IT GOT CLOSER to the trip, some of the parents began to question the length of it. It was sometime near the end of June when Curt Schuppi's mother, asked Jerry about the severe heat that we were going to encounter in the South. Curt's parents unexpectedly showed up at Jerry's house one evening and said, "He can't go."

"Why?" Jerry asked. "He's been training with us for some time now and wants to go."

"Why did you pick Florida, don't you realize how hot it is down there in the summer?" Curt's mother responded. Jerry was a bit taken aback and since he had never actually been to Florida, wasn't sure how hot it really got.

Curt had been signed up for the trip from the beginning and made every practice session. With only a few weeks away from leaving, his misguided mother had decided that she would not allow him to go with us on the trip. No matter what Jerry said to try to convince her to let Curt go, nothing seemed to matter. Good-natured Curt was off our list of Scouts traveling to Florida that summer. Mrs. Schuppi had made up her mind and Curt was devastated. Jerry had to put out a few more fires of apprehension that summer with a few other parents that had also voiced their concerns. However, it was apparent that we were still going to Florida, as clearer heads would prevail.

Ron Herff continued to help with all the preparations for the trip, even though he realized his chances of going had passed due to his accident. His condition had improved dramatically since having his cast removed. Ron was getting stronger by the week with a regiment of physical therapy. We were practicing some of our maneuvers in the church parking lot one evening in preparation for our bicycle rules of the road examination. Ron was sitting in Jerry's green International Scout watching us as we tried to perfect some of our riding skills. "How are you feeling, Ron?" Jerry asked.

"I'm doing pretty well," Ron replied.

"Well do you think you might be able to go with us?" Jerry responded.

"I really want to take this trip and have always wanted to," Ron said.

"We will need to set up a doctor's appointment for you Ron, as long as your mom and dad would agree to it. Are you in if the doctor says you're ok?" Jerry said.

"Yes, I want to go!" Ron responded. The next day Jerry approached Ron's father, Dick Herff. "How would you feel if Ron wanted to go on the Florida trip?" Jerry asked him. His dad was ok with the idea as long as they made a doctor's appointment to have Ron thoroughly checked out.

"He's coming along just fine, but if he gets tired you will have to give him a break," the doctor soon reported.

"That won't be a problem, I will keep a close eye on him," Jerry said. Unfortunately, for poor Curt, his mother's decision to strip him of the opportunity to go to Florida had opened up a spot for Ron to join us. Shortly after his doctor's approval, Ron was put on the trip list and started to train with us. With less than a month left to train, he knew he would have to work hard to prepare for the long ride. He put a lot of effort toward the remaining training sessions and would do well on the trip despite a slight a limp. Ron would ride up near the front of the pack near Mr. Giannini, as Jerry realized that he had some limitations and didn't want to put an undo amount of strain on him.

When June 26, finally rolled around, we all realized what was at stake and that it was an important "make or break" day. I helped to set up a driving course in the church parking lot placing cones in several places throughout the lot. The written part of the test would be administered in the church basement before any riding would take place. If you passed both the written and driving tests, you would receive a Safe Driver License from the Bicycle Institute of America Safety League.

Up to this point, we knew we were going to be tested but no one had any idea that some guy from the state of Illinois, who introduced himself as the State of Illinois Licensing Examiner, would be testing us. Jerry had told us at our last meeting to study hard because if you didn't pass both the written and riding tests you would not be going to Florida with the rest of the guys. From 6:30 p.m. to 10:00 p.m., we were involved in bicycle licensing examinations and road tests with the state licensing examiner. The mood in the church basement all of a sudden got serious and no one dared make a sound. After about 30 minutes of testing, the guy from the state told us to put our pencils down, that our time was up. Fortunately, we all passed both tests and were each promptly issued our Safe Driver License.

The headline from the Herald on Wednesday, July 5, read, "Scouts in muscle tune-up." We were still planning on a four-day excursion with all our gear to the Mississippi Palisades State Park some 130 miles west of Wood Dale. All of us felt that we were ready for a longer trip and anxious to get our bikes out onto the open road to perfect our riding skills. This would be an important test and a way to prepare ourselves for the Florida trip.

Jerry had put us through a rigorous training program in an effort to get us ready for our long journey. We had ridden 20 conditioning hikes. The first 16 were all two and a half hours long. Since we were getting progressively stronger and more confident with our bikes after each hike, Jerry decided to add another hour to our routine toward the end of June. He realized that while on the trip we would need to ride almost the entire day in order to make it to Florida in the 30 days we had allotted.

We had practiced hard for the Fourth of July parade a few days earlier that summer. We were going to be a big attraction, as we would all be riding our new red, white, and blue Free Spirit bikes two abreast down the middle of Wood Dale Road. It was quite a spectacle that day. Nearly everyone from town lined up in the thousands crowding along the roadside, waving and cheering us on. I even saw Billy and his sister Kathy, both on their bikes, smiling and waving as we rode by. Despite the fact that Billy wasn't going on the trip, his spirit of friendship that we had developed over the years would be with me, encouraging me the entire way. The whole town was now behind us, as our trip would surely put Wood Dale on the map. All 32 of us would soon be ambassadors of goodwill, representing our little town, spreading the values of Scouting wherever we would go.

The parade seemed to signify a real turning point in the trip's progress and everyone in our group was starting to feel the excitement and the anticipation of our upcoming adventure, as we got closer to our departure date of July 22. My mother had written on our July calendar the words, "*starting day*," and everyone in my family knew what it meant.

I had discovered a new seamstress in my family and my grandmother was hard at work finishing the tents she had offered to help sew for our trip. We would be organized into groups of three during our trip to Florida and the Mississippi Palisades would be our first experience with each of our groups to test the compatibility. Two Scouts would each carry a blanket and the other boy carried the tent. We shared the blankets amongst the three of us. It was a common practice on our longer trips to have a group consisting of three boys. Unfortunately, that arrangement did not assure that all three would get along with each other. Usually the mix consisted of one older Scout coupled with two younger boys to keep some sense of order.

Although we knew it would be hot where we were heading especially in July and August, we still needed to have a decent blanket since we would be sleeping on the ground most of the time. Our excursion to the Palisades would be our first overnighter with all our gear in tow. My special blanket, that I designed, was made using an old wool army blanket and a white sheet that my grandmother had sewed onto one side. The idea of wool against bare skin didn't appeal to me, but it would keep me dry and the sheet would be more comfortable. The blanket although a bit on the heavy side, proved to be a well-designed system since some of the nights were chilly and it kept us warm but the material was still able to breath.

TWENTY-SEVEN

WE SLEPT UNDER THE STARS at Salt Creek Park the night before we left for our practice trip to the Mississippi Palisades. We took off early the next morning on July 6, despite having a problem getting our blankets dry because of heavy morning dew. We wanted to leave as early as possible to get our mileage in and simulate as many of the conditions we might experience on our trip to Florida. Jerry had a limited amount of time and was able to get off work at the water filtration plant on both Friday and the following Monday. The four day round trip would be estimated at around 168 miles and be our longest bike hike yet.

Equipped with our 10-speed Free Spirit bikes and our new saddlebags, we quickly sped through town, as there was almost no traffic in sight early in the morning. Our tents would take longer to sew but the weather was forecasted to be favorable with no rain. We decided to go without any real shelter except for a few plastic tarps we planned to sleep on. It was a trip all unto itself and we realized that it would be two days out and two days back. We were very excited to be on the open road with all our gear and were determined to make it to our destination and back. Our spirits were very high as we turned west onto Route 64 with the warm sun now at our backs.

We practiced and tried to perfect our road guard system during this trip. It seemed as if it was working well without much of a hitch. The communication between Mr. "G" and the road guards had gotten much better over the past few months and added a higher degree of safety.

We traveled about 45 miles that first day and slept under the stars on a grassy patch we found just outside of Sycamore. I had traveled this same route with my parents many times before on all of our campouts at White Pines. For the most part, Route 64 was flat as we headed further west. The landscape in that part of Illinois is dominated by some of the richest farmland in the country. Thousands of acres of corn and soybeans are grown year after year. An occasional white farmhouse can be spotted tucked away amongst the only stand of trees seen for miles.

We started our training sessions wanting to cover the same number of miles we were expected to travel to get to Florida. Our estimate of the distance was somewhere between 1,200 and 1,400 miles depending on the road conditions we might encounter. We were falling short of that goal since we were forced in the beginning to use our own bikes. When we set off for the Palisades that morning we had every intension of making it all the way to the park. Somewhere along the way, Jerry made the sobering announcement that the distance to the Palisades was too far for us to ride, since he and the other leaders had to get back to work. We had underestimated the time it would take to travel the full distance to the park. White Pines State Park was suggested as an alternate destination as it would be a more reasonable 84 miles in each direction.

When we started to get closer to the park area near the town of Oregon, the topography of the land started to change. No longer were the roads flat and I could hear everyone struggle to shift their gears as we started to climb each hill. The Rock River had cut a massive series of deep valleys throughout the area and pedaling our bikes up all the steep hills proved to be a greater challenge than many had expected. The area is well known for its hilly and heavily wooded terrain. It was one of the reasons the great Indian warrior, Blackhawk, and his band of followers found it appealing. Although I had never ridden a bicycle through the area, I had hiked extensively as a young boy throughout many of the nearby parks. As we passed over the Rock River, I could see off in the distance the massive concrete statue of Blackhawk, soaring 125 feet into the air over-looking the river.

After two days of riding up and down the hills, we finally arrived at White Pines State Park. Before we set up camp for the night, I led our group on a hike into the pine forest since I knew all of the park's trails. We were on a mission during this trip and had a limited amount of time to test all of our skills and systems for the open road.

Everyone in our unit was getting more muscular and increasingly more comfortable on their bikes as a result of all of our training. I was a junior leader and in a group of older boys that ranged in age from 14 through 16. When you add the 11, 12 and 13-year-olds into the mix, it was their attitude that really struck me as being the core of the group's spirit. They possessed a sense of blind ambition where failure in their minds was non-existent or even a part of their vocabulary. They just did it, and rarely complained as they continued to ride day after day during our conditioning hikes. Our excursion to White Pines that weekend would prove to Jerry and all the other leaders that we could make it to Florida. There were four 11-year-olds in our group of 32, and as Jerry would later say, "Golly, they really outdid themselves."

The next morning we got up very early, and after dressing in our full uniforms, marched up to the lodge and had breakfast before heading back home. Throughout the park, concrete fords were constructed instead of bridges, allowing visitors to drive through Pine Creek. The water was a little higher, since it had rained hard a few days earlier and the rangers had just re-opened the fords. The fords are usually less than a foot deep, but this time the creek was still running pretty strong. For an automobile, they posed no problem. A lightweight bicycle would be another issue, as a skinny Mark Titone, would soon find out. He was petrified of riding through the water and was one of the younger 11-year-old boys on a smaller bike. When we finally coaxed him into crossing, he jumped off his bike half way and walked it over the water bridge. He got soaked and vowed the next morning to ride through the water like everyone else had.

Mark had come from a tough family where his father was in the printing business and worked long hours. He didn't have much time to spend with Mark or his five younger sisters. He was a shorter skinny kid and we always called him, "Mouse." Despite his apparent hardships at home, Mark always had a great smile and for the most part maintained a good sense of humor. The fords at White Pines were a real problem for him. As we rode out of the park he stuck with his pledge to cross, but it was clear that he was tentative in his actions and was having some difficulty.

Most of the younger boys were ahead of me in our convoy. I could see Mark start to weave back and forth, as the pressure of the rushing stream had pushed his bike to the right. All of a sudden, he just lost it, and fell over sideways into Pine Creek, becoming completely immersed under water. His bike and all his gear just disappeared under the rushing water, later popping up several yards downstream. The surface of the concrete road was always slippery due to the algae and further exasperated the situation. Billy Mikuls, who was also on a smaller bike and riding close behind, tried to help Mark, but the road was too slick and he wasn't much help. When we finally extricated Mark and his bike from the creek, his eyes looked like they were going to pop out of his head he was so frazzled from the experience.

Mark had taken a bad fall that day and he was still shaken up, but like a good Scout he just got back on his bike and we continued on our way back toward Wood Dale. After pedaling nearly 40 miles, Jerry noticed that Mark was having a rough time riding and was really slowing down. He started complaining of how hard it was to pedal his bike and a few of us noticed that his saddlebags were moving about in a rather strange manner. When we eventually pulled off the road to take a break, Mark's bike just fell over and green creek water came gushing out of his saddled bags. He had unknowingly been carrying a lot of extra weight for several miles up and down all those huge hills near the park.

Mark had ridden all that distance with water soaked saddlebags. Mr. Giannini and his wife had done an excellent job sewing the canvas bags together and we now knew for sure that they were waterproof. As we jumped on our bikes to try to put in a few more miles, I thought that in an odd way, Mark's experience with the fords had helped to prepare him for what would be a grueling trip ahead.

Later that night we were searching for a place to camp as it was beginning to get dark and very hazy. Several large low-lying clouds seemed to be hanging over us covering our faces in a light mist. As we continued to ride, I looked out over the vast expanses of corn and bean fields that stretched for miles. Our visibility was getting worse by the minute and we needed to find a place to camp soon. When we finally stopped by what appeared to be two smaller roads that intersected, the area looked somewhat familiar. We camped along the grassy side of one of the roads, and as the night set in, it became very dark and eerily quiet. There was almost no traffic along the road that night. As the clouds slowly dissipated and the mist began to lift, we all rolled out our blankets onto the plastic tarps. As I lay in my blanket looking up at the vastness of the sky, millions of bright stars appeared revealing more constellations then I had ever seen in my life. We all slept pretty well that night knowing that the trip we were soon to embark upon would test all of our mental and physical conditioning. We were now prepared for what would be the longest organized bike hike in the history of Scouting.

TWENTY-EIGHT

E VERYTHING WAS MOVING much faster now since having returned from our trip to White Pines. Nearly everyone in town could feel the excitement of the trip building.
Several last minute fundraising events had been planned by the
HHY as our estimate of our trip costs had gone up. Even our
route to Florida had now been finalized, and two copies of the
trip ticket were in the process of being run off using the Wood
Dale Police Department's IBM computer. It was an important
document and would serve as our guide, mapping out all the
hundreds of little roads that we would need to travel on as we
made our way down to Florida.

The Wood Dale Association of Commerce and Industry
would hold a dinner and dance on Tuesday, July 11, at Mr.
Duke's Restaurant in Wood Dale. It was described as the social
event of the year by a spokesman for the association to help
the Scouts raise part of the $265.00 each one needed for the
trip. Live music was provided by the popular band, "Summer
Daze." The admission fee for the dinner dance was $10.00. Half
of the proceeds would be allocated to the Scouts to help us purchase the equipment we needed for the trip.

Posters for the dinner and dance were plastered all over
town, as several dignitaries would be present, including former
Illinois Governor William G. Stratton and Wood Dale's Mayor,
Lewis Mazzuca. The association had hoped to raise $800.00 at
the dinner for the Scouts. Tickets for the big event were being
sold at Sievers Pharmacy, Arts Bootery and Forrest Realty.

My mother was always a procrastinator and had scheduled
my required medical exam with Doctor Benoris on July 13. Our
assistant Scoutmaster, Mike Terese, had been telling us for

weeks that all of our doctor's appointments had to be completed no later than July 14. The medical form was due at the upcoming Florida parents and boys meeting. It was an important meeting and would mark the last time all of the parents and boys would be together before our departure on July 22. The final trip fees along with our spending money was also due. I had earned all of my own spending money between cutting grass and my paper route and my father had agreed to pay for the rest of the trip.

The directive from Jerry's handout was clear. Each Scout would be required to have a haircut beginning on Tuesday July 18 to Thursday July 20. This would not be just any kind of haircut either. Our hair had to be cut short, almost crew cut style before the trip. It was a direct order from Jerry. We had scheduled one of our longer bicycle conditioning hikes later that evening from 6:30 p.m. to 10:00 p.m.

Hairstyles were worn longer back then and my hair was no exception despite the fight with my father's clippers. A crew cut was going to be a tough thing to handle. If you didn't get your hair cut short enough, you would have to get it cut again. If you chose not to get it cut or it wasn't cut to the specs Jerry had given to all the barbers in the area, he would cut it himself. His impressions of the people down South were that they were straight laced and that they all had short haircuts. Since we were going to be our town's representatives for nearly 30 days, Jerry wanted us to make a good impression on everyone we met along our route.

Billy and I hadn't seen much of each other that summer except for a few campouts in my backyard. We both missed playing together and still managed to ride our bikes around town a bit when I wasn't practicing for my trip. A heat wave was predicted to hit the area over the next several days with temperatures expected to reach well above 90°F. No one I knew had air conditioning in their house, so we mostly hooked up the sprinkler in the backyard to cool off. Both Billy and my brother's friend, Steve Neuman, had come over to our house early that day. We started to hook up the sprinkler, since the thermometer on our front porch was already reading 82°F. It was well on its way to be the hottest day so far when I said, "Why don't we go to the lake!"

"What lake?" Billy responded in somewhat of a surprised voice.

"Lake Michigan!" I said.

"That's pretty far isn't it?" he replied.

"Come on, we can do it," I said.

So with that, all four of us, jumped on our Frankenstein bikes and were soon heading east down Irving Park Road toward what I hoped would be Lake Michigan at the end of the road. The truth is, I really wasn't sure how far it was. All I knew was that it was at the end of that road from looking at one of my father's maps he had stashed in the glove compartment of his car.

I lead our little group, with Billy close behind, followed by Steve and my brother Mark at the rear. None of us had any real money to speak of. All we knew was that as the day went on, it was getting hotter by the minute and we wanted to swim and cool off in that big lake. I had decided to take my older bike and although the rear tire was a bit on the bald side, I just felt more comfortable riding it. My brother, on the other hand, had chosen to ride his new Stingray. Billy's bike and Steve's were pretty old too, but in good shape.

We had been riding for more than an hour, jumping every curb along the road, when we decided to stop for a break after crossing over the Des Plaines River near Cumberland. My brother said that he was tired and wanted to turn back. Mark was always a stocky kid and never quite as athletic as me, but after a little coaxing from his friend, Steve, we took off again. Once we got past Cumberland, the traffic really started to pick up, so we stuck to riding mostly on the sidewalks dodging several people along the way. I don't think we had even pedaled half way when I looked back and saw that my brother had fallen further behind.

Irving Park Road is a major drag through the northern part of Chicago. I knew the lake was where I had told everyone it was, but I had no idea how many miles we would have to pedal or how long it would take us to get there. Billy wanted to let Mark go back, but I couldn't just let him ride home alone and I was determined to make it there. I was in better shape than the other guys since I had been training on my 10-speed for the past two months. When we finally made it to a major highway that passed overhead, both my brother and Steve were really dragging. The 93°F heat was getting to them.

When we stopped to drink from a water fountain, I could feel somewhat of a breeze that I thought must be coming from the lake. The traffic continued to get busier the closer we got to the city. We would have to change up our lineup coming back, as my brother would not be able to keep up with Billy or me. I wasn't familiar with the neighborhoods we were passing through, but knew that they were a far cry from our little rural town of Wood Dale. We rode past several massive dark stone churches that seemed to be on every other corner with soaring steeples.

When we finally made it to the lake, it felt as if we had discovered a new world. The beautiful blue expanse of the lake was calling us. Unfortunately, where we had planned to swim was not a very safe spot. The lakeshore at the end of Irving

Park Road is lined with massive concrete blocks and boulders piled several feet high to prevent erosion of the shoreline. We weren't going to be denied though, as we had pedaled a long way in record high temperatures. When we reached the lake, we immediately took off our shirts and shoes and jumped off the huge blocks into the icy water. What a great feeling that was. We had ridden our little bikes nearly 20 miles through the heart of Chicago, and would now have to turn around and do it again.

I really had to coax my brother and Steve to keep pedaling on our way back. Despite swimming and resting for about an hour, we had to find the energy to pedal home. It had taken us a long time to get to the lake and now we had to ride back. We had made it! The fun we had that day, as we jumped into the frigid waters of the great lake beat any sprinkler in our backyard.

The traffic heading back had increased along Irving Park Road as we traversed across all the sidewalks through the old Chicago neighborhoods on our quest for adventure. Our bikes were holding up pretty well and none of us experienced any problems with them. We seemed to be making better progress heading home. We rode quickly past the store fronts zipping along on the sidewalks and crossing over driveways. Our little romp bicycling through Chicago was just another one of our crazy stunts that summer. We had a great time, and I was certain it would be something we would remember for the rest of our lives. As young boys, we were full of adventure but often oblivious to the dangers.

When we got back later that night, my mother who was unaware of our whereabouts the entire day was visibly worried. When she told my father about our exploits, he didn't seem all that surprised telling my mother that the route we had taken was pretty safe.

Our final briefing for our trip to Florida that now seemed to be more like a military mission, was held that night at the church basement. Our departure date was fast approaching and was now only a few days away. My excursion to the great lake that summer with Billy would be one of our last great adventures together. I knew despite the fact that he had not trained with all of us, that he could make it to Florida if he wanted to.

TWENTY-NINE

WHEN MY MOTHER woke me up on the morning of July 22, it was still dark outside. She whispered, "Pauly, you need to get up now, it's *starting day*." The muscles in my legs ached from the long ride to the lake and I was slow to get out of bed. The intense heat that had started a few days earlier was not letting up and our first day out would prove to be a hot one. One of the last things my mother would say to me before I left the house was to remember to fill up my canteen. I was excited but a little nervous too. We had been training for this day for two and a half months and now it had finally arrived. I was confident that we would make it to Florida, but I knew it would not be an easy ride, especially through the Smoky Mountains. I said goodbye to everyone in my family, and hugged and kissed my mother and father.

My grandmother gave me her usual wet kiss on my cheek and said, "Be a good Scout!" She had been a big help preparing me for the trip. She was proud of the fact that I was a Scout and had planned on tracking our progress, clipping newspaper articles, and tuning into WIVS, a radio station out of Crystal Lake. The station had offered to cover our troop's progress with a daily radio broadcast.

My younger brother, Michael looked like he was going to cry and I knew I would miss him the most. I had packed and repacked my saddlebags at least a few times and made last minute adjustments to my bike the night before. I lashed the blanket my grandmother had sewn onto the bike rack carefully wrapping it in a piece of thick plastic my father had given me.

Everyone in my family, except my grandmother, would be leaving early on Monday morning heading down to Florida for a stay at the Lago Mar in Fort Lauderdale. When I started down our gravel driveway on my Free Spirit, I looked back to see everyone waving goodbye. I felt my eyes begin to tear up as I knew I would miss my family. For many of us it would be the longest time we would be away from home.

Despite the fact that it was only 5:45 a.m., the heat was already starting to build and the thermometer on my back porch of my house read 80°F. When I turned east onto Irving Park Road, it wasn't long before I made it to the Two Eagles Restaurant. Jerry and a few of the other leaders and Father Thompson, the Associate Pastor of Holy Ghost were already drinking their morning coffee. I was only 14 at the time and hadn't started drinking coffee yet but it smelled good. When I approached the table where Jerry was sitting he stood up and greeted me with a big smile and said, "Are you excited?"

"Yes, I can't wait to shove off," I said.

Mike Terese was the only leader not present at breakfast as he had left earlier in the month to start his basic training in the Navy. He had arranged for a leave and would be joining us somewhere in Indiana or Kentucky later the following week. The other guys started to filter into the restaurant and when everyone was accounted for by 6:00 a.m., Father Thompson stood up and blessed the breakfast and said a prayer. We were all anxious to get on the road but had one more stop to make before we could take off on our long journey. Most of the other boy's parents had gathered at the church parking lot to say their final goodbyes before we could officially shove off at 7:30 a.m. My parents were never big on crowds so they had decided to say their goodbyes in private.

Our caravan of 31 bikes left the restaurant at preciously 7:00 a.m. as Jerry had planned and started heading east toward the church. As we flew past the Dog N' Suds and the old bowling alley, we looked like a well-oiled machine that was now click-ing on all cylinders. I was already thinking about what our first night out on the road might be like. Jerry, who had been named Wood Dale's first "Citizen of the Year," gathered every-one together in the church parking lot for one last talk with all of our parents and well-wishers.

In a short speech, he explained to everyone that we planned to ride through nine states where the Scouts would have an op-portunity to be in direct communication with people from all walks of life. Many of my fellow Scouts had never been out of Illinois and our route would take us through such towns as In-dianapolis, Renfro Valley, Cumberland Gap, Franklin, and Yulee. It would be quite an adventure as we had planned to stop along the way and visit with other Scouts and their fami-lies. The communication would be mutually beneficial Jerry went on to say, and be a kind of "cross fertilization" of ideas and opinions.

Jerry's final message to the crowd would be a statement he would read that his former Scoutmaster, Tony Langfeld, had prepared. *"Exposing the Scouts to the goodness of people and the people to the goodness of Scouts,"* Jerry said, "is the motto of our trip." Several mothers in the crowd began to cry, as it was an emotional speech. We would soon become the youth ambas-sadors of Wood Dale wherever our bicycles might take us. Ev-eryone knew where we were heading but no one knew exactly what conditions or people we might encounter. Since we had only received a few responses to the letters we had sent out to the towns, it was anyone's guess as to the reception we might expect.

How Mr. Langfeld came up with the idea for the motto of our trip is not known, but it was clear that our Scout troop would soon be representing Wood Dale. "People are going to meet you and want to get to know you along the way," Jerry told us before the start of the trip. As we crossed into different states, passing through all the cities and small towns, everyone we encountered was curious and asked a lot of questions. "We are doing something very special and are supporting our community," Jerry told us. "You need to be on your best behavior," he said. His comments would become the mantra for the trip. The entire town was now firmly behind us. What we were attempting to accomplish was important to us as Scouts, but it was also important to the citizens of Wood Dale, and we didn't want to let them down.

The headline on page two in the Herald on Friday, July 21, 1972 read, "Wood Dale Scouts are taking off to discover America." The article went on to say, "Some people claim that our mechanized age has killed America's spirit of adventure. But adventure's obituary may be premature and some twenty-seven Scouts and five leaders from Wood Dale Troop 65 are setting out to prove it."

Emotions were still running high as many of us held back tears when we finally mounted our bikes and rode off on our venture heading east down Irving Park Road. With Mr. Giannini at the head of the pack we made our first turn south onto Wood Dale Road. From there it was as if we had been shot out of a cannon and we quickly flew past the Salt Creek Forest Preserve. We were clearly on a mission. Everything was running smoothly. We were in a perfect rhythm. From the very beginning of our training sessions it had been determined that Mr. "G" would take the lead position. He had a good sense of awareness of the young kids and understood the group's strengths and weaknesses. He never went hog wild with taking off faster than the crew could manage and always kept a steady pace.

Over the years, Mr. Giannini had driven to many different places in the country with his family while on vacation. He had been designated as our navigator and we considered him to be our point man. Jack Froehling who also had a good sense of direction would help Mr. "G" on occasion. We made several stops along the way to make a decision on the route. Usually the lead person would pull over and we would all stop to make sure the route we were on was the correct one. There were only a few of us that had actually been to Florida and certainly, no one in our group had ever taken the route we were following.

We would get information to the front of the line by passing the word up from the back where Mr. "G" would eventually receive the message. The guys were good at passing the message along. There were certain instances where we would need to make a stop. Jerry and Mike Rohl were always at the back of the line where the order was usually initiated. Jerry would simply say, "We need to stop," and with that, the word "stop" began to immediately be passed from one Scout to another until it reached Mr. "G," the number 32 bike. It was similar to a game we played in the early days of Scouting that had originally been developed by General Powell for his scout's reconnaissance missions.

We were only about five or six miles out and still riding at a good clip when we passed the Elmhurst Country Club. Our turn onto North Avenue went without a hitch and we started heading east toward Route 83 where we would soon make a turn to the south. We had been down this same route several times on our training exercises and knew that it would be a good 20-mile run before nearing Palos Park. My bike was working well despite a nagging rear brake problem that I thought I had fixed the night before. I was anxious to really open my bike up and do some cruising. It would be our first long run of the day.

Up to this point, we had been sailing along at a good pace. Everyone's level of enthusiasm was high and our adrenalin had taken over. We all seemed to be on autopilot. Heading toward us, I saw a cop in a green and white squad car start to slow down. It was obvious that we had caught his attention and he was staring at us. All of a sudden, his red and blue lights started flashing. I lost sight of him as our caravan kept moving and I had to keep my eyes on the road. At that moment, I heard Danny yell, "Stop!" and within a few moments, the word to stop was repeated several times up the chain to the front of the group. Our caravan had just been pulled over by an Elmhurst police officer.

This cop was on a mission. After forcing us to stop, he didn't appear to be very friendly as I overheard his heated discussion with Jerry. He was insisting that what we were doing was illegal, saying that we were supposed to be riding against the traffic and not with it. All I could think of was that this guy had apparently never taken a bicycle rules of the road class. We all knew what this ill-advised cop was saying was completely false. We had all just finished a bicycle rules of the road course and had been awarded a safe driver's license.

We knew we were correct but the cop was adamant and said he needed to check it out. Bob Sample, a police officer himself, even talked to him, but he still wanted to check it out. After lecturing Bob and Jerry on a few more bicycle rules of the road, he abruptly left, saying that he needed to talk with his sergeant and ordered us to stay put until he got back. After waiting for 20 minutes, we just decided to take off. Fortunately, we didn't see the cop again and never had any other problems along the way with the police. In fact, just the opposite was true as we would have a few police escorts through some of the towns we would eventually pass through.

Safety was an issue from the beginning of our planning sessions and had been one of Jerry's main concerns. Some of the mothers from the HHY wondered what would happen if a kid were to get sick. Contingency plans were discussed in the event something unforeseen might happen. It was decided that as a precaution, Jerry's mother, Marie, and Betty Rohl, would drive Jerry's truck staying ahead of us some 15 to 20 miles. Jerry's International Scout was new and equipped with an automatic transmission that would be easier for the women to drive.

Although Jerry's mother had never learned how to drive, she and her friend Betty wanted to help our troop in making an emergency vehicle available. We also needed a way to transport some of our extra gear such as spare tires and bike parts. We would also be supported by Mr. Kennedy, a representative from Sears, who had planned on following us with some spare parts of his own for several days. Initially we had thought about setting up repair stations at predetermined points along the route. We soon abandoned the idea because we didn't know when we might need to make repairs or where we might be in reference to the repair stations.

There was a Troop 65 decal on each side of the truck's window making it clearly visible to the police should there be an emergency. It was decided that it would not be safe for the women to drive slowly behind us. Staying several miles ahead seemed reasonable without acting as a crutch for our group. They helped us quite a bit and would go ahead and check out the different communities. Since there were no cell phones back then, this seemed to be the best system we could devise.

Since Mike Terese wasn't able to secure his leave from the Navy until after our group took off, he needed a way to hook up with us. It was determined that Jerry's mother and Mrs. Rohl would transport Mike and carry his bike on the top of Jerry's truck. For about the first week out, we did not have an emergency vehicle available to us. Mike was due home on Wednesday, July 26, and had planned to leave early the next morning and would connect with us along the route.

When we passed over the Chicago Sanitary and Ship Canal, Route 83 took a hard turn to the east where it turned into the Calumet Sag Road. Just as I saw a sign for the Palos Forest Preserve, I started to hear "stop!" coming from behind me. We were riding through a wooded area and the shade would be a welcome relief from the hot sun. We had traveled nearly 25 miles and decided it was time to take our first break. My legs despite feeling tight when I first woke up were no longer sore. The temperature had risen to a sweltering 94°F. We were going through a lot of the water in our canteens and needed to start rationing it, Jerry said.

Turning south onto Route 45 would be our next big stretch of road. It also marked an area we had never ridden to in any of our training sessions. The route so far was pretty flat going and I was struck by how desolate the area seemed. The landscape was dominated by mostly corn and bean fields as far as the eye could see. We were making incredible time, better than on any conditioning hike. I wondered if we could keep up such a fast pace. As we passed through the small town of Palos Park, I was hoping we were going to stop for lunch soon. After riding a few more miles, I saw the sign for the town of Orland Park. Its population on our trip ticket was listed at 4,505 people. We had traveled an astonishing 32 miles in a relatively short period of time. It seemed like a good place to stop as it was about half the distance we planned on covering that day. There were a few small restaurants along the town's main street but only one that was open, so our choices were limited.

It was taking us a lot longer to eat lunch than Jerry had planned. He was getting more anxious by the minute to get back on the road and keep us on schedule. Meals were always an issue, as it was important to keep our costs down. We soon discovered that it took too much time to eat three full meals a day. We made the decision to eat a larger breakfast and dinner and have a snack for lunch. It gave us more money for our two main meals of the day and we could get back on the road quicker after a shorter lunch break. There were times when he had more money than others for our meals, but had to really budget it since we still needed to leave a tip at the restaurant. Meals and tips cost a lot less back then but our budget for them was pretty slim.

Due to a few donations, the final cost of the trip was slightly less than what we had originally estimated. The cost per Scout was $265.00 and we all worked to earn a portion of it ourselves. Included was the cost of the bike at $40.00, our $30.00 in spending money, and $51.00 for our airplane ticket. That left $144.00 for everything else including three meals a day, extra bike parts and repairs, entertainment, and any other incidentals for the 30 days we would be on the road.

Despite the lower cost of the trip, it was still a lot of money in those days, as many families did not make a whole lot. There were four sets of brothers that went on the trip and the cost for those families was particularly high. Some of the boys almost didn't make it. When my friend Danny's mother first heard about the trip, her initial reaction was not very encouraging. "You're not going. How can you expect us to pay for both you and your brother," she said, "think about all the dangers you will encounter!" Danny, who was only 13 at the time, would not turn 14 until sometime after the trip in October. He came from a large family with seven kids and money would be an issue.

Danny was always an industrious guy and had saved enough money to buy his own bike having worked a few odd jobs. He was determined to go to Florida. Jerry took notice and offered to help him raise the additional money he would need to go on the trip. He was able to find a weeklong job for Danny delivering flyers throughout town. The one page flyer was a Wood Dale newsletter that had to be delivered to about 3,000 homes. He would be paid $100.00 for his efforts, Jerry told him. Danny knew that it was a lot of money and took his job seriously. He folded each of the flyers in thirds and placed them in several large brown paper bags that he marked with the street name. Everything we did back then seemed to have a purpose. When we needed money for something, we found a way to earn it. The value of the Florida trip took on a different meaning since the $265.00 needed to go was not just handed to us by our parents.

THIRTY

DESPITE THE INTENSE HEAT that day, we continued to make better than expected time and everyone was in good spirits. We were learning to ration our water and stopping less to take bathroom breaks. Every time someone had to go to the bathroom, we had to stop. We tried to establish certain times to take breaks so everyone could use the bathroom at the same time and limit the number of stops. Each break turned into a big deal as all 31 bikes had to pull over, do our business, and then get back on the road. We were drinking a lot of water in the beginning and it was difficult to hold it until our designated stop. None of us wore hats so the heat beating down on us was intense, hour after hour while riding.

We were traveling east on Route 30 when we shot past Woodrow Wilson Woods, near the town of East Chicago Heights, and had already logged in 47 miles. The road was straight as an arrow and we saw very few cars until we started to get closer to town. As we passed through the next few towns, it was clear that we would have to keep going since there wasn't anywhere suitable to camp in the area. No one seemed tired despite the unrelenting heat. We had trained hard over the past few months, always pushing ourselves to maximize our endurance. Riding this many miles in such a short time period on a flat road, was one thing. However, we knew that once we hit the foothills of the Smokies, the number of miles we would be able to travel would be less. It was clear that we had prepared well and our performance on the first day was testament to the rigorous training. We just kept pedaling, and knew that we were getting close to the Indiana state line.

This time the word came from the front of the pack when I heard Arlin yell, "Indiana!" As we passed over the border into Indiana there was a real sense of accomplishment that we all felt. We stopped in the small town of Dyer, for a short bathroom break. A few of the guys, including Danny Zoubek seemed particularly elated that we had made it to Indiana. "Yes, we're almost there," he thought. Of course, we had only just started out and had nearly 1,200 more miles left to ride. Nonetheless, it felt good to make it out of Illinois into another state, even if it was just the next one over. All of our conditioning hikes had been in Illinois, so it really did feel like we had accomplished something significant at the time.

When we passed through the outskirts of Schererville, Indiana, we finally turned south again, this time our route would take us down US-41. The rural landscape seemed to suddenly change. The road began to get noticeably hillier and was not in very good repair. It looked like a huge patchwork quilt with its hundreds of repairs running in all directions. The sides of the road were a crumbling mass of aging asphalt, the result of years of neglect and the harsh Midwest winters. The shoulders of the road were made of a soft gravel and sand mix. We had to be very careful not to get too close to the edge or worse fall off the road which could prove to be disastrous. Riding up and down the rolling hills was nothing we hadn't already trained for since the hills near White Pines had been a much greater challenge. There wouldn't be another large town for several miles as the corn and bean fields once again dominated the countryside.

When we pulled into the small town of Schneider, Indiana we had ridden an amazing 81 miles. We were all wiped out and hungry. The small town boasted a population of 405 people, a Laundromat, and a saloon that was attached to the Family

Room Café. Jerry wasn't very keen on the fact that the place was part of a saloon, but it was the only restaurant for miles where we could get a meal. The next town south was Lake Village another three or four miles down the road and it had an even smaller population.

It was a hot summer night and the heat of the day had finally taken its toll on us. As we passed over the Kankakee River heading further south on Route 41, the topography and scenery changed quickly. Instead of rolling hills and corn fields there were lots of trees and what appeared to be a large grassy marshland. We knew from our trip ticket that this was the LaSalle Fish & Wildlife Area. The area's forests and marshes are bisected by the Kankakee River and was once part of the Grand Kankakee Marsh. It was like an oasis in a desert of corn and bean fields and a welcome relief from the mundane treeless landscape we had ridden through most of the day.

"Towns along the way have also been notified of the trip so they can make preparations to welcome the visitors," said Mrs. Joy Sykes in an interview with the Herald. Mrs. Sykes was a real organizer with the mother's group and a member of the correspondence committee for our troop. She had been informed by the governors of the states on our cycling route, that all of our camping fees would be waived. Her son, Steve was one of the younger boys on the trip. He was a husky shorter guy who was very energetic and always on the go. He shared some of his mother's traits and was someone you could count on and just seemed to do everything right while in the Scouts.

There hadn't been much of a breeze the entire day. This was only the beginning, I thought. Even as a younger boy I had experienced some difficulty with a mild form of heat exhaustion and had experienced severe headaches in the past. My mother was understandably worried and was always reminding me to drink enough water. The days and weeks ahead would prove to be even hotter.

The road we had been traveling on for the past several miles was four lanes with a grass median strip running between. We would occasionally ride two abreast depending on the road conditions. Since there weren't very many cars on the road we doubled up for several miles. It seemed to break the monotony that I was starting to feel while riding single file. Although I didn't realize it yet, some of the battle to stay motivated and keep pedaling would have to come from within myself. Loneliness was starting to set in, and I needed to stay focused.

We carried plastic ground clothes and the first night out slept under the stars on the grass near a stand of trees in the park. There was a nice breeze that had developed later that night and since there appeared to be no rain in the forecast, we didn't bother to set up our tents. When we finally bedded down that night, everyone was very tired. There wasn't much talk going on, and as soon as we crawled into our blankets, most of us fell asleep quickly. We had expended a great deal of energy and our muscles were sore from having put on so many miles the first day.

Despite the breeze, heavy dew had set in overnight and when we woke up at 6:00 a.m. Sunday morning, a hazy mist had blanketed the area. The dampness from the surrounding marshland had collected on our bedding and the plastic tarp. We tried to dry out our bedding as best we could but at 6:30 a.m., Danny Scott, who was our timekeeper was anxious to get us all on the road. We just rolled up our blankets and the tarps and took off on our bikes hoping everything would dry. We named our first campground the "Dew Drop Inn." Although we had ridden in the rain many times before, I don't think we could have ever imagined how much rain was actually in store for us.

The muscle pains that we had all felt that night miraculously disappeared. We were on a strict schedule from the beginning knowing that we had a set amount of time to make it to Florida. Like clockwork, Danny would get up at 6:00 a.m. every morning and after packing our gear, we would try to pedal about 20 miles before eating breakfast. We didn't pack any food with us so we always had to find a restaurant or small café along the road to eat at. We shot through the town of Morocco after about 16 miles or so but there was no place to eat, so we would have to make Kentland, another 12 miles. Then it started to rain, and it wouldn't stop raining until our caravan would eventually reach the small town of Kentland, some 112 miles from Wood Dale.

When we stopped to put our rain suits on shortly after passing through Morocco, Indiana, it was clear that the rain gear we had chosen would be a problem. None of our rain suits held up very well. We had only traveled another five miles or so when somebody's suit in front of me just tore apart. When we pulled off the road to assess the damage, everyone was complaining about how hot and sweaty they were from wearing the plastic suits.

Already the day was not going as planned. The rain was really slowing us down. Even though Route 41 was a four-lane road, every time a semi would pass us, the wind from the truck speeding by almost blew us off our bikes. You had to really hang on tight to your handlebars and adjust your balance to compensate for the blast of wind and spraying water. Some of us had rain ponchos instead of suits and although they were more durable, they were more dangerous. There was the risk of being blown off the bike when a gust of wind would hit the poncho as it acted like a sail. Nearly everyone was having the same problem, so most of us abandoned our rain gear and just rode until we dried off. Arlin didn't like getting wet, and fortunately for him, his rain suit was made of a more durable plastic, so he decided to keep it.

We continued heading toward Kentland making little progress and getting more soaked by the minute. Just as I thought we were making somewhat better time, I heard "Stop!" from Danny behind me. Jerry had suffered the first flat tire of the trip. He had hit a large pothole square on, popping his tire instantly. We had only fixed a few tires in the rain up to this point so it was a bit of a challenge to get the rubber tube dry enough so we could patch it. After a few failed attempts, we were able to fix Jerry's tire and it was clear that we were not going to make anywhere close to the same mileage we had made on our first day.

Kentland, Indiana was a welcome site and by the time we arrived, it was already lunchtime. We all looked like a bunch of drenched rats that had just crawled out of a sewer. Jerry realized that our entire unit was still exhausted from having put on so many miles the day before. He didn't want anyone to get hurt so he made the decision to start looking for a place to camp.

Just before making the turn east onto US Route 52 we spotted a farmhouse with an open field. It looked like it would make a good place to bed down for the night. The farmer was very nice and allowed us to stay in his barn that evening and gave us some wood so we could build a fire to dry out our clothes. Looking more like a Civil War encampment, everyone was camped out on tarps with our clothes hanging over rafters trying to dry everything out. We were all exhausted and thankful that the rain had finally stopped.

The next morning, I woke up to hear Jerry urging everyone to get up so we could get on the road. We had only covered about 30 miles our second day out and we were all anxious to get an early start. It was really muggy that morning and everything including our bedding was still damp when we packed it. From the overcast skies, it was obvious that it was going to rain again. I could over hear Danny Scott talking to Jerry saying that we had to better pace ourselves.

When we turned onto US 52 our pace started to pick up and it felt as though we had regained our strength. The next town according to our trip ticket was Otterbein, Indiana with a population of 788 people, some 29 miles pedaling distance. We weren't more than five miles out and the blackened sky just opened up and we were hit with a deluge of rain. We had practiced riding in the rain so it wasn't anything new, but this storm topped any previous one, pummeling us with a relentless downpour. We just kept riding. The lightning strikes came with an intensity I had never seen before, followed by the deafening sound of thunder. Our pace picked up and we never stopped even to go to the bathroom until we hit Otterbein.

It was still pouring when we left the little roadside café and our visibility was becoming more and more reduced as the torrential storm was not letting up. Having ditched our raincoats proved to be a good idea but the rain was hitting my face sometimes so hard that it was beginning to blind me. I was worried that I might ride off onto the soft shoulder of the road as I could barely make out the faded white line. We kept riding.

The black plastic wrap used on our handlebars became very slick when it got wet from our sweat or when it rained. The rain wasn't stopping. I could feel my muscles straining just to hold onto my bike as the winds began to pick up blowing more fiercely across the open fields. My leather low-quarter lace shoes were similar to a military style boot and when they got wet, they were like lead weights attached to my feet. At this moment, I was miserable, but knew I had to keep pedaling.

When we pulled into Lafayette, Indiana for lunch at around 2:30 p.m., I noticed the green city sign that showed a population of 47,000. It would be the largest town that we had ridden through so far on our trip or on any of our training exercises. We had already covered an impressive 44 miles that day despite the storm's intensity. The sky was starting to clear up and the rain had stopped, at least for the moment. When we passed Purdue University on the outskirts of town, I could hear Mr. Giannini yell, "Road guards out!" Just as soon as that order was given, one Scout from the front of the pack went to the left and one went to the right, blocking traffic coming from the busy intersection. When we were all safely through, Jerry yelled out, "Road guards in!" and the two Scouts immediately fell back into line where Jerry and Mike Rohl would let them in at the rear of our caravan.

We had expended a lot of energy just trying to hold onto our bikes as we were continuously buffeted around by the high winds. When we stopped at McDonalds for lunch, we were still soaked from head to toe and physically exhausted from the grueling ride. Several of us were in the bathroom using one of the hand driers to dry our socks when Jerry walked in. "What's that terrible smell!" he said. We were all just trying to get our socks dried out. It was a common problem as our leather shoes acted like sponges, retaining all the rainwater and soaking our socks. We had a lot of stinky feet on that trip. A stop at a Mc-Donald's every once in a while was a welcome relief.

It was time to do our laundry since we had such a limited amount of clothes. Half of what we had carried with us was wet. Our next stop would be at a small Laundromat in West

Lafayette where we also cleaned up our bikes. The rain that had been beating down on us most of the day had finally cleared up. We were able to get a weather report on Danny Zoubek's little cube radio attached to his handlebars that he had won before the trip. It was one of six waterproof plastic radios shaped in the form of a small cube that were donated by one of Wood Dale's local businesses. It was a fitting prize for Danny since he was always tinkering around with some kind of radio or other electronic device. He had a real interest in electronics and was awarded his Electronics merit badge sometime before the trip.

The weather for the next few days was expected to be clear but hotter than normal temperatures were predicted. The intense heat was compounded by riding on hot asphalt and bothered all of us. The frequency of rain and the intensity of the storms were becoming more of a problem the further south we went. We were particularly concerned about the high winds that could cause anyone of us to veer out into traffic.

With clean bikes and freshly laundered clothes, we left town just as the traffic was starting to build. Our road guard system would be put to the test. At almost every major intersection for the next several miles, all I could hear was, "Road guards out!" and "Road guards in!" We were anxious to get in some more miles and hopefully find a decent place to camp along the road. Between the bad weather and the traffic, our progress was slower than what we had planned but we just kept pushing on.

When we road into Monroe, Indiana some 10 miles further south along US 52, we stopped to get a drink at the Road Savin Motel. It wasn't long before the owner of the motel who let us use his hose to fill up our canteens, offered to let us camp out on his front lawn. We had only been gone for a few days but as Jerry had predicted, we were already arousing a great deal of curiosity and questions from many of the people we had met along the way.

Dennis Kazmiersczak's mother, Carol, who was another spokesperson for our troop would later report exactly the same story to the Herald. Other moms of the HHY contacted a few of the papers in Chicago, but they said they weren't interested in covering the story. The moms were pretty turned off by this. Undeterred, knowing that this was a big story, Mrs. Patricia Stoll, Jim Stoll's mother, and a member of our correspondence team had made contact with a man who was a rather famous TV and radio personality by the name of Mal Bellairs. Mal had been with Chicago's WBBM radio since 1955, where he spent 15 years as a radio host before purchasing a radio station in Crystal Lake, Illinois in 1969. He would rename his new station WIVS-AM.

Mal had a strong base of listeners and was very popular in the northern suburbs of Chicago, where he was the star of the station. He loved covering human-interest type stories, most of which the larger radio stations would never consider. Mal was intrigued by our story and thought what we were doing was important to the youth of our country. He had agreed to feature us each day in a live broadcast. Anyone who tuned into his radio station could follow our trip's progress. The excitement of our first live radio broadcast scheduled to air on Tuesday morning, July 25 was starting to build with our families and thousands of others living in Wood Dale and the surrounding communities. The Mal Bellairs Show would soon become our troop's "Mission Control."

THIRTY-ONE

WE LEFT MONROE early that morning. We had been instructed to be extra quiet so we didn't wake up any of the paying guests at the motel. Our energy and morale were very good up to this point of the trip. Part of my assigned duties as the troop personnel officer, was to provide a good sense of discipline and help to maintain a high morale for all the Scouts and leaders. So far, we had encountered very few problems while on the road except for our sore muscles and bottoms. Our bikes and other equipment were functioning smoothly and everyone was in good spirits. Despite the aches and pains, we were now ahead of schedule as the result our last push through West Lafayette, Indiana and we hoped to stay there.

Because the radio station was expecting a progress report from our troop on a daily basis between 9:00 -10:00 a.m., we had to locate a telephone each day. Since cell phones didn't exist, it was often difficult to locate a payphone during the time we had agreed to call Mal. Everyone had decided that a different boy each time would explain what happened on the trip the previous day. There were many times we were just out in the middle of nowhere and really had to search for a phone booth. It turned into a kind of game to see who could spot a payphone first. Somehow, no matter where we were, we always managed to call Mal during the time he was expecting us even if it we had to call from the back of a store or restaurant.

The sun had just come up and the skies were once again clear with only a slight breeze. It was still hot but not nearly as humid as when we first started out. It was perfect riding weather and we were making great time according to our timekeeper. Route 52 was a four-lane road and since the weather had calmed down, we decided to double up on the right lane. We had practiced this formation many times during our training exercises so it wasn't anything new. In fact, it was a welcome relief because you could at least talk with your fellow Scouts and relieve some of the boredom you often felt riding alone single file.

Danny Zoubek, who was a responsible Scout, was right behind me so we usually rode double together. I felt much more comfortable with him riding next to me than Arlin. We were good friends, but as long as I had known Arlin, he was always bit of a trouble maker. He was a real class clown but a potential bully, too, and often used his size to intimidate some of the other kids. He never messed with me. He was itching to get into some sort of mischief and it would only be a matter of time, so I had to be on my guard. There was a reason that Jerry had placed him in front of me.

When we rolled into the town of Lebanon, Indiana at around 9:00 a.m. that morning we had already covered 20 miles and were well ahead of schedule. Our next task was to find a place to eat breakfast and locate a payphone so Danny Scott could make our first radio broadcast with Mal Bellairs on WIVS. I had been informed by Jack Froehling, our assistant Scoutmaster, that my report with the radio station would follow Danny's on Wednesday.

Breakfast was quick that day and I had my first taste of grits. I would soon acquire a real taste for grits and other southern cooked food as the trip progressed. Lebanon, Indiana was a big town, so finding a payphone was not a problem. When we called Mal, the first thing he asked Jerry was if we had a good breakfast and if we were all packed up and raring to go. What he hadn't realized is that we had been on the road since about 6:15 a.m. and had already covered quite a distance.

We were following a rigid routine that Jerry had devised where we would awaken each morning at about 6:00 a.m., break camp, and try to leave by 6:30 a.m. We would usually pedal about 20 miles or so before stopping for breakfast at little roadside cafes. After the morning meal, we would pedal onward until around 2:00 p.m. when we would stop at a drive-in for a quick lunch or snack before riding further to locate a sit down place for dinner. With as much energy as we were expending pedaling our bikes, our appetites were pretty big sometimes.

Jerry had entrusted Danny Scott with the duties of being our timekeeper. He was one of the older more innovative Scouts, and a junior leader while on the trip. When Jerry turned the phone over to him that morning, Mal immediately asked him, "Alright, now what's your job again?" You could tell that Danny was a little nervous, but seemed to handle himself well. He explained to Mal that his job was to try to keep the time, and keep the pace, to make sure we didn't get too far behind.

The job fit him well since he seemed to be somewhat obsessed with time anyway, always checking his watch. Jerry had a way of using each of the Scout's talents to best suit the needs of the troop. Danny was a sharp kid but would often make coy and sometimes slick comments. Jerry stood close by the phone to help coach him through the report. Danny always made you think, and usually found an entertaining way to solve any problem we might encounter. For the most part, he was always willing to help and proved himself as a good leader while on the trip.

It was a real fine first report and Mal seemed to get a kick out of us. I think he even wished he could be along for the ride.

It would be a trip that all of us, "Step for step and spin for spin of those wheels would never forget," Mal reported. He thought it was a great project and was impressed with Danny and our progress so far, saying that we were all, "Just a bunch of tigers." According to Danny's report, we were now on schedule and would be soon heading into Indianapolis, about 27 miles away. We had traveled 211 miles so far on our great adventure.

Having had a hearty breakfast and our first radio broadcast under our belt, we hit the road with a vengeance. Indianapolis would be the largest city we would travel through to date with a population of over a half a million people. We had reviewed our road guard procedures and all of our other safety precautions. Once again, we would be hitting a major city at the time of their rush hour. Our route would take us straight through the heart of Indianapolis and past the Indy 500 Racetrack. I had been a racecar fan since I was five years old when I got my first HO road race set for Christmas. The only real car race I had been to was a few years earlier to watch my uncle race stock cars.

When we turned onto Lafayette Avenue heading southeast, the city still appeared quite a distance away although I could see the outline of several skyscrapers. After a few miles, we made a stop while Mr. "G" and Jack took a closer look at our map. We decided that it would be a good idea to shift to a single file formation in anticipation of getting into an area that had more traffic. It wasn't long afterwards that we started to see several old factories and a few dilapidated houses that looked more like shacks along our path. The route we had chosen did not appear to be a very nice part of town.

It wasn't until we turned south onto Georgetown Road and were heading straight for the Indy 500 track that we started to see some older rundown two story houses. A number of families were just sitting outside on their front porches in an attempt to escape the heat. As we got closer to the track, several people started waving to us. One rather large black woman stood up from her rocking chair, and yelled out, "Where ya all goin?"

"Florida!" everyone yelled back.

"Florida?" she shouted out, "on bikes!"

We were really starting to attract a lot of attention wherever we went. When I first caught a glimpse of the Indy 500 racetrack, I was amazed by the size of the massive oval structure surrounding the track. It looked more like a large football stadium than any racetrack I had ever seen. We would soon learn that the legendary track had been built in 1909, and with a seating capacity of 260,000 people, it is the largest facility of its kind in the world. We all wanted to take a closer look at the track, so we stopped at the main gates after turning east along West 16th Street. Jerry and a few of the other adult leaders spoke with one of the guards inquiring about where we might be able to park all 31 of our bikes while we toured the track.

It wasn't long afterwards that some of the track officials from the main raceway heard about us. They offered to buy us lunch in the cafeteria and show us around the rest of the complex. Just when we were ready to leave, they told us that we could take a lap around the track, so they opened it up for us. When we all took off riding as fast as we could around the massive track, it looked like a wall of bikes as we rounded the first turn. Jack who was an incredible athlete had taken an early lead, but I was close behind challenging him the entire two-and-a-half-mile length of the track. The four-quarter mile turns were steeply banked posing a challenge for all of us. The blacktop on the track was softer than the road we had been used to riding on and it was hard to pedal. We were told that the track material was a special blend of asphalt designed to help the racecars better grip the road as they flew around the track at nearly 200 miles per hour. It was a real thrill that day to actually ride my bike around such an iconic racetrack that I had only dreamed about. I wished that I could see a real Indianapolis 500 race someday.

The Indy 500 crew had graciously donated lunch to us. We would soon find out it would be one of many meals and other kind gestures of hospitality we would be treated to along the way. We had budgeted enough money for all of our food, never really expecting anyone to donate any meals to us. There were several times we would skip lunch simply because there was no place to eat, as our route would often take us through some very rural areas. We tried to eat a big breakfast just in case we found ourselves in a situation where we had to skip lunch. It usually just meant that we would have a little extra money for dinner that night. It was Jerry's plan to get the most out of what we had and to stretch the $4.50 a day we had budgeted for our meals.

Jerry controlled the $30.00 of spending money we had brought with us and would only give us a dollar a day. "When it was gone, it's gone," he often said. He knew that if he would have given us all of our spending money up front, we would have been broke in a matter of days. He was always scrambling to get enough singles to give us each the $1.00 per day. He wouldn't give us our allowance until after lunch knowing that we might try to spend it on food.

When we left Wood Dale, we carried enough cash for food, campground fees, and any additional monies we might need for our entertainment or emergencies. Each Scout leader carried $5,600.00. Jerry also carried $700.00 of his own money just in case of an emergency. "Be Prepared!" he would always say.

In addition to cash, the leaders each carried three checks from our troop's emergency fund that we could write up to $500.00 per check. We always had a hefty petty cash account from our various fund raising efforts including our paper drives, where we would typically make between $1,000-$1,400. We were never concerned that someone might steal from us. I suppose it was just another sign of the times. The innocence of our trip was closely associated with the 60's and the early 70's. It was nothing any of us really thought about; we just lived it, and it was evident from the simplest of things, like never locking our doors at night in Wood Dale.

It wasn't long after leaving the track before I started to hear Mr. "G" order the road guards out, as we passed through one busy intersection after another. When we finally turned south onto US Route 31, I think we had gone through almost our entire convoy of bikes using all of us as road guards.

THIRTY-TWO

W E WERE HAVING TROUBLE finding a phone Wednes- day morning once we arrived in the small town of Amity, Indiana, nearly 30 miles from Indianapolis. It was get- ting past the time when everyone from Wood Dale was expect- ing our call so we were getting desperate to find a phone. Anxious to get back on the open road and away from the city, I think we just lost track of time and thought we could make Ed- inburg, another six miles south. Amity was a very small town with a population of only a few hundred people with no down- town or businesses to speak of.

We had an early morning breakfast in Franklin having slept the night under a shelter in Greenwood after meeting up with another Boy Scout troop. They were a great bunch of guys who showed a real interest in what we were doing. It was getting closer to the time were we needed to call Mal, so we stopped at a small white house along Route 31. An older woman was working in her garden and her eyes lit up when she looked up and saw all 31 one of us pulled off the road. Jerry spoke with her and she was very kind and trusting and let us into her house so we could make our phone call.

I could overhear the weather report from Mrs. Sander's ra- dio inside her living room as I prepared to make my call to the Mal Bellairs show. According to the weatherman, the skies were expected to cloud up later in the afternoon but no rain was expected. We were now some 276 miles from Chicago and still pedaling strong when I reported to Mal that the weather was real nice now and there were no sore legs. We were all "doing ok in the leg department," I reported. We were planning on staying in Dupont, Indiana, 62 miles from where we had slept the night before, and only about 15 miles from the Kentucky border. We were making good time on what was mostly flat terrain, but knew that the foothills of Kentucky would be fast approaching.

We were riding at a good swift pace when we made the turn onto Highway 7 near Columbus, making our way toward the Kentucky border. When we first arrived in town, it was later in the day and the clouds were already beginning to build. I didn't sense any rain. Just as we were getting into the downtown area the yelp of a police car's siren startled me. We quickly pulled over to the side of the road and from his microphone, the police officer blurted out a woman's name that I couldn't make out. She wanted all of us to come to her house just up the line and said that the kids could use the showers. It was a rather large white house and she welcomed us by making sandwiches and serving cold drinks. Afterwards everyone thanked her for her hospitality and we continued on our way.

After dinner, some of the Scouts seemed a bit on edge when we jumped on our bikes and left North Vernon on the lookout for a campsite that night. Clifty Falls State Park would be a real push if we were to try to make it, but it was doubtful. We were beginning to run out of daylight. The hills were becoming more frequent now and as we rode up the front of a hill, we would fly down the backside at a good clip. I think Mr. "G" was trying to control our rate of decent thinking that we were getting a little out of control. The entire convoy was starting to slow down.

Arlin was looking off into the distance riding with his arms crossed against his chest when the crash occurred, almost smashing into the rear of Billy Mikuls. Billy had suddenly stopped as he ran into the Scout in front of him severely damaging his front wheel. As Arlin hit his brakes at the last minute to avoid hitting Billy, I tried to steer off the road onto the shoulder to avoid another crash. Billy now in tears, wasn't paying attention to Dave Miller who was trying to slow down in front of him. The damage to his bike had been done and Billy's rim was bent severely and he was not able to pedal much further.

Billy was in Danny Zoubek's group and a good kid, never really stepping out of line, so I think the shock of the crash bothered him. His dad, Frank, was on the troop committee and would routinely camp with us even making one of the trips to Glacier National Park. Through his dedication, Billy would eventually become an Eagle Scout and act as a tour guide on one of the later Glacier trips. His father had sadly passed away of Leukemia the December before the Florida trip, devastating all three of his sons including Bob, who was Billy's older brother and also on the Florida trip.

The sign off Highway 7 near Dupont Indiana read, Broom-sage Ranch, and was located in the southern part of Jennings County. It would be where we would have to stay the night and wait to buy a spare rim. That night, despite the trauma of our first real accident there was a large lake with a beach that we all swam at. It was a welcome relief from the heat and we had a lot of fun that night. There was a large beach pavilion near the lake that the owner of the ranch allowed us to bed down in for the night. It would also be the location of our first traffic court.

With our wet clothes and towels hanging from the wooden rafters of the beach pavilion, Danny Scott, using a makeshift bible began swearing in Billy Mikuls. With his left hand on the bible and holding up his right hand, he took an oath to tell the truth, the whole truth and nothing but the truth. With a little grin on his face, Mr. "G" would put a blanket over his shoulders and he would be transformed into Judge Giannini. Almost everyone took the court seriously because if you were found guilty, you faced a fine that would be taken out of your $1.00 per day spending money. Mr. "G" had a genuine sense of warmth about him and he helped to keep our spirits high. He made a real effort to make everything a lot of fun, even traffic court.

Everyone had made the decision to hold traffic court since some of us were starting to get a bit out of line. Mr. "G" had been appointed by Jerry as the Judge, since he was our most senior amongst us. There was also assigned prosecutors, an arresting officer, and a news reporter that would talk into a screwdriver or anything else resembling a microphone. Then there was the bailiff who would typically call the cases before the Judge. Attorneys on both sides would argue each of the offender's cases. The fine was typically anywhere from five to fifteen cents, but sometimes substantially more for a serious offence like Billy's. After all, his bike had been severely damaged and it would slow down our progress. There was real drama in the courtroom as Mr. "G" draped in his blanket, struck his Crescent Wrench down onto the wooden bench declaring Billy guilty. We would often use the accumulated fines to treat everyone to ice cream.

When we woke up on Friday, the rain had returned with a vengeance and the morning sky was once again lit up with lightning strikes. After having a quick breakfast, we hit the road again. Something however seemed much different with a number of the Scouts as I sensed their mood had changed. Maybe it was the accident or the large hills that some of the guys were having trouble getting over. I wasn't sure. No one had been injured in the accident but it was clear that some of the Scout's spirits had changed overnight. The closer we got to the Kentucky border the more grumbling I was hearing. As the troop's personnel officer, part of my assigned duties on the trip involved keeping a close eye on matters involving discipline and overall morale. I was already having some minor discipline problems within my own small unit of three and wondered if it wasn't spreading to the other Scouts. I was never a proponent of the groups of three as it always seemed that one of the guys was the odd man out. This time it was me, maybe because I was older and the two younger Scouts that I was supposed to look after were beginning to rebel.

We had no choice, each day we would just get up and do it all over again. The further we got into Southern Indiana, Jerry himself started to notice a bunch of guys beginning to complain. They were saying how tough it was, and that they weren't sure if they could make it. Bert Bell was a red headed kid that was forever smiling. He never really created any problems. He had just turned 12 years old a few months before the trip and was clearly struggling with the hilly terrain. The hills were the tallest things he had ever seen and he was getting more and more agitated as many of the older Scouts kept saying, "These aren't mountains, they're only foothills!"

Bert and Mike Fasiang were good friends. Mike was rather mature for his age and serious by nature. He never bucked the system and just kept pedaling, but his younger brother Don, who was riding a smaller bike, was struggling a bit. Even Danny Zoubek, a respected hardworking Scout was quietly starting to question his own endurance and spirit, wondering if we were going to make it. Jerry realized that something had to be done as we had only been on the road since Saturday and had several more days of pedaling ahead of us.

Dogs were becoming more of a problem the further south we traveled. If a dog were to bite anyone of us, it could cause a trip ending injury. There were several incidents of dogs of all sizes and demeanors that would chase us, trying to bite at our legs and feet. All the adult leaders were equipped with squirt bottles filled with a mixture of water and ammonia that they used as a deterrent against the dogs. They would keep the bottles in their drink tumbler and use it on the dogs if they got too close. The ammonia water mixture would usually stop the dogs in their tracks. Nine times out of ten after being sprayed, they would just run back to where they had come from with their tails between their legs and take a leak.

The further south into Indiana we rode, the more complaining Jerry was hearing. He was getting fed up with the Scout's poor attitudes and decided that it was a good time to have a heart-to-heart talk with everyone. He felt that if he didn't talk to the Scouts soon the trip might be in serious jeopardy. Their spirit and willingness to go forward was in question. In his talk, he told us that we were ambassadors from Wood Dale, and that a lot of people were counting on us to make the trip a success. "We can't disappoint them," he said in a firm voice. "We have to do this as a group. Each one of us can help out by carrying their own weight, so that we can all make it," he pleaded, "you guys figure it out." With that, he just turned and walked away, leaving the group. After a few minutes of discussion, Mike Rohl walked over to where Jerry was standing. "They've made their decision, we're going to Florida," Mike said. After that, everyone gave a hundred percent effort. "It had to be their decision," Jerry would later say to the other leaders.

From the beginning, Jerry had some of his own concerns. He had never been to Florida before and had certainly never traveled the route we were on with all these "little roads" as he often called them. His main concern was safety and having never traveled this way before he had some legitimate worries. We would be on the road 30 days not knowing exactly where we would be on any given day. As far as the boys were concerned, he never had any doubt that we would make it. He wasn't worried that the spirit might not be there. It was the not knowing and what might lie ahead that concerned him.

We were now headed down the trail toward Madison. It would be the last town in Indiana we would pass through before crossing over the expansive Ohio River into Kentucky. The closer we got to the river valley the more hills we encountered. It was fantastic and almost like riding on a giant roller coaster as we went up and down the hills. Since the accident, everyone seemed to be a bit more on guard and they were taking special care to keep a safe distance from each other. Our spirits had been lifted by Jerry's pep talk and we were having a great time flying up and down some of the hills, hitting 40-45 mph. We were having a blast and were all pretty much under control; riding like champions.

Tony Langfeld's motto for our trip had become a reality. We continued to be surprised by the level of hospitality that had been extended to us throughout the trip. We tried to be as self-sufficient as possible but the motorists and everyone that we visited with were very courteous and willing to go out of their way to help us. It reminded me of when my father would pull over to help a stranded car stuck in the snow. It was just another example of the way people did things back then.

Everywhere we went, the people in the communities were warm hearted and curious about us, always asking a lot of questions about our troop. Many of the people we spoke with couldn't believe that we were really from Wood Dale and headed to Florida on bikes. They would be anxious to share their own stories too, telling us everything about their communities and often taking us on a tour of their town.

We had received a warm reception from everyone we met along the way beginning with the farmer in Kentland and the motel owner in Monroe, Indiana, where each person had opened their front lawns to us. In his report to Mal that morning, Jerry said the folks that we had been fortunate enough to meet were, "The greatest people in our country." The decision to wear our uniforms helped everyone that we met recognize us as Scouts, and it opened the door for us in many instances.

Just as we pulled into Madison, and were planning on crossing over the bridge into Kentucky, a woman in a black Cadillac flagged us down. She had seen us ride into town and introduced herself as Mrs. Huffman. She was the chairman of another bicycle riding group called the Spokesmiths. She offered to have one of the state police officers who she knew escort us to her home nearby. Officer Sutherland's lights started flashing from his squad car and he escorted us to her house down the road.

When we arrived, we couldn't believe our eyes. Mrs. Huffman's mansion sat on several well-groomed acres. It seemed that wherever we went now, people wanted to treat us to lunch or offer us some other hospitality. Mrs. Huffman's son was a star athlete. There was a room in the mansion dedicated to displaying his trophies. We ended up spending about four hours there, as we swam in the enormous in ground pool, took showers and were treated to a real good lunch of fried chicken and potato chips.

Later that day Officer Sutherland would take us all on a tour of Clifty Falls State Park just outside of town. When we arrived at the park, we really had no idea how beautiful it was going to be. We soon discovered that there were four major waterfalls the highest being some 83 feet that had been created during the Ice Age. The park reminded me a lot of the area around the Vermilion River, where my family's summer home was located.

We had some free time on our hands while at the park to explore. I took off with Danny Zoubek and Billy Mikuls for our own little joy ride. The three of us were sitting on top of a massive hill overlooking the countryside and adventure was calling us. We took off flying down this huge hill at a breakneck speed. The road twisted and turned making a hard bank to the right before straightening out. When we finally reached the bottom of the hill, we were totally exhausted and nearly out of breath from holding on to our bikes for dear life. Once we caught our breath, we all looked at each other and realized that we would have to go back up the hill to join the rest of the guys. It took us nearly an hour in first gear to reach the top where Jerry was waiting. He wasn't very happy with us, but it was sure a lot of fun.

By the time we made it back to the rest of the group it was starting to get late. We rode into Madison and camped that night along the banks of the Ohio River at "The City Campground." It was always a challenge to locate a campsite with bathroom and shower facilities. We were fortunate that this campground was equipped with a full bathhouse and a laundry nearby. Doing the wash was difficult at times since we often camped out in the middle of a field or in a forest somewhere. We had limited supplies of everything and when we took showers the single bar of soap we had, would be passed around. That night after we cleaned up we all walked into town for dinner. It was a neat little town with many historic buildings some dating back to the Civil War. The campground was close to the big bridge we would use to cross over the Ohio River and make our initial push into Kentucky.

Just before bedding down that night, several of the boys seemed a bit on edge despite Jerry's pep talk earlier. A few of the younger guys were still pretty shook up, questioning their ability to climb the hills and were terrified of what looked like a large mountain on the other side of the Madison Bridge. Jerry seemed to be able to console most of the Scouts that he spoke with privately, some who were in tears.

When morning came and we were breaking camp, everyone's spirit had once again been restored. It would not be the last time that Jerry would have to talk with us about overcoming our fears. It was a constant battle and we would have to fight hard not to become discouraged as we made our way toward the mountains. We would all learn on this trip that what we were attempting to accomplish was monumental and historic by all measures. It was a feat that no one else had accomplished to date, especially with so many young people all together in one group.

Feeling discouraged at times during the trip was part of life, and an inevitable aspect of the venture. In order to overcome the obstacles that we were to encounter, we could never give up. We could never quit. The idea of failure or quitting was not an option. Our leaders had instilled in us the fact that we all possessed the ability, determination, and pride needed to make our trip a success. Jerry's teachings had been ingrained in us early in our Scout training. He realized however, that we were still young boys, and that he would have to encourage us to push on, to keep pedaling. We had to finish what we had started, and to do it, "one mile at a time." A trip of this magnitude would continue to pull a great deal of raw emotion from all of us. Four of the boys were only 11 years old at the time, and five of the Scouts would have birthdays while on the trip.

Rick Lee who was our troop's safety officer would make his
report to Mal on Friday morning from the back of a shoe store
in Madison. Having just finished breakfast, "We made a total of
24 miles," he would tell Mal. Mal just figured with having only
covered 24 miles that day, we either had some real problems or
that our social life had gotten in the way. We enjoyed our time
at Clifty Falls State Park and meeting all the nice folks in Madison. Jerry and a few of the other leaders began to voice some
concern over how much time we could spend visiting and touring places along the way. It would be somewhat of a difficult
balance, as we didn't want to insult anyone who wished to
show us their hospitality.

Rick went on, telling Mal that we were getting ready to cross
over the Ohio River into Kentucky and were hoping to make
Frankfort later that night. We were instructed by the Madison
police officer to double up, as he would escort our troop across
the bridge over the Ohio River. It would be the longest bridge
we would cross so far and the shear height over the river below scared a lot of us.

There were five sets of brothers on our trip and Rick Lee,
and his younger brother Steve, were as opposite as brothers
could ever be. Both were real down to earth types living in the
woods in a small cabin with their parents in Wood Dale. As a
family, they did not have much and were raised by their father
to be self-sufficient. Mr. Lee was a bit odd in his mannerisms
and had some strange ways of doing things. He had been a
Scout himself and although the trip would be a financial strain
on the family, he wanted his boys to go. Rick was the older
brother and a serious personality. When he made his report to
Mal, it was all business. He was raised in the outdoors and
could shoot and skin a squirrel without much thought put into
it. He was more leadership material than his younger brother

was however, and had been assigned the duties of safety officer for the trip.

Steve on the other hand was a good-natured kid and more modernistic in his manner even in the games he would play. He could be a little lazy at times though and was one of the first boys to start complaining on the bike trip. He just had an attitude about him sometimes and once he was finished with something, he just figured he had done enough. He was a bit of a loner and often stayed more to himself.

THIRTY-THREE

THE BRIDGE CROSSING that would take us over the Ohio River into Milton, Kentucky was a bit tense for many of us. The aging, severely rusted structure that spanned some 3,184 feet had been built in 1929, and looked more like something I had built with my Erector Set. The shear height of the bridge as it rose over the Ohio River gave all us some pause. It seemed to take a long time to cross as we slowly followed our police escort who was driving only a few miles per hour. The two lanes of the bridge were so narrow that I could almost reach out and touch the steel girders that made up the main structure.

The larger hills that looked more like small mountains loomed in the distance, shrouded in a hazy mist as we rode two abreast. I had always loved climbing trees as a younger boy, but at some point, I became frightened of heights. I didn't dare look down and tried to keep my eyes focused on Arlin's red rain coat ahead of me. Somehow, I managed to snap a picture with my Kodak 110 camera of the long train of bikes ahead of me. More rain had been predicted for the day and there was a slow steady drizzle that had started before making our way across the bridge.

When we finally all made it across, we stopped for a few minutes to study our map and thank the police officer. What I saw ahead of us was surely a mountain, and I wondered how we were going to climb it with our bikes. It was by far one of the most formidable obstacles we had seen on the trip so far. Kentucky was the second state that we had crossed into since the beginning of our trip. We were really on our way, I thought. It was slow going as we crawled up the steep incline on US 421 in first gear, making our way out of the Ohio River valley. It was only the second time since having left Wood Dale that I had to shift to such a low gear on my bike. From the look of the soaring bluffs and terrain ahead of us, I was sure I would be using all 10-speeds of my bike more often.

As we passed through several small towns along our route, I was struck by the sheer beauty of the state with its lush forests as far as I could see in every direction. It was a welcome relief and a stark contrast to the corn and bean fields that had dominated the Illinois and Indiana countryside. Despite our slow climb out of the valley, we were now cruising up and down all the hills and making some great time. Our spirits were high once again.

When we hit Eminence, Kentucky, we had already traveled over 36 miles. Then the skies began to darken. The rain began to come down harder now, hitting me in the face and blurring my vision. When we finally stopped for lunch, we were all soaked. Most everyone, including Arlin, had now discarded their cumbersome raincoats. After stopping for lunch, we decided to alter our original route and headed toward the town of Shelbyville. There we felt we would have a better chance to find a restaurant for dinner. Our original route from Madison to Frankfort would have taken us through some very small towns and it was doubtful if there would be anywhere to eat until we got into Frankfort.

Our assistant Scoutmaster, Mike Terese, was still en route with Jerry's mother, Marie, and Mrs. Rohl. The plan had been to drop Mike off and continue ahead, making an emergency vehicle available to us. They would eventually meet up with us on Saturday, as Mike Rohl reported to Josh Bradley of the Mal Bellairs show. Having now hit more challenging terrain, we were hoping to cover 50 to 60 miles per day. If all went well, we would make Gatlinburg, Tennessee by Monday, the halfway point to Jacksonville, Florida.

As we headed east out of Shelbyville on Route 60 toward Kentucky's capital of Frankfort, the landscape had changed once again. The hills were getting bigger and closer together. The forests had now been replaced by thousands of acres of farm fields with crops of mostly tobacco and hay. White plank fence lines that ran for miles in every direction dominated the countryside where horses grazed on Kentucky Bluegrass. The skies were sunny and the heat was starting to build again.

The capital building was an incredible sight and it was the first thing you saw as we headed straight for it down Route 60 into town. We were moving at a good clip, maybe 35 miles per hour on a steep hill into town. I could hear several of the guys commenting on how huge the building was. Just as we were making a turn to the right, I heard a loud thud, metal hitting metal behind me and then a scream as Danny Zoubek had just driven his Free Spirit over a sewer grate. We were only a few hundred yards from the capital. Apparently, he had his eyes focused on the massive three-story structure and was riding too close to the curb when his bike hit the grate. Stopped cold, Danny went flying head first over his handlebars. His glasses, equipped with clip-on sunglasses were nearly run over. Fortunately, he tucked at the last moment saving himself from a major head injury as he hit the pavement. Unfortunately, his front tire was now a mangled mess, and looked like a figure eight. Danny was always so careful and I thought he would be the last one to have such a bad accident. It was still early in the day and there was a Sears store just down the block from the capital building. We were able to buy a new rim and get him back on the road.

I grew up watching the Daniel Boone television series featuring Fess Parker, which ran from 1964 to 1970. The words of
the theme song, "Daniel Boone was a man, Yes, a big man!"
would forever be implanted in my mind. As a young boy, I always pictured myself as a pioneer and a fierce Indian fighter
blazing trails through the woods. When the Scouts decided to
see his gravesite outside of Frankfort, I was excited.

Daniel Boone first reached Kentucky in the fall of 1767 while
on a long hunt with his brother, Squire. A prominent judge,
from North Carolina, would later hire Boone to blaze a trail
that became known as the Wilderness Road, which went
through the Cumberland Gap and into central Kentucky where
he founded Boonesborough. Despite occasional Indian attacks,
Boone brought his family and other settlers to Boonesborough
on September 8, 1775.

We grabbed lunch at a little place outside of town and were
getting ready to leave when a man from the restaurant approached Jerry. Standing next to him was Pat Malick and two
other Scouts, all three looking scared. They were the only ones
of the bunch who had been sitting in the back room at a table
near a bar. Apparently, there was a tip jar on the counter,
which was now empty. The man was not too happy and had
caught Pat red-handed stuffing some of the change into his
pockets.

Pat was occasionally a prankster and he would often get into
trouble. He was a curious kid, always eager, and the kind that
wanted to be in the middle of things. We once toured a copper
mine and he wanted to know everything about it, asking the
guide seemingly endless questions. For the most part, Pat was a
trustworthy kid, but before the trip he immersed himself in
some trouble that threatened his chances to go with us. To

make matters worse, his dad, Gene Malick, was Troop 65's Committee Chairman.

One evening, about a month before the trip, Jerry got a phone call from Pat's dad saying that he had taken another kids bike. Having stolen it from his friend's backyard, the ever-resourceful Pat decided to spray paint it a different color. When his dad got home from work, he asked Pat where he had gotten the new bike. Pat made up some cockamamie story, but would eventually fess up, saying simply, "I liked it." Well, his dad was pretty upset and called Jerry immediately saying that he better come over quickly as he was on the verge of killing young Pat for his dishonest actions.

When Jerry arrived on the scene, he spoke with Pat and all he had to say was that he wanted the bike. Jerry explained to him that if he wanted a bike he had to pay for it. Pat was a bright kid but didn't really appear to understand the conse-quences of his actions. Jerry was determined to try and make him understand that what he had done was wrong. Later that night, Jerry and Pat went to the house where the bike had been stolen and spoke with the parents. Jerry told them that Pat would pay for a new bike but he would have to work it off. The parents were upset and wanted the money for a new bike right away.

Jerry had a half-gallon jar of coins he had been saving with nickels, dimes, and quarters. He told Pat that he could use the money from the jar but would have to count it out to deter-mine how much money was actually there. He counted out $66.00 in coins. They gave the entire lot to the people realizing that a new bike would not cost that much. Jerry told Pat that he would have to work off the money by pulling weeds and pay him back. True to his word, Pat did just that, he called

Jerry and told him that he had earned enough money and promptly paid him back.

It was a great lesson and was yet another example of the value system that was being instilled in us at an early age. You would have thought that after pulling hundreds of weeds, young Pat would have learned his lesson. Unfortunately, for whatever reason, he had not yet and Jerry was fuming mad when we left the restaurant that day.

When we finally connected with Mike Terese, after leaving Lexington, he had been driving for hours and was tired but anxious to get on the road with us. We had already traveled about 470 miles and were now about to hit even more challenging terrain. The relentless rainstorms and brutal heat had taken a toll on all of us but despite the incident, our spirits were good and our confidence was building. Our group of 32 was now reunited and ready for the next leg of our journey.

After dinner, Mike was briefed on the situation with Pat and the other two Scouts who had stolen the coins out of the tip jar. I'm not sure if it was because he was tired from his long car ride but I never saw Mike angrier than on that night. He gave us all a lecture that lasted several minutes. "We are Wood Dale's youth ambassadors of goodwill," he said. "With this single act of dishonesty, it threatens to derail everything." Everyone was stunned with what Mike had just said, and we knew he was serious. Pat appeared to be on his best behavior after Mike's tongue-lashing and there was never another incident like it.

THIRTY-FOUR

THE FURTHER SOUTH WE WENT the larger the hills got and for the first time I really began to feel a burning pain in my thighs. I had felt some muscle pain when we first took off and had traveled over 80 miles the first night out, but this felt different. It wasn't going away. As we pedaled our bikes over each hill, the sweat from my forehead began to drip into my eyes and they began to burn. The sun was relentless and for hours it beat down on my head. I was beginning to feel dizzy. I was struggling and trying to drink as much water as possible. My clothes and hands were completely drenched in sweat. I could feel my hands start to slip from the plastic wrap around my handlebars, no matter how hard I gripped them.

I focused on my pedaling, trying to time it somewhat, and make the most out of the energy I was expending. We had trained for this trip over a period of two and a half months riding on mostly flat ground. Nothing had prepared us for this kind of terrain or this many miles over an extended period of time. I had been through the same mountain pass many times with my family on our way to Florida, but we were always in our car.

I was determined to make it. As I struggled to pedal up one massive hill after the other, I would push down on my left foot, and then more forcefully push down on my right, taking advantage of my stronger leg to propel the bike forward up the hill. Even though I was with a group, as I pedaled onward, feelings of loneliness were beginning to set in. Despite my technique, my muscles still ached. After several hours of nonstop pedaling, I began to put myself into a sort of meditative state and started to develop a rhythm with my pedaling. It was the only way for me to overcome the pain and loneliness I was feeling. I would be 15 years old in just a few more days and was in the best physical condition of my life. I knew that I could make it to Florida and was now more determined than ever. I kept telling myself that nothing was going to stop me.

I had not really thought about Billy since we had taken off that first day but I started to feel his presence, and could hear his voice encouraging me to not give up. Whether he realized it or not, all the things we had done as young boys from our chase games and the bike ride down to Lake Michigan, had helped to prepare me for this trip. His enduring spirit of never giving up was instilled in me. I wondered what his sister Kathy was doing, too, and if she missed me. I was beginning to miss them both.

My mind was focused on my struggle to pedal up what was now the longest and steepest hill I had ever ridden up on a bicycle. Every muscle in my body strained and ached as I shifted my Free Spirit into first gear. I stood up this time pressing down as hard as I could on my pedals turning the crank ever so slowly. It was tough going, but up the hill I went with each rotation of the bike's wheels.

I began thinking about a story my dad had told me while sitting around a campfire at White Pines. It was February 12, 1951 and my father who was only 14 years old at the time was hiking cross-country with a group of older boys, near the Indiana Dunes State Park. They were heading out of the Dunes by foot from a cabin on the lake where they had stayed that night. It was cold, bitter cold, and the wind was slicing into his eyes causing his tears to run down his cheeks, freezing them almost instantly. He began to whimper and then moan as it was so cold his entire body started to hurt. The night before a sudden snow squall, common to the snow belt of Northern Indiana had dumped 18 inches of snow. The sun had melted the top portion, and then the temperatures plunged, quick freezing the crust above, leaving a sheet of thin ice. Each step was an agonizing high lift of one leg, a tentative momentary hold on the surface, and then his foot would break through the ice and plunge into the snow, covering his knees.

Their cars were parked at the state park, which was closed for the winter several miles away. My father was not properly dressed and by far the youngest boy. Wearing only a pair of rubber goulashes over his shoes, an old Navy Pea coat, and a pair of wool gloves, he was sorely equipped for such an arduous hike through the snow. The small group had been walking now for three hours and stopped, huddled together in a clump of hemlock trees. They all agreed that they were in trouble. For the moment, they were out of the wind.

They were attempting to hike out one day earlier than anyone had expected them to because several of the boys, including my father, had come down with a strain of the flu. It had severely weakened him. There was talk of dying, and the possibility of freezing to death. One of the Boy Scouts had a thermometer that read - 23ºF. A few argued that they should turn back; that the three hours it would take to walk back were shorter than the rest of the trip. Being the youngest and least experienced, my father gave no input. He had stopped thinking and was just hurting.

Others argued with the group's patrol leader, John Redockavich, that his reading of the compass was wrong and that they were not even going in the right direction. No one knew what wind chill factor was back in those days and there was only one compass. My father's only thought at this point was that he was going to die. John offered to help anyone who wanted to go back to the cabin, but he was committed to taking the four sick boys to where the cars were parked. Leadership is an amazing thing my father thought. No one turned back. They began slowly walking again with the target of four more hours of hiking and the thought of being safe at the cars.

One hour later, my father's body gave out as he lay down in the snow and quit. Everyone else kept moving forward. John came back and sat down next to my father. "Get up Rega," he said.

"I can't, John. I shit in my pants. It's running down my leg and freezing. I can't walk three more hours," my father responded.

"Neither can I," John said, "but I can walk one more step, and so can you."

"What good is one more step?" my father cried out in an anguished voice. He felt he had been defeated.

"We can always walk one more step, Rega, and after you do that next step, that will be true," John said. "We are not three hours away from those cars."

"How far are we, really?" my father asked.

"A lot of one more steps, but you can do them one at a time, so get your shitty ass up Rega, and take one more step with me," John responded.

Sometime, after the sun had set and five and a half hours later, the shivering group of Scouts stumbled into the Indiana Dunes parking lot. My father was not the only one John had given that same talk to, just the first one. The lesson that day of, "one step at a time" had been a simple one, but resonated with each of the Scouts and would benefit my father throughout the rest of his life, and help him navigate through other tough times. "Don't give up!" he would often say to me.

After passing through Richmond, Kentucky, the hills in the distance were starting to look more like mountains the closer we got to them. The horse pastures that we had gotten accustomed to seeing were now fewer in number as we inched further south toward the mountains. Rain had been predicted and was now threatening to return as the skies began to darken and the winds started picking up. We wanted to reach Renfro Valley some 56 miles from where we had camped the night before. When it started to pour, we were still heading south on Wilderness Road only about 10 miles away from our destination. The climb was slow and we could only pedal about three mph. It was painful. My legs were aching and all I could think of was my father's story, and I kept telling myself, "one step at a time, don't quit!"

When we finally got to the top of what must have been the first real mountain we had climbed, the clouds were right on top of us. The fog was so dense that I could barely see Arlin, only catching glimpses of him as we started to fly down the back side of the mountain. A few minutes into my ride I hit a break in the fog and caught a quick view of the valley below. I was shocked to see just how high up we were. I heard Jack Froehling several bikes in front of me, yell out, "40 mph!" Jack's bike was one of four that had been equipped with a speedometer. I was scared, and held on tight to my handlebars just in case I would have to make a quick maneuver to avoid hitting Arlin.

It was the steepest downhill grade that we had encountered and we were all pumping our brakes to control our decent. I could hear the constant squeal of rubber brake pads against the wet metal rims. As we got closer to the bottom of the mountain, I could see the faint outline of a few buildings. When the word came from Arlin that we were stopping, I heard a loud pop, followed by laughter from a few of the guys in front of the line. Jack's rim had apparently gotten so hot from pumping his brakes that his tire just blew.

We were completely soaked. It was still pouring like crazy with no letup in sight. I was cold, and started to shiver as I rustled through my saddlebags looking for my red jacket. At this point, we just needed a place to get out of the rain and try to get warm. The higher up in elevation we went, the colder and damper it seemed to get. We had landed in the small town of Renfro Valley, and after fixing Jack's flat we located a restaurant downtown. While we were eating dinner, a man introduced himself as the station manager for the local radio station WRVK, and invited us to sleep over with them. It was a neat place that was air-conditioned and got us out of the rain. We slept that night in the lower level control room. In the morning, the D J spoke with all of us while he was on the air. He asked each of us to give our names while he questioned us about the trip. They were nice people, and after our broadcast, they provided us with breakfast, so we could get back on the road.

We had been trained to do most of our own maintenance on the bikes, but Mr. Giannini and Jerry would usually tighten our spokes. If someone had a loose spoke, Jerry would encourage the kids to tell him right away, so it could be fixed. Safety was imperative and Jerry had instilled in us that it was important to keep our bikes in tiptop condition to avoid an accident from a loose nut or something. We had several flat tires and breakages along the way and when someone did get a flat, a team of us would converge and fix the tire in just a few minutes. We would then blow it up with one of our CO_2 cartridges to the required 60lbs of pressure and be on our way. After our broadcast, we left the studio that morning only to find Mr. "G" adjusting all of our bikes spokes. He would always attend to his bike last. It was just his way. He wasn't selfish and was always willing to help others in need.

THIRTY-FIVE

THE SKIES WERE CLOUDY when we left Renfro Valley and headed deeper into the forest and the Appalachian Mountains. We would be pedaling right through the rugged countryside of the Daniel Boone National Forest, with its steep forested slopes and sandstone cliffs. We had covered some 520 miles on the trip so far. Inch by inch, foot by foot and mile by mile, we continued onward heading down the road on our bicycles. Later that afternoon, the rain returned with a vengeance soaking us once again. This time the storms came quickly and ended just as quickly as they had appeared. The warmth of the hot sun felt good on my water soaked body and my wet cloths slowly began to dry as we cruised up and down the mountains. My shoes never completely dried out at the radio station, and I figured wet feet would just be something I would have to get used to. Every one of us whether we liked it or not, was learning to adapt to the conditions.

We were making good time and only a few hours outside of Corbin, Kentucky when several of the Scouts said that they were getting hungry. After a few more miles, we stopped at a small white building built into the side of a hill. The rusty sign in front of the building read, "Hamburgers 25 cents," "Fries 15 cents." It appeared to be a big enough restaurant with enough tables and chairs to seat all of us. Jerry and Mr. "G" went in and asked the people at the restaurant if they could cook up enough hamburgers and fries for everyone in our group. They said it wouldn't be a problem. Once we sat down, it took forever to take our order and even longer for some of us to get our burgers.

Just as we were getting ready to pay our bill and make a push toward Corbin, the owner of the restaurant, looking agitated, confronted Jerry and handed him a napkin with some writing on it. One of the Scouts had apparently written a note to one of the waitresses that read, "You will never see us in this greasy spoon restaurant again." Everyone was immediately ordered to fall in and Jerry demanded that who had ever written the note to step forward and admit it. No one said a word. "We know what table it came from," Jerry said, "so you had better fess up." Another minute or so went by and Danny Zoubek raised his hand saying that he had written it. "A crummy nickel would have been better than this note!" Jerry responded, in disgust. Danny was usually a good Scout but he could be a bit of a practical joker too, and it would get him in trouble sometimes. After that, Danny had to apologize to the waitress and the owner. It was Jerry's way of making us accountable for our actions and keeping us in line.

We were only about a half hour outside of Corbin, when Dave Miller who was one of the 11-year-olds was not getting up the hill fast enough and was starting to hold us up. Then he fell out of line and just started throwing up over his handlebars. Jerry thought at first that it might be heat stroke. He told the rest of the group to go ahead saying that when Dave felt better they would catch up. Dave was always a decent kid and had come to us at 11 years old. He would be one of three to turn 12 while on the trip. In the beginning of his Scouting days, it seemed that he would forever screw up. He often tried Jerry's patience and was always testing the limits of the rules. This time however, things were different and Jerry knew he was in trouble.

After a few minutes, a young man in a red pickup truck stopped and asked Jerry if he needed any help. Nearly everyone back then was friendly and would offer their assistance. Jerry realized that Dave was not getting much better and put their bikes in the pickup and they continued on toward Corbin.

Then Danny Scott got sick and a few others. A local gas station owner noticed that we were having a problem and closed his station so we could set up camp under the canopies. As the evening set in, nearly one-half of the outfit appeared sick and were throwing up and having severe bouts of diarrhea. Jerry was concerned and called the local police department and told them that he felt that he had a problem. They immediately dispatched two ambulances and several police cars to the gas station and told Jerry to take the seven worst kids to the hospital to check them out.

The scene that night was chaotic as several of the guys were loaded into ambulances and police cars. The cops started questioning Jerry asking him what restaurants we had eaten at in the past several hours, trying to narrow down the source of the problem. They told him they would investigate the restaurant where we had eaten the hamburgers. Mr. "Giannini's" son, Jeff, was one of the boys that got really sick. After realizing the severity of the situation he decided to stay back with the rest of the troop, while Jerry accompanied the sick boys to the hospital.

Whatever was causing the other guys to get sick had not affected me. I was trying to help the boys that weren't feeling well by bringing water around in a bucket to keep everyone hydrated. Our camp looked like a scene out of a Civil War movie with our tents and blankets hanging over ropes that we had strung to make shelters for everyone that was sick. Danny Zoubek was scared that he might get sick, too, and hunkered down in his sleeping bag worried that the trip might be over. It wasn't until much later that night when I got sick too, but I wasn't feeling nearly as bad as some of my fellow Scouts.

When the Scouts arrived at the hospital, the doctors checked them out. They were diagnosed with a severe case of bacterial food poisoning. They knew we had eaten hamburgers earlier in the day, and explained that it was most likely the result of an E. coli bacteria originating from tainted and improperly cooked hamburger meat. The hospital gave the kids meds along with enough supply for the rest of the troop and whoever else might need it and released them from the hospital.

On one of my many trips to the bathroom, I overheard Jerry talking with Mike Terese, saying that in more serious cases, there can be kidney failure and even death from an E. coli infection. That scared the heck out of me thinking that some of us might die. I kept what I had just heard to myself not wanting to scare anyone. Despite the fact that we tried to be careful wherever we ate our meals, it could have happened to anyone. The restaurant we ate at was simply not equipped to feed 32 Scouts. The doctors theorized that some of the hamburgers had been properly cooked bringing the meat up to a temperature that would have killed any bacteria present. However, it was clear that was not the case with all of the burgers explaining why only some of us got sick.

The next morning after the poisoning, most of the Scouts were not very energetic. One of the local motels in Corbin opened their pool to us so we could recuperate. We all realized that we had a close call, and were thankful that there weren't any serious complications that could have resulted in someone's death. By the time Ken Mauer would give his report to Mal we had not eaten breakfast yet. That was unusual for us since we typically would be on the road by 6:30 a.m. and eat an early breakfast. Not everyone got sick, but nearly everybody was drained from either having been sick or tending to everyone else. Like Danny Zoubek and a few others, Ken had not been affected by the tainted hamburgers. He was one of the younger boys, who rode a smaller bike. He was always full of energy and a real dynamo, getting up and down all those hills without too much trouble. He rarely complained about being tired and was a good member of the crew.

Later in the day, everyone had perked up and was itching to roll. At about 6:00 p.m. in the evening after dinner, we took off out of town winding our way further south. We must have all felt better because by the time we pulled into Williamsburg, we had ridden 20 miles. We had located a campground just south of town that had a small restaurant and a few cabins. We quickly rolled out our plastic tarps and our blankets and camped out in a grassy field under the stars. We were now only a few miles from the border of Tennessee.

We were adapting as we went along sometimes having to alter the route on our trip ticket. We had lost valuable time because of the food poisoning incident and needed to try to make it up somehow. After studying the map, we concluded that our original route that would have taken us through the Cumberland Gap into Virginia would be too time consuming and strenuous. It would have required us to ascend Cumberland Mountain, some 3,380 feet in elevation. The painstaking climb would have taken us several hours especially under our weakened condition. We decided that heading straight south down Route 26 into Williamsburg was a safer choice. There would be better facilities including medical care should anyone else get sick. The doctor at the hospital said the effects of the bacteria could hit some of us later who had not yet experienced any symptoms. We didn't want to take that chance. Our new route would soon take us across the Tennessee border sometime early Wednesday morning, August 2.

The last few days had been tough on everyone not to mention our parents who had heard for the first time yesterday that we had been food poisoned. It wasn't something you wanted to hear knowing your son was over 500 miles away from home. "We're back in business so to speak and we're now doing real fine," Jerry reported to Mal in an attempt to calm the worried parents. We now had an emergency car close by and that seemed to help ease some of the tension with our parents.

The advance car proved to be a big help the rest of the trip and they would usually check in with us in the morning to drop off replacement parts before heading on ahead of us. The wash load was so bad sometimes because of our limited amount of clothes, that the women would occasionally do our laundry for us. Usually we would just wash them out ourselves using a pump at a campsite somewhere. That night after dropping off some replacement tires, Jerry's mother and Mrs. Rohl decided to stay at one of the cabins at the campground. Everyone was still a bit on edge after the poisoning a few days earlier and Jerry didn't want to take any unnecessary chances.

Mal Bellairs was very helpful to us and would sometimes relay personal messages from friends and family members. His personal interest in our trip was very genuine. He saw the real story in our adventure, choosing not to just cover what would be our success or possible failure. He was with us the entire way supporting us from start to finish. He was our "Mission Control."

People in Wood Dale and the surrounding towns were captivated by our trip and were listening to Mal while we reported our progress each day. Our exploits gave him and his new radio station some more notoriety. "I'm really enjoying myself and wish I had a story like this to talk about each week," Mal commented during one of his broadcasts. We knew people would be expecting our call and always made a good effort to make the phone call on time.

We awoke Wednesday morning to a heavy fog cover. Everything was wet. It was something we were starting to get used to. It almost felt as if we were riding through a rainstorm the higher up in elevation we went. We quickly broke camp, packing away our damp blankets, and headed straight for the restaurant. Everyone seemed fine that morning. It appeared that our appetites had returned, and we polished off several platters of pancakes and bacon before hitting the road. By the time we took off heading for the Norris Dam about 60 miles away, the sun had burned off most of the fog. It was predicted to be another hot day with temperatures hitting 100°F.

THIRTY-SIX

WHEN WE ARRIVED at the dam, we were in awe of its massive size. There was another Scout troop there and the park ranger took us all on a tour. The enormous concrete structure stretches 1,860 feet across the Clinch River and is equipped with two 50,000-kilowatt generators. The Norris Dam was built by the Tennessee Valley Authority creating Norris Lake, the largest reservoir on a tributary of the Tennessee River.

After the tour, some of the Scouts from the other troop came over to where Danny Zoubek and Pat Malick and were standing and starting asking them about our trip. A few minutes into the conversation, one of the boys from this troop pulls out a cigarette from his shirt pocket and lights up. Just as the Scout starts to take his first puff, one of the leaders from the same troop walks over and lights up, too. I could see the shocked look on Jerry's face from where he was standing about 20 feet away. He didn't look very pleased. Not wanting to make a scene, Jerry let the madness go on for several more minutes until he had seen enough and said, "Ok guys, we need to get rolling." We said good-bye to the other Scouts and took off down the road on our bikes.

As a young Scout, Jerry would occasionally smoke a cigar, but he always left the campsite to smoke them. He knew it was wrong then too, but this was different. To allow a young Scout to smoke in the presence of a leader, who was also smoking in front of the other Scouts, was unconscionable and irresponsible, Jerry thought. He would occasionally catch a kid smoking and would call the Scout's parents and was often shocked by what they would say. "Is it about him smoking," they'd ask, "well how many packages did he smoke?" Smoking was very common back then, but when anyone of us got caught, the leaders came down hard on the Scouts. It was often left up to Jerry, as our Scoutmaster, to deal with the kids and try to prevent them from smoking. He had a neat way to outsmart us and often did some fun things to discipline and teach us a lesson at the same time.

The temperatures had risen to a sweltering 102°F by afternoon and we had already suffered two flat tires. As we started our trek through Knoxville, Tennessee, the traffic became noticeably heavier. We seemed to have a knack for hitting the largest cities during rush hour. We weaved our way through town passing by one busy intersection after the other dodging cars and buses. I could hear Mr. Giannini yelling, "Road guards out!" followed by Jerry's order of, "Road guards in!" By this time in the trip, our safety systems were working well and it was routine, as everyone knew what they were doing.

It was getting late and we needed to find a place to eat soon and locate a camp along the road somewhere outside of the city. We had stopped for a break at an American Legion Hall parking lot. Jerry and a few of the other adult leaders walked across the street to a gas station to ask for directions to a restaurant and where we might be able to camp for the night.

Pat lit up first, then Danny. They had apparently bummed a few cigarettes from the troop at the dam and just figured they would smoke 'em. It wasn't too long after they lit up that a few other Scouts were asking to lite up, too. Problem was, there were only two cigarettes, and Danny and Pat were smoking them. Mike Rohl had been keeping his eye on Danny the entire trip, figuring he would catch him smoking eventually. He had been caught in the act once before, while out on a campout several months ago. Mike was gunning for him. Pat had been known to have taken a few puffs in the past, too, so when Mike caught them both smoking in the corner of the American Legion parking lot, he had hit pay dirt. To make matters worse, Mike Terese was with him. It wasn't good, and Danny and Pat were immediately read the riot act and would soon suffer the consequences. After a brief pow-wow with Jerry, it was decided that the boys would have to send a letter to their folks explaining the situation.

When Steve Sykes gave his report from the restaurant on Friday, we were only about 12 miles outside of Gatlinburg. We had been on the road nearly 14 days, and a few of the Scouts were beginning to get a little homesick. For some, it had been the longest time they had been away from their families. The bacterial infection had hit Steve pretty hard. He was one of seven boys that had been taken by ambulance to the hospital. He reported to Mal that morning his stomach and health was ok now. However, it was obvious from his response that the ordeal had shaken him up.

We stayed that night under a pavilion at the Meridian Baptist Church just outside of Knoxville. There was a water faucet next to the church where we all washed out our clothes. At dinner that night everyone's health seemed to be back to normal now and we were fully recovered.

Someone from McDonald's had heard about our trip and contacted Dennis Kazmierczak's mom saying they wanted to donate safety flags to the troop. When Mrs. Miller and Mrs. Kazmierczak connected with us that night at the restaurant, they were amazed by our manners and how quiet and well behaved we all were. They praised Jerry for the remarkable level of discipline he was able to maintain.

We mounted all 32 white fiberglass flagpoles to the left side of each of our bike's front tires. The bright plastic orange and blue flags would add another level of safety as we prepared to cross over the Great Smoky Mountains. The flags looked pretty good and did make us more noticeable to traffic. They may have added a bit of extra safety but were somewhat of a nuisance too. The fiberglass poles that the flags were attached to seemed to always be in the way when we mounted our bikes. The added flapping noise of two plastic flags constantly whipping in the wind was annoying.

It was a nice gesture on McDonald's part, but I'm sure it helped them with their advertising efforts more than it helped us. There were occasions when we would come in to town and stop at one of their hamburger stands. After seeing all their flags on our bikes, they would often donate lunch to us. There were no chicken sandwiches or salads back then, and the Quarter Pounder had just been added to their menu that year. It was a decent place to go to eat on a Friday when my dad got paid. It was a real treat when there were only hamburgers and cheeseburgers. Their fries were fried in animal fat and the burgers were all beef, or at least a better grade of beef, and both tasted great!

When we woke up the next morning, we were raring to go. We packed up the bikes quickly and just took off logging in 20 miles before stopping at a little restaurant outside of Pigeon Forge. We were beginning to line ourselves up to climb the Great Smoky Mountains. With the huge mountain range now clearly in our sight, the excitement was building by the minute. Everyone was in fine spirits.

THIRTY-SEVEN

I HAD BEEN TO GATLINBURG before with my family on our way to Florida, but never on a bicycle. When we rode into town later in the afternoon, the little village was bustling and there were people and cars everywhere. Our road guards were being kept busy once again. We had planned on camping just outside of town, where we would soon begin to prepare ourselves for the great climb over the Smoky Mountains. Gatlinburg is the gateway to the Great Smoky Mountains National Park and is well known for its many tourist attractions from Ripley's Believe it or Not Museum to go-carts, mini golf, and giant slides.

The busy area is in stark contrast to the park itself with its lush ancient forests and abundant wildlife that consists of over a half million acres and eight-hundred and fifty miles of hiking trails. Fly fishermen come from all over the country to fish for the park's native Appalachian brook trout in its many rivers and streams.

Almost everywhere, we went that night there was someone playing a guitar or harmonica and singing a country tune. After touring the town, we had dinner and headed back to camp to start working on tuning up our bicycles. We ran a methodical check, thoroughly inspecting each bike's mechanicals including the brakes and tires and putting on new brake pads on most of the bikes. I was personally on the team that ran the inspections being a bit older and a junior leader. I seemingly always had some oil or grease on my hands from fixing my bike or a fellow Scout's bike. We changed out several tires and tightened nearly everyone's spokes. It would be a long arduous climb that would take several hours to reach the top. We wanted to be prepared.

Our path would take us straight up through Newfound Gap on US Highway 441, the lowest drivable pass through the Great Smoky Mountains National Park. Before the park was developed, Newfound Gap was an undiscovered pass two miles east of Indian Gap, and was thought to be the lowest pass over the mountains. For centuries, the Cherokee walked the old Indian Gap Trail between the present day towns of Cherokee and Gatlinburg.

The road is marked with mile markers starting at Gatlinburg and ending in the town of Cherokee, North Carolina. Newfound Gap Road begins on US 441 at the last stoplight on the southern edge of Gatlinburg. Starting at an elevation of 1,400 feet above sea level, the road ascends nearly a mile high to Newfound Gap at an elevation of 5,046 feet. The narrow stretch of road is 33 miles long cutting across the center width of the park to the town of Cherokee on the North Carolina side of the Smoky Mountains. Cherokee is located in the Qualla Boundary, where the Eastern Band of Cherokee Indians reside and have maintained a cultural heritage dating back centuries.

Jerry had been to the outdoor play, "Unto These Hills," a number of years earlier with his family and wanted all of us to experience it. The play was first produced in 1950 and follows the triumphant story of the Cherokee from the first contact with Spaniards in 1540, searching for gold, to the infamous and tragic Trail of Tears in 1838.

We wore our full dress uniforms to the play and boarded a large bus in Gatlinburg after dinner and began our climb through the mountains on Newfound Gap Road. I had been through the same mountain pass with my family several times. As we slowly headed up the winding narrow stretch of road toward the mountainside theater in Cherokee, I began to take special notice this time. The grade at first didn't feel that steep. After passing the first of what would be several overlooks, there was loud clunking noise followed by the sharp sound of metal grinding on metal. The bus lunged suddenly forward as I was pushed hard back into my seat. I could see our driver; an older man quickly shifting gears. The bus was now struggling to climb up a much steeper grade of the mountain. I could see a faint outline of the massive mountain before us, the top shrouded in a misty blue haze. I began to wonder for the first time if we could really pedal the entire way up to the top.

When we arrived at the Mountainside Theatre in Cherokee, it was just before sunset and we were running a little late. We were quickly ushered to our seats and I was amazed by the massive 2,800 seat outdoor theater. The seating area was shaped in the form of a semicircle and cut deeply into the side of the mountain.

A woman who was sitting just below us had started to talk to a few of the younger Scouts, asking them where we were from. When she found out that we had ridden our bikes all the way from Illinois, she commented saying, "You all have such short haircuts and look so sharp. Most of the boys from this area usually wear their hair much longer, and are not as well kept," she said. Well, with hearing that, the Scouts said, "See Jerry, we didn't need to get our hair cut so short!" From Jerry's expression, you could tell that he was proud of all of us.

When the show started, it was pitch black and I couldn't see a thing. Then I began to hear the faint sound of Indians chanting off in the distance. They just seemed to come out of the smoke that had been illuminated by a bright light overhead. One by one dressed in brightly colored costumes, the Indians would appear dancing and chanting across the stage. I imagined myself dancing with them as my father had done in the Order of the Arrow. It was an incredible show that featured 1,500 actors and lasted about three hours.

It had started to drizzle when we woke up early the next morning, just as we were beginning to break camp. By the time we rode into Gatlinburg the rain had already stopped. We had a quick breakfast of grits, pancakes and bacon at around 6:00 a.m. Afterwards, Jerry ordered all of us to make one last check of the tension on our spokes and to make sure all of our tires had 60 pounds of pressure. We left town at mile marker 1, and started the climb up the mountain in an effort to beat the traffic.

During our last report to Mal, at "Mission Control," we told him that we might not be able to contact him during our climb through the mountain pass. We had anticipated that there would not be any payphones along our route. He understood having traveled through the same mountain pass himself and said, "We'll just have a period of blackout while you go behind the moon."

Our route on Newfound Gap Road would take us through the mountain pass, pedaling about 15 miles straight up a sheer grade, and then we would come down the other side of the mountain to Cherokee. A total run of approximately 33 miles. We would have to get over the mountain in one trek, Jerry told us. When we entered the Great Smoky Mountains National Park, we pedaled for just a few minutes before stopping at the Sugarland Visitors Center to make final adjustments to our bikes.

The same drive in a car usually takes about an hour depending on traffic. We would be pedaling about 3 mph up the mountain, and estimated that it would take us approximately seven to eight hours just to get to the top of Newfound Gap.

Then we would have to come down the other side of the mountain. When we left the visitor center and mounted our bikes to start the climb, everyone was excited. We had trained hard in preparation for the trip. With as many miles as we had put on traversing all those hills, we were now in very good shape. There was no grumbling from anyone; we were on a mission to climb over this mountain and we were going to do it no matter what!

From the Sugarlands Visitor Center, we began our long ascent up the mountain. I was in third gear and my bike seemed to be handling the pressure on the sprocket without too much trouble. Jerry had been concerned about the pressure the steep climb might cause on our sprockets and spokes. He theorized that the combination of weight between our equipment and that of each Scout could cause a catastrophic failure of the gearing systems, if there was too much pressure.

Newfound Gap Road runs parallel to the Little Pigeon River. I spotted a few fishermen walking the banks, casting their lines into the crystal clear water. I had fished the same river a few years earlier with my father and younger brother, Mark. As I started to make the long climb, I wondered how everyone in my family was doing. I had promised my mother I would write to them once they arrived at the Largo Mar Hotel in Florida.

The grade was beginning to get much steeper now. As I shifted my bike to second gear, I began to feel the muscles in my legs start to strain a bit. Still it wasn't too bad. We just kept pedaling, moving up the mountain, all 32 of us, ever so slowly, and our rhythm was now in perfect sync.

The view from my bike was spectacular as we continued our climb through the heart of the mountains with the view of the valley below. I had hiked and camped throughout many parts of the park with my family in the past but this experience was much different. It was exhilarating and I could feel a bit of fear come over me the higher we went. I began to take more notice of how lush and green everything was. In the distance, I could see a brown sign signifying the Campbell Overlook was just ahead. It looked familiar to me as we had driven by it in the bus on our way to the play the night before. Suddenly, the grade became much steeper, and I immediately shifted into first gear, now standing up pushing down hard with each rotation of the crank. I noticed we were coming up on mile marker 4, when I heard Dave Miller, several bikes ahead of me, grumble something as he was struggling to shift his bike into a lower gear.

I began to feel very small as the mountains before me rose up several thousand feet, before disappearing into the misty cloud cover. The rain earlier had created a smoke-like bluish haze that enveloped the tops of the tallest mountain peaks. We had learned while at the play Unto These Hills, the Cherokee name for the area is, "Shaconage," meaning "land of blue smoke."

I heard Danny behind me yell, "Stop!" and shortly afterwards, we pulled over into the parking area of Campbell Overlook. The spot looked familiar since we had passed the same overlook the night before during our bus ride up the mountain. It would be the first of many stops we would make. I was glad we decided to rest as my legs were starting to really ache. The views from the overlook were spectacular. Mount LeConte, the third largest peak in the Smokies dwarfed everything else in sight. Large groves of sugar maple trees used by the early settlers for sugar and syrup, dominated the valley's landscape below.

The climb was getting much more difficult the further up the mountain we went. We would not come to another pullover for at least another two and a half miles of pedaling up what was now a much steeper grade. I could hear Danny Scott talking with Jerry, saying that, we had to start making better time. When we all mounted our bikes to resume the climb, I noticed there were now several more cars on the road. The narrow two-lane road had a 45 mph speed limit, with lower limits in some of the more curvy areas.

As we made our way further up the mountain, several cars were now beginning to pass us. It was making me a little nervous since the road has so many curves in places. Some of the cars were passing us at high speeds often on blind corners. We were all now standing and pedaling in first gear, and everyone was struggling, but kept pushing on. About 45 minutes after leaving the Campbell Overlook, I looked over my shoulder and noticed a line of several cars behind us waiting to pass our convoy.

When the park ranger pulled us over, his lights were flashing. He stopped traffic in both directions of the road while he spoke with Jerry and Mike in the rear. "There's a two mile line of cars that don't want to pass you," he said to Jerry. We were still a distance before the next pull over and the ranger wanted the cars to be able to pass us. He told Jerry that he wanted us to stay parked along the side of the road until he could direct traffic around us. "You still have a pretty long ride up, the ranger went on to say, "but I'm more concerned about the long ride down since the traffic in the park is getting real heavy."

"We don't have to worry about that, we can get up to 60 mph," Bert said, smiling. The ranger looked shocked.

"Well, you will have to slow down; the speed limit is only 35 mph!" the ranger replied. Bert was being serious, as we had approached that speed a few times before, but on a lesser grade.

Our next stop would be at the Chimneys picnic area just past mile marker 6. There was nowhere really to park, just lots of little pull-offs with picnic tables and grills. We needed to rest so we pulled off into one of the smaller areas and parked our bikes. Several of us headed over to the Little Pigeon River that cut directly through the picnic area. The riverbanks were lined with many different kinds of trees but I was awed by the giant hemlocks, which were remnants of the old growth forests.

We had been told by the locals, while at breakfast, that it was a popular area of the park, especially around sunset since bears often frequented the area. Jerry had instructed us several times before to stay as far away from the bears as possible, and never attempt to feed them. My father's voice resonated in my mind as I recalled his words of caution regarding bears during our family camping trip around Lake Michigan.

After a short break, we got back on our bikes and continued our trek up the mountain. It was at this point in our climb that the road took a sharp turn to the north looping around and then back to the south. We knew that going up the mountain would be an extreme challenge. The pressure that was now being placed on the crank and being transferred to our spokes was beginning to worry Jerry. Prior to the climb, we had discussed that we might have to walk the bikes up a part of the mountain. Still we all kept riding, all still in first gear.

I could feel my bike straining and I could hear it creaking under the pressure each time I pushed down on my pedals. I was now standing upright pedaling as hard as I could and using every muscle in my body. I was using the same technique I had devised earlier thrusting down hard on my pedal with my stronger right leg followed by another push of my left. It was working but not nearly as efficiently as it had while riding in the foothills. I wasn't sure how much longer I could sustain myself pedaling like that. I was in good shape but this was an extreme test of my strength and will power. I wanted to do it, and I kept telling myself, "I can do it, don't give up."

By the time we made it to the Chimney Tops Lookout just before mile marker 9, I was completely exhausted. My thighs and calve muscles were burning. I was experiencing muscle fatigue and didn't know how much longer they would hold up. I was one of the older boys on the trip too, and couldn't imagine what some of the 11-year-old boys were feeling. I was spent but knew we still had several miles to go. It seemed as if the climb would never end. The further up the mountain we went the cooler it got. That was a welcome relief, as I was completely drenched in sweat. My clothes were wet to the touch and my feet felt like they were burning up.

When I got off my bike, I felt like I had no legs under me to support myself. It took several minutes of stretching and walking around before I felt normal again. The next rest area would be the Cove Hardwood Roadside before we would encounter our next challenge known as the "loop." The speed limit for the loop was 20 mph and for good reason. In order to alleviate the extreme slope of the mountain, engineers with the Civilian Conservation Corps in the 1930's cut a tunnel where the road had to make a switchback, looping back atop itself in order to stair step its way up the steep slope. From the pictures I had seen at the visitor center, the loop looked like something I had built with my racecar set.

The climb after the loop was very steep but seemed manageable and I felt at this point we could make it to the top. About a mile or so up the road there were several cars that had stopped. Apparently, several black bears were on the road blocking traffic. We all decided to get off our bikes and take a closer look. I saw a woman ahead of us jump out of her car and start to run toward us. She looked agitated by the time she got to where Jerry was standing and started yelling at him. "How dare you let these kids be exposed to all these bears! You should get back in your cars!" she said.

"We don't have any cars, we're riding our bikes," Jerry responded calmly. I don't think the lady believed him, apparently thinking he was rude and stormed away. We had to wait several minutes for the bears to clear the road, so the cars and people could proceed up the mountain. We were unable to pass so many cars riding up the mountain at such a slow pace.

Shortly after reaching mile marker 10, our speed up the mountain was now significantly reduced to only about 1-2 mph. We pulled off near the Alum Cave Trail a few minutes later. According to our trail map, we were now about four miles away from reaching the top of the mountain. It didn't sound like a great distance to travel but at the pace we were now moving, it would take forever to reach the top. The road was becoming much steeper the closer we got to Newfound Gap.

If our bicycle hike up would be anything like our bus ride the night before, we were in for some serious mountain climbing. I think the bus must have used every gear it had in its arsenal as it struggled mightily to reach the top. At one point, I thought we had come to a complete stop before suddenly jerking forward, finally reaching the top of the mountain pass. Going down the mountain was even more terrifying as the bus on several occasions felt like it was about to career off the side of the cliff. The driver the whole time was struggling to slow the bus down frantically pumping his brakes. I couldn't see any smoke, but I could definitely smell something burning. I figured it must be the brakes heating up.

This section of the road would prove to be the most challenging and would put our training to a test pushing the limits of our endurance and the mechanical capabilities of our bicycles. The vegetation was beginning to take on a new look. I started to notice different types of trees and bushes growing along the mountainside. The lower elevations were dominated by a mixture of sugar maples and northern hardwoods. The higher up we rode the forest was coming alive with more spruce and fir trees. A ranger at the campground had told us that the Fraser Fir and Red Spruce are the dominant trees above 4,500 feet in elevation.

The next rest area wouldn't be until Morton Overlook, about three and a half miles straight up the mountain. The task ahead of us looked daunting and there was a question as to whether we could even pedal up this stretch of the road since it was so steep. As Jerry and the other leaders were talking about our options, several of us started to explore a bit. As we headed up along a steep trail called Arch Rock, we heard a loud scream back by where our bikes were parked. It sounded like maybe one of the Scouts yelling, but I couldn't make out what all the commotion was about.

We flew back to the parking lot and saw Arlin running as fast as he could, heading straight toward us. A few other Scouts were right on his tail. He had a look of terror in his eyes as he ran right past all of us screaming, "There's a bear!" About 200 feet away from where we were standing, I could see four large garbage cans that were overflowing. Near the area where Arlin had just come from, there were several people, all screaming, "Bears!"

Arlin was once again living up to his reputation as a real goofball who always wanted to be at the center of attention. He had apparently seen a few bear cubs playing near the garbage cans and decided that it would be neat to try and feed them. It was exactly what Jerry had told all of us not to do, but Arlin was determined. As he reached his hand out holding a piece of candy he had found on the ground, a much larger bear appeared from behind the garbage cans and started walking toward him. Having been taught not to run from bears, Arlin stood frozen, not moving a muscle. Then the huge bear weighing more than 300 pounds lunged toward him. He took off running for his life. Everyone knows not to mess around with a mother bear and her cubs.

When we all finally calmed down after the incident, it had been decided that the strain on our bike's mechanicals would be too great to continue our climb. We would have to walk the final four miles up the mountain. From his days in the army and having worked on large helicopters, Jerry understood something about torque. He tried to explain to us that his decision to walk the bikes up the last stretch of the mountain had something to do with the amount of torque that is placed on the chain when it turns the rear axle. The increased amount of strain on the wheel would be so great that it could potentially snap the spokes. The risk was too great, Jerry thought.

The last four miles was a real hike as we slowly pushed all 32 bikes up the mountain. The road made a sharp turn to the east as we continued our long trek up what was the steepest part of our climb. I started to hear some grumbling ahead of me as a few of the guys were near exhaustion. We kept moving, walking one-step at a time. About an hour or so into our climb, the road made a big loop around, turning us in a more southwest direction, curving wildly snaking its way closer to our destination.

When we finally made it to the overlook at Newfound Gap it was around 2:00 p.m. I was never more tired in my life, every muscle in my body ached. It was emotional. We were all excited and knew that we had just done something few others had ever accomplished. We had climbed over 3000 feet, straight up into the clouds, conquering the great mountain, on a bicycle! Overcoming such a great hardship had lifted up all of our spirits. We knew that climbing the Smokies would be a tough part of the trip and a tremendous challenge. Our training had paid off, and our confidence level and spirits were never higher.

There was no place to buy lunch at the top of the mountain, so Jerry's mother and Mrs. Rohl had made peanut butter and jelly sandwiches for all of us. We rested for a short time after eating and then started to run a number of checks on our bikes. The extreme pressure on the rear wheels from the climb had loosened several of the bike's spokes. Making sure they were properly tightened was critical to heading down the mountain safely. If anyone was to crash due to loose spokes or their wheel collapsing at 40 to 50 mph, it would be catastrophic. Someone could be seriously injured or even die.

THIRTY-EIGHT

THE VIEW from Newfound Gap was breathtaking with lush green forests of spruce and fir trees as far as the eye could see. I observed several massive mountains clothed in a shadowy white haze off in the distance. I felt like we were on the top of the world. Even the temperatures were much lower. Our reward for reaching the summit would be to ride down the other side, freewheeling the entire way until we would have to eventually slow down and stop. That would be something easier said than done, as we would soon find out.

Mr. Giannini, our point man, went down the mountain first. Then, one at a time, a few of the younger guys went down, all spaced apart by five-minute intervals. "We don't want the Scouts passing each other," Jerry said. Ron Herff went next followed by Jack Froehling and a few others. "Do not ride the brakes," Jerry warned Arlin. "The rims will over heat and you might blow a tire." It wasn't a very comforting thought, as I was getting ready to ride down the side of a mountain at 50 mph. I was next in line. Just as I was getting ready to shove off, I could hear Jerry giving a few of the other Scouts last minute instructions. "Sit up to slow down," he told them.

The wind had picked up when I took off pedaling down the mountain. The temperature had dropped another five degrees and was noticeably cooler. Rain was expected later in the day and the clouds were starting to build "Pump the brakes to slow down," Jerry said, as I shoved off. If the rims were to heat up too much, the tires could blow. It had already happened to Jack's bike coming into Renfro Valley, so I knew it was possible.

I made my first turn to the east after passing the Oconaluftee Valley Overlook and started to pick up a good amount of speed. It wasn't long before I came up to my first car. Without any hesitation, I passed him without too much trouble. There had been no directive on passing cars and the further down the mountain I went, the more cars I passed. Each time I zoomed by, there was always the same look of shock on their faces. I figured if I didn't pass them, I would have to apply more pressure to my brakes. I didn't want to heat up the rims too much. At this point in the trip, most of us were pretty adept at riding our bikes, so to pass a car was not a big deal. I still felt a rush of adrenalin each time I did it.

I started to feel myself speed up and sat up for the first time in an attempt to slow down. It didn't seem to decrease my speed that much, so I started to pump my brakes. It was an exhilarating feeling, as I flew down the mountain. I estimated my speed to be about 45-50 mph with the wind in my face. I knew from the trail map that just ahead was a giant S-curve. I would have to start slowing down soon as the series of turns would reverse my direction twice before hitting a long straightaway. When I came out of my last turn in the switchback, I could see Jack ahead of me, slowing down. When I got close, he started to pick up some speed and we were really flying. "Fifty-five mph now!" he yelled out. "My speedometer is buried!" I figured we hit at least 60 mph as we both flew down the mountain. Jack started to slow down saying that he needed to fall back and make sure everyone else was coming down the mountain safely.

We were no longer "greenhorn bicyclists," Jerry said before we all headed down the mountain. It was a good thing too as riding down at breakneck speeds took a great deal of skill and balance. It was unlike any rollercoaster ride I had ever been on.

All of those foothills and smaller mountains helped to strengthen our bodies. I shot past the Oconaluftee River Trail having slowed down a bit. The muscles in my arms began to ache from holding on to my handlebars so tight. I was coming around a slight bend in the road and I spotted two large black bears off to the side feeding on some berries. There were no cubs that I could see. I just kept riding and didn't slow down.

So far, everyone seemed to be getting down the mountain safely. Jerry went down last. He had a speedometer on his bike and like the rest of us was soon clocking speeds of 50-55mph. When he came upon his first car, his speedometer read 51mph. He wasn't into speed like many of us were and would pass the cars very carefully. Our ascent up the mountain had taken nearly seven hours. We estimated that our decent would take each Scout only about 45 minutes.

When I passed Collins Creek Picnic area, I was getting tired and decided to pull off the road for few minutes. I laid my bike down in a little nook in the grass and rested my head on my saddlebags. About four minutes later, I saw Danny Zoubek come flying down the mountain, wild eyed, and hanging on for dear life. He must have been going at least 60 mph from the looks of things. I didn't dare call out his name for fear that it might distract him. Five minutes later, Dennis Kazmierczak, with his white blond hair and looking just as crazed as Danny, flew right past me. Neither of them saw me. It appeared that he was going faster than Danny! Shocked at the speeds these guys were traveling, I didn't utter a word and decided I should get heading back down the last stretch of the mountain.

When Jerry finally came rolling in to where we had all stopped, Mr. Giannini was happy to report that everyone had gotten down the mountain safely without incident. Incredible considering the age of some of the younger boys and the speeds we were traveling. We each had our own harrowing story to tell about our adventure coming down the mountain that day, and would talk about it for several days afterwards. We all agreed that it was a very intense experience and the most exciting time of our lives. The bicycle hike through the great mountain pass had taken us all day. We were all wiped out, and still needed to find a place to eat dinner and bed down for the night.

We camped that night near the town of Cherokee, North Carolina. When we woke up on Sunday morning, Jerry was the first to wish me a happy birthday. It was August 6, and I was now 15 years old, a relatively old-timer in the Scouts. Most boys did not last that long, as other more pressing things would often get in the way and Scouting became a secondary interest. I was still motivated, having achieved the rank of Life in July, and now my mind was set on reaching the rank of Eagle.

Our plan was to try and make it into Franklin and then on to Highlands, North Carolina before eventually crossing the border into Georgia. From Cherokee, we were still traveling on US 441, or the Great Smoky Mountains Expressway, as it is called. At first, our ride out of town wasn't too bad but then the topography and the road changed dramatically. I was forced to shift to a much lower gear and once again employ my pedaling technique.

The road had been cut right into the side of the mountain leaving a jagged face of solid rock that had been shattered by the use of dynamite. I had never seen so many waterfalls all in one area, some cascading over the side of the mountain and onto the road. At one point, I stood up to pedal, making only marginal headway. It was slow going as the mountains in this area were still very steep. The road was narrow and was getting steeper every turn we made as it snaked its way through the mountains. By the time we reached the small town of Sylva, we had pedaled only about 16 miles and were already exhausted.

That night, a few miles outside of town, we set up our small orange tents for the first time. The tents by design did not have a flap to close up the opening. As good Scouts, we set them up with the front facing east, as rain was predicted. The campsite we chose was spectacular, nestled high up on a grassy ridge surrounded by the pristine forests of the Great Smoky and the Blue Ridge mountains. With the Great Smokies now off in the distance, it was a clear reminder that the climb was now behind us.

There was a beautiful sunset that night. I took a picture of our campsite as everyone was scurrying around setting up camp. My Kodak 110 captured a picture of the yellow orange glow of the sun reflecting through our nylon tents. As the sun began its slow decent and finally disappear behind the mountain pass, I knew it was a site I would never forget. The picture was now stored in the cartridge of my trusty 110. It would be a memory caught on film of our great achievement.

Keith Gregrow was a husky good-humored kid, and like Arlin was always joking around. We had nicknamed him, "Eggroll," and he seemed to get a real kick out of it. However, as funny and good natured as Keith was, he was suffering that night from a bad toothache. It had been building throughout the day and was getting worse by the minute. He was in such agony that Jerry knew he needed to do something quick. The next morning we were lucky enough to find a dentist in Sylva. "It looks pretty bad," the dentist said. "The tooth is infected and it's impacted. I will have to pull it. Normally I would get the infection under control before pulling the tooth, but it seems as if you guys need to get on your way. My suggestion is that you let me pull it." To make matters worse, it was a permanent tooth.

Jerry felt that he had no choice and made the decision to have the bad tooth pulled and gave the dentist permission. Keith took it all pretty well despite the agonizing pain. It was such a different time dealing with emergencies regarding kids back then. Jerry had been assigned responsibility for the boys when out on our camping trips. He would always call the shots, and the parents knew that and accepted it. The last word was always Jerry's.

THIRTY-NINE

S EVERAL DAYS had gone by and there was no mention of the smoking incident. Danny thought that Mike Terese had forgotten about it and he was off the hook. We were stopped at a small souvenir shop along the road near Sylva, North Carolina. Mike pointed to the picture post cards and said to Danny, "Okay, it's time." Danny filled out the post card, addressed it and bought a stamp. Mike read the card, in which Danny had confessed to his parents about smoking, and told him to drop it in the mail. The outgoing mailbox was a shoebox on the counter near the cash register. Mike watched him put it in the box. Everyone was buying postcards, including me, as I had promised my mother I would send her one.

As we mounted up and got into formation, I saw Danny run back into the store. I thought maybe he was making a last minute bathroom stop or something. In all the commotion to get back on the road, no one else seemed to know he was gone. Danny was on a mission with ulterior motives. He knew he didn't have a lot of time before someone would notice him missing and blow the whistle. Danny's parents were strict disciplinarians. He was afraid of the punishment that was sure to come if they read the postcard; so he removed it from the shoebox and threw it in the trash. No one except his brother, Steve, ever knew.

I guess when I dropped my postcard in the same shoebox; I must have forgotten the postage. Amazingly, my parents received it at the Lago Mar Hotel in Fort Lauderdale, Florida. It was stamped with "Postage Due 2 cents." Having successfully crossed over the Smokies, I wrote to them saying, "We're pretty sure that we will make Florida now!" Up to that point, no one really knew if we were going to make it to Florida or not. The idea that we might not was never really talked about. Certainly, Jerry never discussed the possibility. He had instilled in us a sense of adventure. High adventure type trips was something Troop 65 was known for. "We have the ability, determination and pride to do this," Jerry would say. Having been in the military, he always had a well thought out plan in order to successfully execute each trip. Sure, there was some grumbling from some of the Scouts complaining about the foothills in Indiana, but that had been several days earlier and Jerry was able to resolve the issue.

My first inkling that we might not make Florida was while we were at a restaurant in Gatlinburg, Tennessee. Standing in the hallway, I overheard a rather disturbing conversation between Bob Sample and Mike Terese. Bob, who was usually a positive guy, was expressing his doubts to Mike regarding our chances to make Florida. He was saying that we needed to make better time and were falling short of our goal. I was a little bothered by their discussion and tried to put it out of my mind. I was determined to make it to Florida, and I would continue to do my best to do my part, and get us there.

Our radio blackout had lasted two days, since there were no telephones in the Smoky Mountains and Mal's broadcast did not air on Sundays. When Jeff Giannini, would give his report the morning of August 7, our parents and everyone else that had been following our progress were anxiously awaiting our report. No one had heard from us since the great mountain climb and they were understandably concerned. Mal was just as excited about our whereabouts as our own parents were. He knew that if Jerry could get to a phone, he would hear from us. Jeff was Mr. "G's" youngest son and had been on a mission to prove himself ever since we had left Wood Dale. He desperately wanted to be able to do some of the things his older brothers had done in the Scouts. His wiry build and the fact that he would occasionally get roughed up by some of the other boys, seemed to motivate him. Jeff had a pleasant personality and was always easy to get along with. When he gave his report, he had a big smile on his face. He knew that he had done something special, something even his older brothers had not.

So far, despite a few arguments among some of the Scouts, it was a happy excursion. We had been away from home now 17 days. It was the longest period of time any of the boys had been away from their families, and the longest trip in the troop's history. There had been 16-day trips previously, but somehow this trip was different. It would be the first time Jerry would have all the Scouts together for a full month.

"Everything is going along just fine," Jerry reported to Mal. "I think they're all making it through with flying colors, living together, and working together. They have a few arguments sometimes, as boys often do, but they always work things out and keep going right along. They're all in the best of spirits and doing real well," he said.

In an effort to make up some time, we decided to make a course correction avoiding the route from Franklin, North Carolina to Highlands, North Carolina. We had been told by the police that the roads were extremely steep in that area and unlike any we had seen before. The roads were very narrow with several hairpin turns cut into the side of the mountain, making it difficult for cars to see us. With safety on his mind, Jerry didn't want anyone to get hurt. It was determined that the time it would take us to navigate through this treacherous area would be better spent on a less dangerous road. Our new route would take us from Franklin, North Carolina through the small town of Clayton, Georgia into Westminster, South Carolina. It had been a wise decision as we made almost 50 miles that day. We were now past the halfway point to Florida having ridden our bikes over 700 miles.

When we crossed into Georgia early in the morning of August 8, it marked the sixth state we had passed through on our bicycle adventure. We were now angling toward Anderson, South Carolina and eventually into Westminster, South Carolina, a hike of about 57 miles. The hills were starting to level off a bit and we were starting to make good time. Dark rain clouds were beginning to build late in the afternoon. I could see some lightening off in the distance and it looked like we were heading straight into yet another storm. We kept pedaling.

By the time we rode into Westminster, South Carolina, the winds had picked up quite a bit and I could feel my bike start to get pushed around every time there was a strong gust. We pulled into Martin's Restaurant and Motel for supper just as the rains began. That night Mr. Martin offered to let us sleep in his downstairs dining room. Everywhere we went, people continued to be very open hearted. They took us in, under their roofs, refusing to allow us to sleep out in a field somewhere.

The next morning, the rains had subsided and we took a quick swim in Mr. Martin's swimming pool. We picked up our clothes that had been washed the night before by Jerry's mother and Mrs. Rohl. After breakfast, we headed toward Abbeville, South Carolina, some 61 miles away. In his report to Mal that morning, Nick Herff, would tell everyone listening that the troop was in fine heath and the temperature would be a steamy 100°F. "Pretty hot for pedaling a bike," Mal commented. Since the hills were now beginning to level off somewhat, we had hoped to make some good time that day. We were now angling for the ocean.

Our health, as Nick reported, was never better and the strength in our legs was testament of that. Despite a few saddle sores and some muscle aches, we were all toughing up and could pedal our bikes 60 miles a day without any trouble. Some of the guys even had to slit their shorts because the muscle build-up in their thighs had made them fit too tightly. We were now able to hit a hill at 3-5 mph and climb them like nobody's business. It was a stark contrast to when we first started out where biking up the hills in Indiana, posed a real problem. Each day that went by, we were becoming more in tune for the riding that lay ahead of us. "When we start hitting flat lands we should be able to hit 80, 90, even 100 miles a day without any trouble," Jerry reported to Mal.

"Just a bunch of tigers," Mal responded.

FORTY

THE HEAT was really starting to bother me and I was beginning to feel lightheaded. The temperature had shot well past 100°F and sweat was dripping down my forehead into my eyes and stinging them. Our path down Route 24 would take us through the town of Anderson, South Carolina. We would cross over Lake Hartwell on two long bridges. The massive reservoir was one that we had hoped to swim in and escape the heat.

The further out from town we traveled, the road was deteriorating and had several large potholes and cracks. We had been down roads that were in poor condition before, but this section was about the worst we had seen. It was unusual as the further south we traveled, the better the roads got. I was able to dodge most of the bad spots in the road, hitting only a few of the cracks. Several of the other guys weren't as lucky though.

I could see a few hundred yards ahead where the road had apparently been repaved. Several pieces of equipment and large machines were parked off to the side. They were in the process of resurfacing the road. I heard somebody behind me yell, "Oh no!" Just then, I glanced over my shoulder and saw Dennis Kazmierczak, who was several bikes behind me veer off the road. When he hit the ditch, his saddlebags went flying, and so did Dennis, head over heels over his handlebars. The impact of his front tire smashing into the side of the ditch had caused it to totally collapse. I heard Danny yell, "Stop," and we all pulled off to the shoulder of the road. Dennis, who usually had a smile on his face, was still lying in the field laughing at what had just happened. Jerry had witnessed the entire crash and didn't think it was all that funny, but was thankful Dennis hadn't been seriously injured. After looking over his bike, Jerry thought his spokes were too tight contributing to the collapse of the rim.

In the past, when someone blew out a rim, there had been a larger town close by. This time, we were in a remote area and the closest town with any real population was Anderson, South Carolina, some 15 miles away. Our safety vehicle had planned on heading into Abbeville, South Carolina, to alert them of our passing through, so they wouldn't be any help. We needed to get Dennis back on the road as soon as possible. We always carried at least seven spare tires and inner tubes on our bike racks, but carrying an extra rim was out of the question.

We were all standing in the field next to the mangled bike, brainstorming, trying to figure out what to. That's when one of the older boys blurted out, "Let's make a tandem bike!" It was an ingenious idea and that's exactly what we did. We removed the bent up wheel and hooked the front fork of that bike onto the back of Bob Sample's bike. The three-wheeled contraption worked, and balancing ever so carefully, Dennis and Bob took off. Wobbly at first, they headed down the road toward Anderson, pedaling in unison.

The entire trip so far had been a lesson about self-reliance and perseverance, with an attitude of never giving up. We had become very self-sufficient along the way. Faced with a difficult situation, we calmly thought through the problem, never once panicked and came up with a solution. Our preparation and training as Scouts had once again saved the day.

By the time we found a place to swim, I felt like I was going to pass out from the extreme heat. Several of us just jumped in the lake not bothering to put on our swim trunks. After lunch and having reconnected with Dennis and Bob in town, we took off for Abbeville, South Carolina, feeling refreshed and invigo-rated by the cool water. We were determined to make the 63 miles we had set our sights on before the accident.

FORTY-ONE

WHEN WE GOT to the outskirts of Abbeville, South Carolina on Tuesday, August 8, it was about 3:30 p.m. The
odometer on Jack's bike read 867 miles. Just as I saw the sign
for the town, I noticed an Abbeville fire truck speeding our
way with several firemen hanging off the sides waving at us. It
wasn't too long afterwards that they stopped and said that
they had been asked by the mayor to guide us into town. When
we got to the town it appeared that everyone was waiting for
us. Earlier in the day, when Jerry's mother and Mrs. Rohl had
informed the town of our arrival, they said that they had received our correspondence a few months before and were already waiting for us.

The hospitality we had experienced throughout our trip was
remarkable. We saw people in many different walks of life and
were amazed at the level of kindness they showed us. Several
folks we met along the way opened their hearts and even their
homes to us. Jerry was always worried how we might behave
in those situations, but we were always well mannered. Kids
just acted differently in those days as discipline was more ingrained. There was usually a parent at home during the day to
enforce the rules enacted by your father. If you got out of line
while in the care of your mother, you could bet that your father would be well versed of the situation by the time he got
home. Then all hell would break loose. Fathers were more
feared back then, and you never talked back to them since your
life might be in jeopardy. At the very least, a swift and brutal
beating often with a belt or a stick across your bare ass was in
order.

The radio at the restaurant blurted out a report from the UPI World News, something about Vietnam and getting our "nose bloodied," with losses in Saigon and Cambodia. It was a stark reminder that the war was raging and our soldiers were still dying. We had not even seen a TV since we had left 19 days earlier and only occasionally had listened to a radio. The town of Abbeville had just treated us to breakfast and it was getting close to the time of our report with Mal. When we left the restaurant to take a tour of the town, the news had now switched to Frank Sinatra singing, "Fly Me To The Moon," one of my father's favorite songs.

"Abbeville is one of the nicest places we've been to. The people are real friendly," Jim Stoll reported to Mal Wednesday morning. "They've got a lot of things to see and it's really pretty." The Abbeville townsfolk were exceptional and everyone was very accommodating and friendly.

Jim was quite the dynamo in the energy department and always seemed to have a smile on his face. He was the perfect choice to do the report on Abbeville. Despite his jovial personality, Jim and I were usually more serious minded. We were in the Scouts for the fun of it, but you could also count on us in an emergency. Jim was known for not being afraid of trying new things and was a smart intelligent Scout.

The summer before our trip, we were sitting around a campfire at Starved Rock State Park when Jerry decided to play a familiar game of, "what if." He was trying to prepare us for some tragedy or event that could occur in our lives. The game was fun and we always learned something that could potentially save a life someday. It was pitch black out that night. There was no moon. As the fire roared, I glanced up and could see the reflection of the fire's flames bouncing off everyone's eyes, now fixed on Jerry. "What if a flying saucer were to fly over the horizon and come down somewhere close?" he said.

"We stay together and no matter what, don't get on board!" Jim responds quickly. That seemed to make a lot of sense to the rest of us, so we went on to the next, "what if" question.

"We are all traveling in a small plane when all of a sudden there is trouble and we have to make a crash landing. What do we need to do in order to survive?" Jerry asks. Some of the Scouts blurt out, "Start a fire using some of the fuel from the plane's wing."

"That's a good idea, but how do we start the fire without matches?" Jerry said.

"We go find the plane's batteries and some wire and create a spark," Jim responds. Jerry thought that was a neat solution, but that was just the way Jim was, always using his head.

The night we arrived in Abbeville, the town treated us to a nice dinner and kept the municipal swimming pool open until 11:00 p.m. for our use. After our dip, we all took showers and spent the night on the lawn near the pool next to the city hall. There were many things to see in Abbeville, as it was an old Civil War town, rich in history. The town was founded in 1785 and the buildings in the square had been preserved and appeared to be frozen in time.

Our first stop was a tour of the historic opera house where they let us go back stage. "It was really fun and we learned that the building was made just in the right way, so you could hear what a person was saying, no matter what corner of the place they might be in," Jim told Mal in his report. Next, we went to see the monuments marking "Secession Hill." It was here, on November 22, 1860, that a meeting was held to launch South Carolina's secession from the United States of America. One month later, South Carolina became the first state to secede.

The police chief had taken a real interest in our troop and gave us a police escort to the Coca-Cola bottling plant where we were all treated to a cold bottle of coke. Afterwards, he was insistent on wanting us to see the Burt-Stark Mansion. Mary Stark Davis, or "Miss Mary," as she preferred to be called, was the only resident of the mansion. She was 87 years old at the time of our visit, still in good health and even drove a car occasionally. The police chief took care of her and had the keys to her house, since she would often lock herself out.

Near the end of the Civil War, Confederate President, Jefferson Davis, who was fleeing south from Richmond, stopped for the night in Abbeville. He stayed at the home of his friend, Armistead Burt, a former Speaker of the House. It was here that he would hold a final council of war with his cabinet, reluctantly agreeing to dissolve the Confederate government, ending the War Between the States.

In 1900, J.S. Stark, a banker, bought the old house and he and his wife restored it to its original state. They even returned the bed that Jefferson Davis had slept in to its original location in the house. Mary Stark Davis, daughter of Mr. and Mrs. Stark, would eventually inherit the home upon the death of her parents.

After our tour of the mansion, we road our bikes over to the Abbeville Hospital where they treated us to a good meal of fried chicken, corn on the cob and hot biscuits. The local radio station, WABV was owned by Mr. George Settles, who was fascinated with our trip. He invited us to talk on the air. He was a neat person and reminded us all of Mal. With our tour of the town ending, we headed over to Trinity Episcopal Church, a massive structure that had been built in 1859, with a steeple rising above the ground some 120 feet. We climbed up several flights of stairs to the top of the steeple and proceeded to ring the original church bell. With so many Scouts wanting to participate in the ringing the bell, it rang for a long time.

The final part of our visit would lead us to the police station. The Abbeville Police Department showed us around the station, locking a few of us in a cell. They also demonstrated how tests are given to suspected drunk drivers using a breathalyzer. They showed us a neat machine called a Teletype, and sent a message to the Wood Dale Police Department, saying that we were okay.

It had been one the friendliest receptions we had received so far on our trip. The people of Abbeville were some of the nicest, most hospitable people we would meet along our way. As a farewell gesture, the mayor presented each of us with a key to the city saying that we would always be welcome.

It was about 3:00 p.m. when we finally mounted up and rode out of town. We had traveled less than a mile when the police chief came upon us with his lights and sirens blaring. He wanted to tell us that the Abbeville newspaper had printed a story featuring our troop on the front page. He had brought a copy for each of the Scouts. Everyone was so good to us that we just couldn't get away, and had to say our goodbyes again, before we would eventually be on our way toward Augusta, Georgia.

FORTY-TWO

OUR ORIGINAL PLANS when we woke up that morning in Abbeville was to hit the road and cover the 63 miles we had figured it was to Augusta, Georgia. Since we had spent so much time visiting, our plans would have to be altered. Improvising and changing our route when we saw fit was something we were getting very good at. Danny Scott reminded us that we were still several hundred miles away from Florida and our final destination of Jacksonville. It was his job to keep us focused on our goal.

Our plan from the beginning had been to reach Jacksonville by August 18. There, we would arrange for a bus to take us to the Kennedy Space Center for a tour. On Sunday morning, August 20, we would all board a Delta Air Lines jetliner, and fly back to Wood Dale. We had organized and planned well for the trip, and for the most part, despite a few hiccups along the way, everything was going smoothly. If all continued to go well, we would be in Georgia later that evening or early the next day.

The thermometer read 103°F now. With the sun beating down on us for so many days in a row, my brown hair had now turned almost completely blond. None of us wore hats and the constant exposure to the sun had turned everybody's hair a lighter shade. The further south we rode and the deeper into the back roads of South Carolina we got, the more run-down shacks I saw along the road. The people seemed friendly enough and usually waved to all 32 of us as we streamed by returning the gesture. What gave me some pause, however, was the occasional shotgun sitting next to the person as they sat waving from their rocking chair. It was as if we had stepped back in time. Almost every house we passed seemed to have a dog that would usually come running out after us. After we would hit them with our ammonia and water mix, they would stop almost immediately in their tracks, take a pee and run back to where they came from.

As we came up over a hill, there was a junkyard on our left and strewn about were hundreds of rusted out cars and old tractors. I noticed a few German Shepherd puppies playing in the front of an old run down building. If it was a house, it was pretty nasty with several windows broken out and pieces of rusted sheet metal acting as a roof. As we flew past the shack and began to pick up some more speed heading downhill, somebody behind me screamed, "Dog!" That's what we were supposed to do if any of us saw a dog, so it would give the adult leaders enough time to get out in front of it and hit him with their ammonia spray. This time the alert came too late and a huge black and tan German Shepherd was heading straight for us in full stride.

We had all hit a speed of around 40 mph heading down the hill. When the dog's head crashed into Bob Mikuls's bike, her timing must have been off in an attempt to bite Bob. Her snout had got caught in the spokes of his front wheel and she instantly let out a loud yelp. Bob's eyes just about popped out of his head, as he struggled not to fall. The dog was finally able to free its nose from his spokes. Somehow, she managed to land under the crank hanger of his bike where he dragged her for a short distance, until finally running her over with his rear wheel. His momentum going downhill had saved Bob from an ugly crash. The Shepherd, now whimpering, limped back to where her puppies were still playing, licking her wounds.

There had been some wild dogs we had encountered along the way protecting their turf, but mostly we saw domesticated ones intent on attacking us. We stopped a few miles down the road to take a better assessment of the damage that had been done to Bob's bike. Surprisingly, it hadn't been damaged that much from the collision, except for a few bent spokes in the front wheel that we were able to fix. It was incredible that he hadn't crashed. Somehow he was able to stay upright and on the road despite dragging a 100 pound dog under his bike. When Bob's father died of cancer the December before our trip, it had taken a real toll on his state of mind. He seemed distant and didn't speak very much during the entire trip. The dog attack didn't help very much, and it was pretty clear that he had been shaken up.

Our social life had gotten in our way of pedaling and we weren't making very good time. We had eaten much more than we normally would have over the past few days and everyone was acting a bit sluggish. The people of Abbeville had been wonderful to us, rolling out the red carpet. I think they must have thought we were all a bit on the skinny side when we arrived, and just kept feeding us.

We wound our way along Route 28, a two-lane country road that brought us through the heart of the Sumter National Forest. It was a beautiful ride with dense forests of trees on each side of the road. When we got closer to the small town of McCormick, South Carolina, a double set of railroad tracks paralleled the road. I hadn't thought about Billy for some time, but the sight of the tracks reminded me of the time we got caught by the Wood Dale Police putting stuff on the tracks. I realized now how irresponsible we had been and that someone could have really gotten hurt. I wondered how he and Kathy were doing and missed my marathon kissing sessions with her, and riding my bike around town with Billy.

I think Jerry figured we needed a break after the dog attack, so when he spotted Strom's Drug Store on Main Street in Mc-Cormick, we got the word to stop. It was a neat place that featured a turn-of-the-century soda fountain with ice-cream cones, floats, and old-fashioned cherry cokes. The shop owner was a nice man and told us that we should be on the lookout for gold in the streams nearby. We thought he was joking until he told us the story about William Dorn, who in 1852, had discovered the second-richest vein of gold in South Carolina history, on the site where the town of McCormick now stood.

It was later in the day when we left McCormick and were now just a few miles outside of town, coming into Plum Branch. The hotdogs and ice cream we had eaten for dinner was a fitting treat after the dog attack, and Bob and the rest of the guys seemed to be in much better spirits. After riding several more miles out of town, the skies started to darken as another storm approached. It was getting dark fast and off in the distance I could see several teepees burning saw dust. Jerry had told us that it was the result of all the logging in the area. The further we pedaled down the road the darker it got and the glow from the fires became more intense.

Something caught Bob Mikuls's eye and he just stopped riding. He was mesmerized with the fires and wouldn't move. Without any warning, he had stopped pedaling, got off his bike and was holding it upright staring out into the direction of the fires. Danny Zoubeck, stopped and tried to encourage him to get back on his bike. "Come on, Bob, its ok, let's go," he said. He didn't move a muscle, seemingly oblivious to Danny's presence. It was clear that something serious was ailing him. He didn't utter a word or even look at Jerry who was now trying to get him going. We had gotten used to Bob not saying much to anyone during the trip, but when he did speak, it was usually something significant and often important.

Bob was 15 years old while on the trip and a junior leader. He was a dedicated Scout and had done a neat demonstration several months earlier, before one of our winter campouts. He took a large Mason jar and filled it with water and then to everyone's surprise poured the entire contents of the jar into his sleeping bag. "This is the amount of water released from your body into the sleeping bag during the night," he explained to all of us. "We should all wear pajamas when we sleep in our bags," he said. Bob was very meticulous in his ways and had done his research and taught us something important that would benefit all of us on our campouts.

It was clear that Bob wasn't planning on going anywhere very soon. It was getting darker by the minute and we needed to locate a campsite quickly before it became pitch black outside. Realizing that we had to act fast, Jerry instructed Mike Rohl, to take charge of the back of the convoy. He told Mr. "G" to continue with the rest of the group and look ahead for a place to camp. He would stay behind, and wait for Bob and plan to catch up with us. It was out of our normal protocol to split up like that, but the circumstances called for Jerry to make a split decision. Without question, we all just followed his lead.

The only way Jerry could get Bob to move was to start to bike ahead of him making him aware that he was going and encouraging him to follow. Jerry got about a city block away and Bob still had not moved. His eyes were fixed on the burning teepees. A car came up alongside Jerry gesturing him to pull over and stop. "You know there is a guy behind you," the man said.

"I know, I have him in my sight," Jerry responded.

"You should be careful out here, there are a lot of Rednecks out here!" the man replied.

"Ok, thanks," Jerry said. When Bob eventually got going, it had been several minutes since the rest of the crew had taken off. By now, it was almost completely dark outside and the only light was from the glow of the fires and the moon reflecting off the road.

The camp we had chosen was not one of our best sites. It was an old abandoned schoolyard plagued with tall grass and a lot of weeds. After the sun went down, we were getting desperate to find a spot to camp along the road. When Jerry finally reconnected with the rest of us, he told us what the guy in the car had said about Rednecks. "Jerry, do you know what Rednecks are?" a few of the Scouts asked.

"No," he replied. When the boys told him what they were, he felt silly afterwards, admitting he thought certain it was some sort of wild animal lurking in the woods of South Carolina, ready to pounce on unsuspecting Scouts.

Just as we were crawling into our blankets, it started to drizzle. When we woke up the next morning, the skies were still cloudy and everyone's bedding was wet. The temperature had cooled down since yesterday, dropping below 100°F and was a welcome relief. We all seemed pretty energized and raring to go. Normally, we would have tried to dry out our bedding but that morning we just packed up our bikes and headed out along the trail.

We had only ridden about three miles when one of the boy's tires was getting low on air, so we stopped to fix it in the small town of Parksville, South Carolina. There we met with Mrs. Parks, who was in her front yard rounding up a few stray chickens. When she spotted our convoy parked along the side of the road, she walked over and offered to help us. She told us that her husband had founded the small village of 168 people as a family community some years earlier. It seemed no matter where we went, and no matter how large or small the towns were, the people continued to open their arms to assist us.

We stopped for breakfast at a little restaurant just outside of Clarks Hill, having pedaled 17 miles. The weather was starting to clear up and the temperatures remained cool. Everyone was hungry when we stopped. The hotdogs and ice cream, although good, did not really fill us up like the fried chicken and biscuits we had the night before. After breakfast, we made a few adjustments to our bikes and headed further south.

Mrs. Parks, like so many others, was very curious about us and asked a lot of questions about our trip. Jerry's eyes were beaming with joy as he told her how impressed he was with all his boys, saying how we would just get on our bikes and keep riding every day. "Every time there's a turn in the road, we see something new, or meet somebody else," he said. He was clearly proud of his boys, and we were proud of him too, and were grateful that he was our leader.

FORTY-THREE

AUGUSTA WAS FINALLY in our reach with only about 16 more miles to pedal, but it felt like it took forever to get there. I started to notice several areas of reddish colored dirt and sand. I had seen some of it before while on my family vacations, but always from our car. The further south we got, the redder the dirt became. Mr. Giannini, who had been to this part of the country before, explained to us it was due to iron in the soil. When we crossed over the Savannah River on Route 28 into Georgia, it was about 4:00 p.m. We made a quick stop just past the bridge to repair a tire that kept losing air on Rick Lee's bike. We were all in good spirits, knowing that we were getting closer to the last leg of our journey.

We were coming into a particularly bad section of Augusta, Georgia, but we didn't know it. It was rush hour and probably the worst time to be traveling in an area that we weren't familiar with. Our road guards were very active and it appeared that nearly every intersection we went through we needed to use them. I never enjoyed riding through the big cities and Augusta seemed to be about one of the busiest. There were cars and people everywhere. We had all been instructed to be on our guard and stay alert for cars and people and anything else that might cross our path. I was anxious to get back to the country roads as soon as possible, so we wouldn't get killed by a car or some wacko in one of Augusta's worst sections.

Bob Sample knew something about police procedure, and called the Augusta Police Department informing them of our situation. Without hesitation, they came to our aid. The first officer that showed up said that they would escort us to a safer place. He commented on the traffic jam that had been caused as a result of gawkers stopping to check out our caravan. Thirty-two bicycles traveling through town was something I'm sure none of them had ever seen before. When the second squad car showed up, the officer who seemed to be in charge asked Jerry what direction we had come from. "The north," Jerry said.

"Wow, you never want to be in that area! Did you experience any problems?" the cop replied looking shocked.

"No," Jerry responded. "The people were all out on their balconies, waving and asking us were we were going. We didn't have any issues." It was obvious that the cops were anxious to get us out of the area as soon as possible and told Jerry to get all the boys ready to ride, as they would provide a police escort.

"No matter what, make sure the kids stay together, so nobody gets killed!" the cop said.

Although curious, no one ever really bothered us along this particular route or the entire trip. "Do not shift your gears; we don't want anyone to derail," Jerry instructed all of us before we took off. With the police leading the way, we continued through the center of town. All was going smoothly until Dave Miller, decided to shift his gears. Immediately, his chain flew off lodging itself in between the two front sprockets. With the chain now binding up his gears and unable to pedal, Dave had no choice but to pull over. That meant our entire convoy of 32 bikes had to stop. We had just entered into one of the busiest sections of downtown Augusta. The cops that were escorting us didn't realize that we had stopped. They had to make a U-turn to get back to where we had pulled over. Now almost in tears, Dave kept insisting that he hadn't shifted gears, but Jerry knew better. He was upset with Dave, and it was one of the few times on the trip where Jerry yelled at one of us.

In addition to his canteen, Jerry also carried a tool pouch around his waist. It took us several minutes to free the chain. All the while, the traffic kept building. Finally, Steve Zoubek, who was always very handy with tools, was able to pry the chain loose. All in all Dave, was a good-natured polite Scout, and for the most part tried to do his best on the trip.

Once we were able to get back on the road, the traffic that had been building was now almost at a standstill, and looked more like a giant parking lot. Our police escort took us around the stopped cars and we were eventually able to take an alternate route avoiding most of the traffic. When we turned down a side street at the end of the block, I could see several people standing around two white vans. Our convoy soon came to a halt. A woman and two men, one who was carrying a large TV camera over his shoulder rushed over to where we had stopped. The woman introduced herself as a reporter from the local radio station. She immediately began asking some of us questions about our trip. The two men ran past where I was standing and started interviewing and filming a few of the other Scouts further back in the line. They had apparently been alerted to our escort through town and wanted to cover what must have been a great news story at the time.

After a few minutes, the police officer gestured that we should get moving. The cameraman and the rest of the press continued to follow us, now running and filming our procession through town. We all felt like celebrities and got a big kick out of our newfound fame in Augusta.

A few of the boy's bikes needed parts that we weren't carrying. Once we reached a safe area on the outskirts of town, we pulled over to thank our police escort and continued on our way. A few miles down the road, we stopped at a bicycle shop where we met the owner, who was an avid cyclist himself. He had ridden cross-country on a few occasions, and wanted to help us by donating the parts that we needed. After a few more adjustments, we were once again on our way. It was getting late and we still needed to eat dinner and hopefully get further out of town and find a place to camp for the night. Rain was once again forecasted. We stopped for dinner at a restaurant called the Alamo, just south of town. They had heard about us on the radio and took a real interest in our trip.

Our plan had been to try and make it to the town of Waynesboro, Georgia about 20 miles or so out of town. It was getting dark and the traffic along Route 56 was beginning to get heavy again. The road eventually turned into more of a country lane and started twisting and turning for several miles. We spotted a farmhouse and a large barn near an open field after riding about 10 miles. The farmer said that we could sleep in the pasture next to the barn. If it were to rain as was predicted, we could bunk down in the barn. That night we were all exhausted from riding through Augusta. Almost as soon as we rolled out our blankets onto the plastic tarps, we fell asleep, never bothering to start a campfire. In the middle of the night, I woke up to go to the bathroom and saw a bright flash of lightning off in the distance followed by a loud clap of thunder. That woke nearly everyone else up and Jerry said that we needed to move into the barn. Just as everyone got situated, it started to pour.

When we woke up the next morning, it was gloomy and still drizzling outside and nobody wanted to leave the shelter of the barn. We were on a strict time line though. We really had no choice but to pack up and ride through the rain. The roads were now mostly flat and we figured we could put on a decent number of miles despite the rain. We had just packed up our gear and were planning on heading out along a curved part of the road. We could see the headlights from the traffic coming toward us heading into Augusta. As we started to assemble our line, we heard a big bang and saw a large white truck flipped over on its side, skidding across the wet pavement. Sparks were flying everywhere as the metal from the truck had met the asphalt road. Jack Froehling yelled to a couple of the guys to grab a first aid kit and a blanket. By the time they made it over to the truck, the driver had already crawled out of the cab and was apparently unhurt. He had taken the turn too quickly, I heard him say to Jack, and just lost control of the truck. Thankfully, no one else was injured in the accident.

Steve Zoubek reported to Mal that we had been sleeping un-der the stars when it started to rain. It rained throughout the night and never stopped until early that morning when we sat down to eat breakfast in Waynesboro. We were once again soaked to the gills. My shoes absorbed so much water that I'm not sure if they had fully dried out from the last time it rained. Having turned onto US Route 25 outside of town, our path would now take us further south. We would eventually turn east angling more toward Savannah, Georgia.

Savannah is where we thought, we might get our first glimpse of the Atlantic Ocean. Many of the guys had never seen the ocean, and we hoped to do some swimming and maybe even some fishing soon. After breakfast, we connected with Route 24 taking us on a more southeasterly track heading toward Sylvania some 36 miles away. There we had a quick snack and were back on the road on our way to Springfield, Georgia. At this point in the trip, we had gotten used to the ex-treme heat and were doing a much better job of rationing the water in our canteens. As a result, we weren't taking as many bathroom breaks. It was hot, with the temperature now over a 100°F again, but nobody was complaining. We just kept pedaling. We all had a renewed level of energy, knowing we were getting closer to Florida, our final destination.

We had stopped for dinner and as nighttime approached the temperature had cooled off considerably once the sun started to set. When we mounted back up on our bicycles, we were greeted with a tailwind and went clipping along at about 20-22 mph. We were making great time. That night after dinner, we bedded down in a little roadside park a few miles outside the town of Springfield, Georgia. We had set a new record for miles covered in a single day, having traveled a distance of 82 miles. The ride seemed effortless. We were all proud of our accomplishment and slept soundly under the stars. Each day that went by we were getting more and more confident in our riding abilities. I had not heard a single complaint for several days.

FORTY-FOUR

F EELING LIKE we were on a mission, we jumped up early
the next morning, broke camp quickly and headed for the
town of Rincon, Georgia, where we hoped to find a place to eat
breakfast. The heat and high humidity was already beginning
to build at 6:30 a.m. when we took off. Like clockwork, we road
for about eight miles before spotting a little place for breakfast
just as we hit Rincon. The city of Savannah was now firmly in
our grasp with just another 26 miles or so to pedal. It would be
where the road would finally meet the ocean.

The terrain was now flat with row after row of peach trees
as far as I could see. Thousands of acres of farm fields were visible, growing mostly peanuts, cotton, and the now familiar tobacco plants. Nearly every farm had at least one or two
chicken coops, but there were a few that had several hundred
all lined up and on top of each other. It must have been feeding
time when we drove by early that morning, because their loud
"cluck, cluck, cluck" was almost deafening. Later, Jerry said it
was because they had just laid their eggs. We all laughed,
thinking that was funny.

The headline from the Herald on Sunday, August 14, read,
"Bikers gain a following." We had come into a more wooded
area along the road just a few miles outside of Rincon. A
farmer was being pulled along in a small cart by a horse. "How
many horse power?" Danny Zoubek yelled out.

"Just one," the farmer shouts back with a grin on his face. As
we came to a slight bend in the road, we passed a white farmhouse and a large barn off in the distance. We flew past several
horses grazing behind a white wooden fence. I think we must
have startled them a bit, as a few lunged backwards away from

the fence where they were chewing on some grass and took off running.

"Did you hear that!" Danny yells up to me, thinking that he had just heard thunder. There wasn't a cloud in the sky. The horses came upon us fast from the right side. At first, they were on the shoulder of the road running along with us. You could hear their hoofs pounding on the soft shoulder and definitely feel their presence, as they got closer. It felt as if they were chasing us, maybe thinking we were just another herd and wanted to join us. Up to this point, we had witnessed a few accidents with cars and trucks driving off the road. We also had been attacked by several dogs along the way. This was the first time we had been chased by horses.

I knew they weren't wild horses, since I recognized a few of them and their markings from the ones behind the fence. The further up the road we got, the more nerve racking it became, as I tried hard to stay focused on the road ahead and keep riding. No one dared to stop. They ran alongside of us for about a mile or so, mostly on our right side and the shoulder of the road. We were really hauling on our bikes out of fear they might run over us.

Finally, after several minutes of terror, two men and an older woman wearing cowboy hats appeared. The farmers were racing down the road in a green Jeep yelling something, trying to round up the stampeding horses. They were having some difficulty getting them all corralled, and the faster their Jeep sped up, the faster the horses ran toward us. It reminded me of an episode of Wild, Wild World of Animals, which I had watched a few months back. Two guys in a similar looking Jeep were chasing after a rhino with a tranquilizer gun that had escaped from a preserve somewhere in Africa.

As the Jeep sped closer to the horses, one of the farmers clapped his hands and with that, dust went flying everywhere and the herd instantly came to a screeching halt. The woman jumped out of the Jeep first. She was getting ready to throw a rope around one of the horse's necks when something must have spooked them. They took off again, this time into the street at a full gallop heading toward us. I had counted at least 12 horses. Since they had stopped for a moment, we were now able to outrun them. We just kept pedaling as fast as we could and didn't stop until we were several miles down the road.

A few of the guys were still a little shaken up by our experience. When we road into the small town of Garden City, Georgia, Jerry spotted the Pixie Drive-in, and signaled us to stop. It was a hot day and I think he thought we all deserved an ice cream cone after lunch. Despite the fact that ice cream was one of Jerry's favorite treats, it was usually reserved for a special occasion, like one of the boy's birthdays. The city of Savannah was only a few more miles up the road.

As we approached the city, we passed several car dealerships and a few old factories. We continued to wind our way further into town. The closer to the Savannah River we got, we were feeling the presence of the ocean nearby. We had another 20 miles or so to go, but there was a distinct smell of fish and salt water in the air. The scents were familiar to me as I had been to the ocean many times before.

Savannah was the most beautiful city we had seen so far. It had many historic buildings and parks, lush with trees and flowers of nearly every color. Having cut grass since I was 10 years old, I took special notice of the carefully manicured lawns and bushes. Some of the boys were getting their first glimpses of palm trees and the huge oaks dripping with Spanish moss that lined many of the streets. When we reached the banks of the Savannah River there were numerous barges and large ships, some that looked to be several stories high.

We had received special permission from the city to camp in Morrell Park on the riverfront near "The Waving Girl Statue." It was a newly erected bronze statue of Florence Martus, in honor of her 44 years of service as greeter to all the ships and boats entering the Savannah port. Loneliness had initially led her to wave a handkerchief by day and a lantern by night at sailors, as they glided past her island home on the Savannah River.

After securing our camp on Saturday near the statue, we walked downtown to grab a bite to eat. I ate frog legs for the first time in my life and loved them. Tasted just like chicken, I thought. Many of us stayed up late that night watching the ferryboats and huge barges traveling up and down the river towing in larger ships. There were several taverns in the area, something that Jerry was not all that keen on in regards to our chosen campsite. A live jazz band played well into the night at one of the nearby bars.

Danny Zoubek and I both stayed up a good part of the night talking about some of the girls we had seen earlier entering the taverns across East River Street. Secretly, we wondered what it would be like to pick up a girl like that. We were at that age when girls were starting to become interesting to us and the action around the bars that night had piqued our curiosity.

Sunday morning, we hiked into town for breakfast and then headed over to the historic district of Savannah to see several of the city's attractions. Mark Titone would later report to Mal on Monday, August 14, that he had been in awe of the fantastic Cathedral of Saint John the Baptist, a massive church built in 1896 with twin steeples. Like many of us, Mark had been intrigued by all the ships and boats in the area. Later that day, we went on a tour of the Ships of the Sea Maritime Museum. We were amazed by the many beautiful scale model ships and their plaques that described each ship's history.

After our tour of the town, we took a rest break, and some of the boys went fishing in the river and caught a few fish. We had not seen the ocean yet, since the city was a good 17-mile hike to the beach. Later that afternoon, we said our goodbyes to Savannah and headed south out of town on Route 17 toward Midway, Georgia. According to our trip ticket, it would be about a 31 mile hike to the town where we had planned on having dinner and search for a campsite.

Traffic was heavy through this section of town and our road guards were once again getting a good workout. The city and its numerous squares were spectacular and I caught myself not paying as much attention to the road as I needed to. We had all been riding well and everyone was in high spirits and very confident in their riding abilities. A few times along the trip, I had witnessed Arlin riding with no hands, crossing his arms over his chest. He was always a bit of a daredevil and I didn't think too much about it, but knew it was dangerous. Something in one of the parks had caught my eye and when I looked back at the road, Arlin was flying through the air like Superman and disappeared headfirst into a clump of bushes near the side of the road. His front tire had hit a sewer drain and collapsed on impact catapulting him into the woods. The bike flipped over a few times before coming to rest in the grass next to the shoulder. I could hear the screech of rubber on metal from my rear as everyone behind me was desperately trying to stop.

I'm not sure if anyone else knew what had happened to Arlin, until he emerged from the bushes with a big grin on his face, clasping his right hand. "What the heck are you doing?" I asked him smiling. He never saw the drain and admitted to Jerry that he had been riding again with no hands. He had in- jured his hand in the crash and it started to swell up almost im- mediately. He was lucky that he didn't land in the street where he could have been more seriously injured. Thankfully, we were still close to Savannah and could buy a rim at the local Sears store and get him back on the road. I always knew that it was just a matter of time before Arlin had a major crash, so I wasn't surprised when it happened.

FORTY-FIVE

AFTER REPAIRING Arlin's bike, we took off again pedaling further south and deeper into Georgia along US 17/25. When we crossed over the Ogeechee River, the water was a dark brown color and the lush vegetation growing along its banks looked almost prehistoric. We pulled into the town of Richmond Hill and stopped to take a break after knocking off nearly 21 miles.

Cruising down one of the main roads into town there were several houses on both sides of the street. We were pedaling along at a good clip, when I saw a woman a few houses up the road open her front door. Just as she raised her hand to wave at us, her screen door flew open and a large black German Shepherd ran out of the house. He was heading straight for us tearing across her front lawn and into the street. Just as I yelled, "Dog!" an oncoming car blindsided him, sending him flying several feet into the air before landing in front of the stopped car. Looking disoriented, the dog jumped up and limped back to where the woman was standing and crying hysterically. We never stopped and just kept riding. It all happened so fast that none of our leaders even had time to pull out their bottles of ammonia spray. This was the second attack by a large dog in the past week and several of the Scouts were pretty shaken up.

We stopped at a gas station further down the road to use the bathroom. Jerry and several of us walked over to a drug store a few doors down to get a snack. We were getting ready to check out when a woman approached Jerry introducing herself as a nurse from the local hospital. "You have a very sick boy on your hands," she said. She had been observing Bob Mikuls, and noticed that he was having a problem. Jerry knew that Bob had a rather serious psychological condition and admired his courage for going on the trip in the first place. It had been his decision to go with us knowing that it might be difficult for him. The dog attack, a few days earlier, had really taken a toll on Bob's state of mind, and I think this one may have just sent him over the edge.

We were now only a few miles from our destination, but Jerry didn't want to take any chances. He explained that because of Bob's condition, he would not be able to make the final miles of the trip with us. Everyone felt bad for Bob, and we knew as a group that he had made it. We all had a great deal of respect and admiration for him and were happy that he had made it as far as he did. Our emergency vehicle was able to transport Bob to the Jacksonville airport to fly him back to Illinois. It was a sad day for all of us to have lost a member of our group, but we knew it was the best thing for Bob.

Later that day, we pushed on toward the town of Midway, flying by one of the black and yellow US Highway 17 signs. The diamond shaped signs had become familiar to us along the road that was now called Ocean Highway. It was a mostly flat expanse of road with grassy, white sandy shoulders. Several miles out of town, the traffic had died down, so we decided to double up along a stretch that was a four-lane highway. The road was now lined on both sides with dense forests of tall pines and oak trees draped in moss. The further south we rode, I began to see areas of marshland that spread out across the landscape for miles. Despite the pine forests, I would see an occasional palm tree and it was beginning to feel more tropical the closer to Florida we got. We were now riding parallel to the coast of the Atlantic Ocean, but had not had an opportunity to get a glimpse of it yet. We were all anxious to see the ocean and kept pedaling, getting closer and closer to our destination with every push of the bike's pedal and rotation of the crank.

A few miles up the road, I could see two orange diamond shaped "Road Work Ahead" signs. Up to this point, we really had not experienced many delays due to road construction. There were a few rough patches in the Midwest, but we had expected that due to the harsh winters. The bad stretch of road in South Carolina where Dennis had wrecked his bike was un-usual, as the roads down South were generally in good condi-tion.

Sunday night, we stayed in the historic town of Midway on the beautifully landscaped grounds of the Congregational Church. We went to a neat seafood restaurant downtown and many of us had a good meal of steamed shrimp and corn on the cob. It was a real treat on our limited budget, but since there had been several people along the way that donated meals to us, we had a little more money to spend that night.

We had already pedaled 20 miles further south on Monday morning having reached the small community of Eulonia, Georgia. "Everybody is very fine, and doing great," Mark Titone reported to Mal. We had been sailing along together and away from home now nearly 24 days. Having only called home twice during that time, many of the boys were getting a bit homesick. The Wood Dale City Hall would occasionally pass private messages from the Scouts to one of the mothers, who would in turn forward them to the boy's families.

We had planned to put on 80 miles that day which would bring us just north of the Florida border. Having already ped-aled 20 miles, we were all pretty gung-ho and in "high spirits," Jerry reported to Mal. We really didn't know what was going to happen once we reached Jacksonville on Tuesday, but fig-ured that we would have plenty of things to do with trips planned to the Kennedy Space Center and St. Augustine. We were all anxious to get a chance to finally swim in the ocean, and spend some time at the beaches.

"Every day they just hop on their bicycles and are raring to go again. No one ever complains about the distance that lies ahead of them, they just keep riding on. Every time you turn a bend in the road, you see something new," Jerry reported to Mal that day. The trip had been a real education for all of us. We had met so many wonderful people along the way that had helped us. In many cases, they provided a meal or even a place for us to sleep. We rode into towns that most of us had never been to before, and into the lives of so many people.

The nature of the trip had given us the opportunity to speak with people in different walks of life and hear their stories. They were always curious about us, and usually amazed by our courage to have taken on such a challenge. As young boys, we were curious too. We had learned something about each person's life for whom we had come in contact with. In most cases, we had also learned something new about our country. In the end, it was our youthful curiosity that was the driving force behind our success, enabling us to keep going. We all wanted to know what was around the next bend or turn in the road.

Scout Master, Tony Langfelds's vision for the trip had come to fruition as our troop had in fact been exposed to the goodness of people, and the people to the goodness of Scouts. "You're never lost in our world. It's been a real way to reassure everyone's feelings that our country is the greatest place in the world to be living," Jerry concluded in one of his last reports to Mal.

When we pedaled into Darien, Georgia, on Monday afternoon, we were greeted by a police car and a fire truck that gave us an escort through town. We were treated to a swim at a motel in a pool with an Artesian well that went down some 200 feet. The water was crystal clear and very cold, but it felt really good after having already bicycled almost 33 miles in 95°F temperatures. After a nice lunch, we mounted up and continued on our journey, knowing we were getting close to the Florida border.

Pedaling through the town of Brunswick, Georgia, our convoy was forced to stop as a massive ship was passing under the expansive Sidney Lanier Bridge. We were in awe, as we watched the middle section of the bridge being raised allowing the ship to pass, as it made its way to the Atlantic Ocean. When we finally reached the top of the bridge, I could see for miles in every direction. We had never been closer to the ocean at this point in our trip.

After a hair-raising passage over the enormous bridge, our path took us on a sharp northwesterly direction along Jekyll Island Road. Just after we rode under a section of US Interstate 95, I noticed several orange construction signs. The section of road that we were riding on had now switched back to Route 17/25 and appeared closed ahead due to construction. We could see that large sections of the highway were completely torn up and there was no way we could ride our bikes on the road.

Having all passed our bike safety exam, we knew that bicycles were not allowed on the Interstate. Realizing that we might not have any choice, Jerry called the Georgia State Police and explained our situation. They said it would be ok for us to cross a 14-mile section of Interstate 95, but that we would have to ride on the shoulder of the two-lane highway. The temperatures had been rising throughout the day and had now exceeded 100°F. The road, having been repaved a few months before, was still fresh asphalt and was very soft. It was extremely difficult to ride on. The thin tires on our bikes seemed to sink into the pavement as we slowly inched our way toward the Woodbine exit. It took us nearly an hour of hard pedaling to reach our destination.

We were all completely exhausted and drenched in sweat. It had proven to be one of the most challenging parts of the trip. Woodbine, Georgia, was a nice little town with a population of only about 850 people that had been named the "Home of Georgia's Official Crawfish Festival." Driving further into town, I noticed a blue sign indicating an evacuation route, and knew we were getting closer to our Florida destination. That night we camped out in a park just north of the town near the Satilla River. It would be our last night in the state of Georgia.

FORTY-SIX

THE MOSQUITOES WERE PRETTY BAD that night and we were running low on insect repellent. We decided to build a bonfire to try to ward off the relentless attacks. Our discussion around the campfire was lively, and it was clear that each one of us wanted to go first. We finally decided that we would park our bikes and line up shoulder-to-shoulder and take one big step across the border, making our first destination into Florida together.

"The Scouts are fine," Jerry Lettenberger reported on Tuesday, August 15, from Kingsland, Georgia. We were now only about five miles from the Florida border. Jerry was a "happy-go-lucky" guy and nothing ever seemed to bother him. His lively personality was filled with the Scout spirit and he had a great attitude throughout the trip. He loved bicycling up and down all the hills, and told Mal that he was still planning on riding his bike when he got home. I'm not sure if Mal really believed him. Despite the 100°F temperatures, Jerry loved it when the trucks flew by, cooling him off. He reported that he was having a lot of fun.

Everyone was in high spirits that morning, anxious to make it to the Florida border. We felt as if we were astronauts going round and round the moon, getting ready to make a landing. It would be the first time many of the Scouts would see the ocean and get a chance to swim there. We were just about to come in and everybody was getting their sites fixed on our final destination.

Earlier that morning, when we pedaled out of Woodbine, we passed the Georgia Girl Drive-In, on US Highway 17, but none of us even thought about stopping. We were all pumped up and just wanted to log in several miles before eating breakfast. Our energy was high and we were once again on a mission. We had a quick breakfast in Kingsland, Georgia, and after Jerry's report, we jumped on our bikes and took off once again. Our pace was fast.

It wasn't long until we were crossing over the tea-colored St. Marys River, a natural boundary between Georgia and Florida. As we approached the top of the bridge, I saw a large light pale green sign with big silver letters spelling out, **"FLORIDA"** just a few yards past the concrete railings of the bridge. The ten foot high sign equipped with its own lighting system, had a backdrop of five towering palm trees and a maze of decorative concrete blocks rising another three feet above the sign.

When I first got a glimpse of the Florida sign, I could feel tears begin to well up in my eyes, knowing that we were about to achieve something great. It was something that no other Boy Scout troop in the history of Scouting had ever accomplished. There was an incredible feeling of achievement and relief that we had finally made it!

We had planned on crossing the border at the same time, but since the river was the dividing line it would have been next to impossible, unless we stopped traffic in both directions on the narrow two lane bridge. After parking our bikes, we walked over to a point near the sign and we all lined up, shoulder-to-shoulder. At exactly 11:00 a.m., Jerry gave the command, and we all took our first symbolic step over the border of Georgia into the state of Florida. We had all made it safely into Florida after pedaling over 1,200 miles on our bicycles, traversing through eight states.

Other than a few palm trees planted around the Florida sign, the landscape looked more like an extension of Georgia's pine forest, than the entrance to the tropical paradise we were hoping to see. We still had another 35 miles to go before we would get into the heart of Jacksonville, our final destination. There we would see many palm trees and a Florida that we had all dreamed about since having left Wood Dale nearly a month before. We planned to stay the night in Jacksonville, and travel outside the city on Wednesday. Our excitement was growing as we would head toward the beaches and see the ocean for the first time, and get a chance to swim.

The Welcome Center was a short walk from the Florida sign. Jeff Bandel, who was always a bit on the mischievous side, had wandered off and came back with a cup of orange juice in his hand. After taking several pictures, we all left our bikes and walked down to the Welcome Center to claim our cup of free orange juice. I don't think orange juice ever tasted so good to me than it did on that day.

When we left the Welcome Center, we hiked back to where our bicycles were parked and took off. We continued quickly down US 17 passing through the town of Boulogne, Florida. For the next several miles, there were souvenir stands and small motels lining both sides of the highway with billboards advertising everything the Sunshine State had to offer the traveler. We had learned from one of the attendants at the Welcome Center that US 17 was part of what was now considered the old Dixie Highway. Prior to 1960, and long before the Interstates, almost all southbound travelers entered Florida through the town of Boulogne.

We had pedaled only a few miles out of town, when a man and a woman pulled up alongside of us and started waving and honking their horn. We had spurred a lot of curiosity along the way, so we really didn't think anything about it. It was then that Mike Rohl said, "I think we're short one bike." We had always made a count to make sure everyone was present before we took off. However, this time in all the excitement of reaching Florida, we apparently had left one of our own behind. Dave Miller, had somehow been left behind. Earlier, he had parked his bike behind the green Florida sign. We never saw it when we shoved off. He had been taking a last minute bathroom break and when he came out of the Welcome Center, we were already several miles down the road. Dave eventually caught up to us since we had stopped, after realizing we had left him behind.

We were really flying now and making great time. There was no rain in the forecast and the temperature had dropped below 100°F for the first time in quite a while. The lush landscape nearly mirrored that of Georgia's with soaring pine tree forests stretching for miles on each side of the highway. We had made it into Florida ahead of schedule. Jacksonville was now in our sights; we were all pumped and full of energy. When we pedaled into Becker, Florida we had covered almost 24 miles in what seemed like record time. We were hungry but none of us wanted to stop for very long. After a quick snack, we jumped back on our bikes and headed for the little town of Yulee. It was a friendly little village. We stopped for a bathroom break at a motel, and the owner offered to let us swim in his pool. We had been riding all day and were pretty hot and sweaty, so a cool swim was a great relief. I think Jerry figured it would be a good way to clean us all up before meeting the mayor and all the folks in the big city of Jacksonville.

Jacksonville would be the second largest city that we would ride through with a population of 198,000 people. Our road guards would be kept very busy. After pedaling a few miles out of Yulee, it was a straight shot to Jacksonville on a very flat stretch of US 17. The landscape and vegetation was beginning to change quickly. The lush tall pine forests had now been replaced with smaller trees and bushes that dotted large expanses of open grassy fields and marshland.

At some point outside of the city, US 17 became Main Street and the traffic was getting heavier, but still manageable. I could see the outline of the city's large skyscrapers off in the distance. After crossing over a stretch of the St. Johns River, we headed straight into the heart of Jacksonville. My heart was pumping as I heard Mr. "G" order out the first of many road guards. They would stay busy until we reached our final destination. We continued our procession down Main Street until making a turn to the east on 1st Street. After passing a large park, we took a turn south onto A. Philip Randolph Boulevard heading straight toward the Jacksonville City Hall.

The city was very clean. I hadn't seen so many beautifully landscaped parks and mansions since having left Savannah. There were lots of palm trees and other colorful bushes and flowers, some I was familiar with. When we arrived at the Jacksonville City Hall, the officials must have been waiting for us. Almost as soon as we parked our bikes, several people, a few who were dressed in suits approached Jerry and began talking with him. The city hall offices were located on the first floor of a very tall building near a small skyscraper.

At the request of the mayor, we were asked to camp on the front lawn of the city hall, so everyone in Jacksonville would have an opportunity to see our Scout campsite and meet us. It would only be the second time since having left Wood Dale that we set up our tents. This time, we pitched them on the city's front lawn that consisted of a plush St. Augustine grass. Several residents of the town began stopping by our campsite to congratulate us on the completion of our journey. It was big news in town. It wasn't soon afterwards that we were being interviewed by several newspaper men and a TV crew. It was quite a spectacle to see that many orange nylon tents set up in front of the Jacksonville City Hall.

When we first arrived on the city grounds at exactly 6:00 p.m., Jerry took his last odometer reading for our trip, and recorded that we had pedaled 1,253.7 miles. It was an amazing feat and a tremendous accomplishment knowing that we had just completed the longest organized bike hike in the history of Scouting. We had been instilled with the Scout spirit at an early age, beginning with our involvement in the Cub Scouts. Our boyish curiosity and boundless energy was blinded to the challenges and hardships that lay ahead of us on a daily basis. We possessed a strong will to succeed and persevered without thinking of the consequences. We were determined from the beginning that no matter what; we were going to make it to Florida! When we arrived at the steps of the Jacksonville Florida City Hall, we had accomplished our mission and had done it together as a troop.

Once we had committed ourselves to going, there was a lot of pressure on us to make the trip a success. The moment we began planning to go, there was no turning back. We were going to ride our bicycles to Florida. The community of Wood Dale rose to the challenge, getting behind us to help make our dream a reality. Mal Bellairs took a keen interest in the trip and acted as our Mission Control. His radio station had followed our progress daily from our very first broadcast in late July. He allowed everyone who wanted to listen in, "ride along" with us as we traveled foot by foot, and pedal by pedal through eight states. As Wood Dale's "Youth Ambassadors of Goodwill," we could not let anyone down including our parents, who had all come together to make our trip a success.

Since having turned the front lawn of the Jacksonville City Hall into a campground Tuesday night, we took in a much-deserved rest. We all had saddle sores and aching muscles from riding so far. Although sore, the muscles in my legs and upper body had never felt stronger. The city officials were very accommodating and donated a small car, so we wouldn't have to use our bicycles to run errands in the village. With all the excitement of reaching our final destination, we were completely wiped out, both physically and emotionally.

That night, we met several city residents who were curious to learn more about our trip. After a nice meal at Morrison's Cafeteria, we hiked back to our camp where we were met by a reporter from another Jacksonville news station. We bedded down early with the anticipation of a big day on Wednesday. It promised to be full of fun activities, including a long awaited trip to the ocean.

FORTY-SEVEN

ON WEDNESDAY MORNING after a hardy breakfast, we were invited to the mayor's office for a special ceremony to meet him and several city council officials. Jerry was presented with a brass key with the city's emblem embossed on it. They also provided us with a commuter bus, so that we could travel to our planned excursions over the next few days. Our first trip would be later that morning where we would head down to the beaches. Many of the Scouts would see the ocean for the first time and we would all get a chance to swim.

Later that afternoon, we boarded our bus and headed a few more miles further south down the coast to the town of Jacksonville Beach, where we had lunch. The city officials were very friendly and allowed us to stay in a park district cabin right on the beach. While we were eating, a few men dressed in military uniforms walked into the restaurant. They took an interest in us and introduced themselves as members of the US Coast Guard saying they were stationed nearby and wanted us to join them. The whole contingent went down to the docks and I couldn't believe how big their ship was! It wasn't long before they offered to give us a ride and we were heading out to sea. During our one-hour excursion, we all got a chance to take the wheel of this massive Coast Guard Cutter.

When I first spread my blanket out onto the floor that night, I noticed something big and brown shoot across the top of the blanket and disappear into some of my clothing. We had all spread our blankets out and were planning on sleeping on the concrete floor. There were several massive Palmetto bugs, some as big as small mice that lived amongst us in the cabin. They got into everything and scared the heck out of me and my fellow Scouts. Jerry said that they loved to live in the palm trees and got huge because of the warm weather and abundance of food.

Palmetto bugs weren't the only large insects we had encountered while on our trip. My first encounter was with a moth that flew right in front of my face while I was riding my bike. I dodged it, thinking it was a small bird or something. It wasn't uncommon for us to get hit in the face with different kinds of insects while we were riding our bikes. We were riding along a lonely stretch of highway 17 in Georgia, just outside of Savannah. I hadn't seen a building or even a car for miles, just dense forests on each side of the road. Dusk was setting in and we were cruising along at about 30-35 mph when something big hit me and bounced off my left shoulder. I nearly lost control of my bike, dodging several of these gigantic brown moths, with fuzzy bodies that appeared to be four to six inches in diameter from wing tip to wing tip.

During our first night at the cabin, Jack Froehling took us on a night swim. Several of the guys didn't want to go in the water out of a fear of sharks. My father had always warned me about the dangers of swimming in the ocean at night, saying that it was a bit risky. We didn't swim for that long after a couple of the guys swore they had seen a large black fin pop out of the water. Many of us retired early and were tired having swam all day.

Jack, who palled around with Mike Rohl, decided it was time for a practical joke. I was still awake and watched while the both of them spread shaving cream on the hands of several Scouts who had fallen asleep. Taking a foot long piece of fuzzy grass they had found near the beach, they tickled each of the Scout's faces. Almost instantly, the sleeping Scouts rubbed their hands on their faces spreading the shaving cream all over and woke up to hear us roaring in laughter. All hell broke loose, after that, as a massive shaving cream fight ensued.

Jack was living up to his reputation as "good-natured Jack." He was always a comical guy and a real screwball at heart. He loved to clown around and knew exactly how to loosen us all up. It had been a long and sometimes arduous trip, but now it was time to relax and enjoy ourselves. We were having the time of our lives and realized that our great bike hike to Florida would soon be over. It was an adventure of a lifetime and something that we would never forget, as long as we lived.

The cabin we were staying at was out in the boonies and we were unable to locate a telephone on Thursday morning. It would only be the second time since our reporting began with Mal that we would miss our call to him. Media coverage of our arrival into Florida had been intense since we arrived. Several TV and radio stations had featured us. Nearly every newspaper in the area had printed a story of our great adventure. Everywhere we went now, we were being treated like celebrities. After breakfast, we headed to another ceremony in our honor, where the mayor of the city of Jacksonville Beach would present us with a key to their city.

We were all anxious to get back down to the beach, so we hopped aboard our bus and headed toward our cabin where we would spend all day at the beach. "We're having a real fine time down here," Jeff Bandel reported to Mal on Friday. Jeff was a good-natured kid, wiry, and energetic, who went willingly with the flow of things. He was amazed at the size of the waves that practically drowned him after one took him under. "I finally learned to keep my mouth shut," he reported to Mal, after swallowing his first real dose of salt water.

We were having a ball swimming in the Atlantic Ocean. The headline from the Herald at home that same day read, "Florida greets WD Troop 65." Unbeknownst to us, members of the mother's group and several residents from Wood Dale were busy organizing a surprise "Welcome Home" parade in the honor of our troop's 1,254-mile odyssey to the Sunshine State.

On Friday morning, we took off in our bus for a daylong tour of the Kennedy Space Center. It had been a few years since I was there and a lot had changed since the first moon landing in 1969. We took a 48-mile bus tour of the space center and learned quite a bit about the future of space flights and the suits the astronauts wore while walking on the moon. We saw the fourth largest building in the world where the massive Saturn V rockets were being built. I had forgotten how huge the building actually was. After our tour, we were awarded physical fitness certificates from President Nixon. That night, we stayed at the Jacksonville USO facility where the army men usually sleep.

After we had breakfast on Saturday morning, Jerry and Ed Goscinski gave our last radio broadcast and report to Josh Bradley who was in for Mal at WIVS. "They're really having a time," Jerry reported, "nothing is impossible."

"We're on our way to the city hall to get our bikes all ready to go to the airport," Ed reported. Ed was a good Scout, always eager to learn the Scouting ways. He had come from a Romanian family that emphasized strong family values and discipline. When Josh asked him if he would take the trip again, Ed with his wry smile and familiar accent responded simply by saying, "I wouldn't mind doing it again." His level of enthusiasm was beginning to spread throughout our ranks and several of us said that we, too, would take the trip again. Later that day, our last excursion in Florida would take us to the historic town of St. Augustine.

When we arrived at the Jacksonville International Airport that night for our return flight the next morning, the airport official from the port authority had instructed us to sleep on a narrow strip of grass near one of the runways. Jerry did not like that idea, thinking it was dangerous. He worried about what might happen if one of the planes were to skid off the runway and kill us. Worse yet, he was concerned that one of his kids would sleepwalk onto a runway and be killed instantly by an oncoming plane.

We had delivered our bikes earlier that evening and they would be flying back on a 747 late that night. After hearing Jerry's concerns, the airport official suggested that we camp in an area further away from the runways. It wasn't much better as it was where the state would bring and camp prisoners on the chain gang. It was a desolate area of the airport where two small ponds flanked a small strip of grass and an old abandoned building lay in ruin.

It was getting late and the temperature that day had been a muggy 92°F. The heat didn't seem to let up despite the fact that the sun was just about to go down. The mosquitoes were getting fierce. Mike Rohl and Jack Froehling had started to spray insect repellant on us, but quickly ran out before being able to spray everyone. Several of the Scouts just hunkered down in their sleeping bags trying to escape the relentless onslaught of mosquitoes now swarming the camp. The airport authorities said we couldn't build a fire as it would potentially distract incoming planes trying to land.

It was our last night out and the camp was a bit tense, as the constant noise from the planes overhead would make it difficult to fall asleep. Several of the Scouts had never been on a plane before. The sun had just gone down when several firemen from the airport approached our campsite driving a large white tanker truck. They had come out to help us fill up our canteens. We spoke with them for quite a while as they expressed an interest in our trip. Just as they were getting ready to leave, we could hear a loud noise off in the distance that sounded like a dog barking. "Are there dogs loose in the area?" Jerry asked sounding somewhat alarmed.

"No, those are alligators!" the firemen replied. "Make sure you keep the kids away from the ponds, especially at night!"

Well, to say the least, Jerry and most of the leaders did not sleep all that well keeping a close eye on the troop to make sure no one wandered off in their sleep. We were all on the lookout for any alligators that might make their way into the camp. We slept close together, as the barking sound took on new meaning. At about 2:00 a.m., I saw Danny Zoubek, who had gone to bed earlier crawl out of his sleeping bag. I kept an eye on him thinking he might be sleepwalking or had forgotten about the alligator threat. The barking had long subsided. It was dead silence as there were no airplanes landing or taking off. Not even a cricket could be heard. It was that quiet.

As Danny stared up into the night sky, it hit him, "This is almost over," he thought, not believing we did it. Many of us, for the first time were beginning to realize the same thing. With the trip nearly over, our journey as young men was really just beginning, as our lives had been forever changed. We had been away from our homes now nearly a month and had achieved something great, having completed the longest organized bicycle hike by any Boy Scout unit in the 62 year history of the organization.

FORTY-EIGHT

E XHAUSTED BUT EXCITED about our journey home, we awoke the morning of August 20 to a bright sunny sky that would be perfect for flying. Before hopping onto our Delta Airlines jet, one of the flight attendants took our troop's group picture next to the plane. Flight 902, was scheduled to leave Jacksonville, Florida at 9:00 a.m. and arrive at O'Hare Airport at 10:03 a.m. Ironically, our flight back home was more than 30 minutes late due to a mechanical issue with the plane.

When we walked off the airplane and took our first steps into the terminal at O'Hare Airport, we were instantly met by ABC and WGN TV camera crews wanting to interview us. A female reporter from ABC interviewed Dave Miller first, followed by Danny Zoubek. For the most part, we had gotten used to the media attention having been interviewed several times throughout the trip. This time however, we were caught off guard. We had just returned home and weren't really expecting all the TV coverage. With our story now being broadcast throughout the entire Chicago area, we were overwhelmed. We were now celebrities in our home town and were star struck. "You're never away from home when you travel in our country," Jerry told the reporter from WGN TV News.

Our bikes were outside the terminal cordoned off by a red velvet rope with several flags hanging down. The dads had installed a new set of marker flags on the bikes for our final hike home. We were soon greeted by our fellow Scout, Bob Mikuls. Undaunted by his setback and still having the Scout spirit, Bob had gone to O'Hare with a number of the dads to help assemble his own bike, so he could ride with us on our final leg of the trip.

The final 10 miles of our long journey would be one of the most exciting times of my life. It was a beautiful sunny 88°F day when we shoved off for our final ride together riding two abreast down Mannheim Road. Our escort was led by Wood Dale's Fire Chief, William Stanek, and the Chicago Police Department. When we reached the Bensenville city limits, their police department took over the escort duties.

We were all dressed in full uniform anticipating a reunion with our families. With our contingent of 32 bicycles once again complete, we continued our trek west down Irving Park Road. Several TV camera crews in vans were in hot pursuit having followed our convoy. I could see several people standing along both sides of the road waving at us. When we approached Route 83 and Irving Park Road, I noticed fellow Scout, Curt Schuppi. He was sitting on his bike with a big smile on his face waving to us from the bridge. Everybody had felt bad for Curt, when his mother suddenly pulled the plug on his chances to go on the trip. Without hesitation, Jerry signaled him to come into the group and join us for our final ride into town. Curt's smile beamed as he quickly pedaled toward us taking his place in front of Jerry and Mike Rohl. Curt was once again part of the trip, and rightfully so.

We had now been met by members of our own Wood Dale Police Department who would bring us the rest of the way home. I began to see more people standing by the road waving and cheering us on. Just ahead, there were several people standing in the road, some that I recognized as other Scouts. They were lined up behind fire trucks and police cars that had their lights flashing. We were unaware that a parade in our honor had been planned by Mrs. Kazmierczak and several other members of the mother's group. Anxious family members and city officials lined the streets of Wood Dale in anticipation of our pending arrival. The welcome home parade began near the Wood Dale and Bensenville border and was led by Mr. Kazmierczak, serving as the Grand Marshal. Following directly behind him in another car were members of the Wood Dale Lion's and Junior Woman's Clubs.

As we got closer to the railroad tracks at Irving Park and Wood Dale Roads, there was a loud blast from one of the sirens on a fire truck ahead of us. The entire group took a column right marching north down Wood Dale Road. I could see Billy with a big grin on his face standing next to his sister Kathy waving as our convoy crossed the tracks. We soon passed Sievers Pharmacy that had a big "Welcome Home Troop 65" banner displayed outside their doors. A few boys on the baseball fields next to the pharmacy stopped playing ball for a moment and waved as our convoy rode by. There were hundreds of people lining both sides of the street now. It appeared as if the entire town had come out to welcome us home.

With sirens blaring and lights flashing, the Wood Dale Fire Department and Civil Defense Unit had shown up in full force with all of their equipment to greet us. Leading the way and marching in perfect unison, were our fellow Scouts from Troop 65, wearing their full dress uniforms. They were followed closely by Cub Scout Packs 34 and 410. Boy Scout Troop 60 and Girl Scout Troop 308 had also come out to support us and marched proudly down Wood Dale Road. Their leaders barked out a familiar cadence as they proceeded toward the Wood Dale Junior High School.

As we approached the final stretch of road that would mark the end of our trip, we knew that we had done something quite extraordinary. It was an irreplaceable moment of time. I had tears in my eyes while several of the other boys cried, overcome with emotion. We were in awe as we witnessed thousands of people from our hometown waving and cheering our return. It was as if we were astronauts returning home from a mission to the moon, and greeted with a ticker tape parade. Our hometown's enthusiastic reception was an amazing tribute to their loyalty and dedication to us. Without their help, we would have never been able to accomplish such a great feat.

When we pulled into the parking lot of the Wood Dale Junior High School, there were hundreds of people standing everywhere. I noticed my dad right away standing off to one side of the school gym taking pictures. Just as I was beginning to raise my hand to wave, he smiled, gesturing a job well done. The Redwood Sage singing group from Chicago had several of their instruments and a speaker system set up on the bed of a large white truck. A microphone was set up nearby and Mrs. Kazmierczak was testing the sound when we arrived.

We parked our bikes all in a single file order in the school lot just as we had in all the previous 29 days whenever we stopped. As soon as we dismounted, we were immediately surrounded by our parents and other family members anxious to greet us. Everyone from my family was hugging me and my grandmother gave me one of her wet kisses, and said she was proud of me. Several of the boy's mothers wept as they held onto their sons tightly, not wanting to let go.

We had received a hero's welcome from the entire town. There were many local officials on hand including the troop's Committee Chairman, Gene Malik, who served as Master of Ceremonies for the event and Father William Thompson, who would open the festivities with a prayer. Welcoming us home, Mayor Lewis Mazzuca congratulated us on our stamina, and said that our efforts had special significance to the city. "Your outstanding achievement with this trip has put Wood Dale on the map. You have made that one giant step forward for our city," Mazzuca said.

FORTY-NINE

WHEN I FINALLY made it down to the Vermilion River after having located all of my fishing gear, the temperature in my car read 82°F. Just as the weatherman had predicted, it was a new record for this late day in October. My mind had traveled far that day, and I was getting excited about the prospect of catching some fish. It had been nearly two years since I had been down to the river, and I missed the peacefulness and the beauty of the surrounding landscape and wildlife that it had provided me over the years.

I couldn't stop thinking about the great bike hike to Florida and the many lessons my father and the Boy Scouts had taught me that made it all possible. When I had discovered the trip pictures and my certificate, I was instantly taken back to a much simpler time in my life that was now long gone. My annual fishing trips to the Vermilion always seemed to help me regroup and allowed me to relax and focus on the important things in life.

Having had an opportunity to reflect over the past several hours, I now realized that the bike trip to Florida had had a very deep and profound spiritual meaning. The trip had meant a great deal to me at the time, and my understanding of those feelings was now clear. It was the ultimate challenge for me, and one that I had been in training for both mentally and physically for a long time.

When I rounded the long bend in the river heading further north, I lost sight of the 178 bridge. I sat down to take a rest and began to think about the many canoe trips I had taken down the river with my dad and some of my friends. A few years after leaving the Boy Scouts, I was planning a trip down the river with my younger brother Mark, and a few of our friends. I was short on some camping gear, so I contacted Jerry to see if I could borrow a few of the orange nylon tents we had used on our Florida bike trip. He was always good about that kind of thing, and immediately said yes, knowing that I would return them in better shape, than which I had received them.

The Vermilion was raging, nearly reaching the seven-foot mark on the gauge of the Lowell Bridge pilings. All four of us, including me and my brother Mark, and our friend's, Billy and David, were experienced canoeists. We made the decision to make a go of it and try to run the rapids and exit the river near the Oglesby Bridge. The last time I had canoed the river when it was this high, was when I was with my father several years before, and almost died.

We had made it safely downriver to Wildcat rapids, the only Class III rapid on the river. The first time I ever saw Wildcat was when I was canoeing with my father several years before. I was so frightened by what I saw, that I refused to go over it. When I finally got enough courage to run the rapid the following year, my father and I crashed head-on into a massive boulder instantly sinking our canoe.

Wildcat is an intense rapid. The Vermilion River narrows into a single chute only about 20-25 feet across. It then drops four feet into a raging mass of whitewater that can easily sink a canoe. Despite our many years of canoeing experience, none of us that day made it through the rapid without tipping. We each tried it twice with the same result, and were swept down the river, trying desperately to hold on to our swamped canoe.

We were all sitting up on the rocks, having lunch, contemplating a third try when we saw a canoe upriver that didn't look like it was going to stop before going over Wildcat. We had been down the river dozens of times and always beached our canoes upstream before attempting to run the rapid. Wild-cat was always a little different depending on the level of the river. Normally, we would try to stay somewhat to the left of the massive boulder in the middle of the rapid. However, because the river was so high, there was no other way to go except straight through the middle.

When the man and women came shooting over Wildcat in their canoe, I noticed right away that neither of them had life-jackets or helmets on. Their canoe hit a huge whitecap in the middle of the rapid and went airborne; completely flipping it upside down, and dumping both of its passengers into the swirling whitewater. For a split moment, both the man and woman disappeared under the water. I saw the woman pop up a few seconds later, just as their aluminum canoe came crashing down onto her head, driving her completely back under the water. The man was nowhere in sight and with the canoe now covering the woman; David yelled out, "Get a canoe!"

Acting on pure instinct, I ran and jumped into my canoe, paddling as hard as I could toward where the couple's swamped canoe had been swept down the river. The water was still very turbulent and there was white foam everywhere on top of fast moving brown river water. I was being carried further down the river and saw the man crawl up onto the far bank, but I did not see the woman. About two minutes went by without any sign of her. I kept looking.

Just when I thought she might have drowned, I saw what looked to be a blonde head of hair rising to the surface. I immediately reached down and grabbed the top of her hair. With her head now completely out of the water, she was panicked, gasping for air, and grabbing at my arms and the side of the canoe. I quickly calmed her down and told her to hold on to the side of the canoe so I could get her to shore. When I finally got her safely to the bank where the man was standing, I was met by my brother Mark, David and Billy. The woman thanked us and said that it was the last time she was coming up for air before giving up.

The many years of canoeing with my father and the training I received with the Boy Scouts, all had contributed to saving a life that day. Even though I had pulled the woman out of the water, it was my brother Mark, David and Billy that were there to back me up and jump into their canoes, too, and come to my aid. I had acted on David's urging, and with a selfless act of bravery, we had saved a life.

Our bicycle adventure to Florida had marked an end to many things other than the trip itself. It ended a time when that same group would ever be together again in that same setting and time or purpose. The great Florida crossing marked an end to a trip that could only be described as an amazing feat of courage and great teamwork. It was our moon landing. It was never about fame, it was about conquest. Could we do it? The answer was yes, with a great amount of preparation, we could and we did; to the best of our ability, a true mark of a Scout.

"I keep thinking this has got to come out as one of the greatest experiences for these boys. I would put this up with any amount of education, any amount of travel, any amount of history. Just getting to know people and getting to handle yourself, take care of your own personal problems, to work with a group and in co-operation. I just can't say enough for an organization that puts itself through a thing like this."

Mal Bellairs, (Former radio talk show host) 08/11/72

About the Author

Paul Rega began his writing career in 1980 while attending Western Illinois University as a staff reporter for the Western Courier. Upon graduating with a degree in biology and journalism, he spent the next 30 years in business having started his own executive search firm in 1984. His passion for writing stayed with him throughout his business life and he started writing his first book in 1994. He published, "How To Find A Job: When There Are No Jobs" in December 2011. The book was an instant success and hit #1 on Amazon's bestseller list for job hunting books in March 2012. He currently lives in a small town along the Gulf Coast of Florida where he is working on his next book.

Made in the USA
Las Vegas, NV
16 June 2021